TRUE STOREY

TRUE STOREY

MY LIFE AND CRIMES AS A FOOTBALL HATCHET MAN

PETER STOREY
WITH WILL PRICE

MAINSTREAM
PUBLISHING

EDINBURGH AND LONDON

Copyright © Peter Storey, 2010
All rights reserved
The moral right of the author has been asserted

First published in Great Britain in 2010 by
MAINSTREAM PUBLISHING COMPANY
(EDINBURGH) LTD
7 Albany Street
Edinburgh EH1 3UG

ISBN 9781845965846

No part of this book may be reproduced or transmitted
in any form or by any other means without permission
in writing from the publisher, except by a reviewer
who wishes to quote brief passages in connection
with a review written for insertion in
a magazine, newspaper or broadcast

A catalogue record for this book is available
from the British Library

Typeset in Baskerville and Bliss

Printed in Great Britain by
CPI Mackays, Chatham ME5 8TD

1 3 5 7 9 10 8 6 4 2

To Danièle, for never losing faith in me; my dad, Edwin, I hope I made you proud and I apologise for the shame; my sons, Peter, Anthony and Jamie, I love you all, and Natalie – wherever you may be.

Contents

	Introduction	9
CHAPTER ONE	Bloody noses, dirty knees	13
CHAPTER TWO	North Bank boy	17
CHAPTER THREE	A proper shift	26
CHAPTER FOUR	Real pukka job	31
CHAPTER FIVE	Elland Road nutter	38
CHAPTER SIX	Wright and wrong	46
CHAPTER SEVEN	All about Mee	55
CHAPTER EIGHT	You know what to do, Peter	64
CHAPTER NINE	Wembley woe, Fairs Cup fun	74
CHAPTER TEN	When love breaks down	84
CHAPTER ELEVEN	Double delight, double despair	90
CHAPTER TWELVE	I'll always have Sheffield	98
CHAPTER THIRTEEN	Alf's kind of animal	111
CHAPTER FOURTEEN	Three Lions on my shirt	126
CHAPTER FIFTEEN	Howe sad	135
CHAPTER SIXTEEN	Falling at the final fence	147
CHAPTER SEVENTEEN	Losing the plot	153
CHAPTER EIGHTEEN	From the top to the bottle	159
CHAPTER NINETEEN	Mr Nice and the Fulham trip	173
CHAPTER TWENTY	Going down	186
CHAPTER TWENTY-ONE	Behind bars	196
CHAPTER TWENTY-TWO	Video nasty	206
CHAPTER TWENTY-THREE	French renaissance	220

Introduction

I was slagged off unmercifully because of my abrasive playing style, labelled the bastards' bastard, an assassin and a thug. Some of the abuse was vicious, but it never caused me to lose a moment's sleep.

It was a super career at the top as far as I was concerned; 16 years with Arsenal, where I made over 500 first-team appearances, a little niche in history as a member of the side which did the Double in 1970–71, and 19 international caps for England.

Yet so much rubbish has been written about me, so many lies and half-truths peddled as 'fact' relating to the crime which blighted my life, and I'd already had it at the back of my mind for some time to set the record straight when Hollywood actress Mercedes McNab, the daughter of my old Arsenal colleague Bob McNab, introduced me to a couple of British guys she knew in Los Angeles. They were very keen to turn my life story into a film, and we reached the stage of discussing scripts before the deal went cold when they failed to get financial backing.

Fortunately, several things then occurred to act as a catalyst for this book, which I sincerely hope you enjoy.

First, I was living comfortably in the south of France when it was announced, mistakenly, that I was so hard-up I'd had to sell my medals on eBay for £28,000. That niggled away at me; it seemed whenever I read anything about myself, it was inaccurate.

Second, I was in a bookshop looking for a decent autobiography, spotted an effort by an England international still in his 20s and despaired. I wasn't going to learn anything from that either about the game or the player which I didn't already know, and said as much to my wife, Danièle, who challenged me: 'But your life has been so crazy,

Peter, why don't you tell everybody what *really* happened?'

Third, I was approached by a journalist, Will Price, who convinced me I had a cracking tale to tell, and he knew as well as I did that while my professional career with Arsenal and England had been played out for very public consumption in front of thousands of spectators, I had never before spoken about the seedy side of my life after football.

A decade ago, *Match of the Day* magazine printed their Shifty Fifty, a list of the biggest bad boys in the game – and I took no pleasure in being at number one, with a citation reading:

> Not necessarily the most famous of our collection, however, considering the diversity of his crimes, possibly the most notorious. Having admitted boozing and womanising during his playing days, the madness took over when he hung up his boots in 1977. Perhaps his biggest crime was that football just wasn't enough for him.

I wanted to write this book primarily to explain the 'madness' fully for the first time, and particularly how so much of it was interlinked, and while I consider myself to have been a career sportsman, I most certainly was not a career criminal.

I'm going to reveal how I was sentenced to three years in jail for conspiracy to counterfeit gold half-sovereigns, and got banged up again for smuggling pornographic videos into England from Rotterdam in the spare tyre of my Suzuki Jeep, quite apart from receiving a suspended sentence and £700 fine for running a brothel, the Calypso Massage Parlour, in Leyton High Street, east London.

There was also my conviction for negotiating with a crook to buy two cars, a Mercedes and a BMW, which I had on hire-purchase at my Starline minicab firm, the almost inevitable bankruptcy, plus ludicrous accusations of headbutting one traffic warden and driving my car recklessly at another.

As tough as I'd been on the pitch, I was weak and foolish in as much as I confess I was attracted to the brash, flash lifestyle enjoyed by smartly dressed thieves who frequented my pub, the Jolly Farmers in Islington, the way they always seemed to have a pretty girl on one arm, a pocketful of ready cash and plenty of time to indulge themselves.

I hope I don't come over too much as a bitter old pro, although I fear I haven't been totally successful in conveying just how much enjoyment simply playing football gave me for a vast proportion of

INTRODUCTION

my club career. Put it down to frustration; Arsenal should have won much more in terms of trophies in the 1970s.

I must thank Will Price, of the *Daily Mirror* and *The People*, for his professionalism, diligence and constant good humour in helping me complete this book.

Thanks are also due to several former teammates who have had some kind words to say on my behalf, notably Bob Wilson, Frank McLintock, Bob McNab and Eddie Kelly; literary agent David Luxton for his invaluable support and taking care of contractual matters; Bill and Sharon Campbell, Fiona Atherton, Graeme Blaikie, Helen Bleck, Alex Hepworth and Kate McLelland at Mainstream for their enthusiasm and skill; Dominic Sutton and Peter Mason, a couple of devoted Arsenal fans who helped jog my memory by providing some vital statistics; Mark Baber of the Association of Football Statisticians; and particularly the *Daily Mirror* picture desk (mirrorfootball.co.uk) for sourcing some splendid nostalgic action shots of me in my prime.

But I could never thank Danièle enough. Quite apart from being a wonderful, gentle, tolerant woman, she is an extremely gifted landscape artist. Given a fraction of her talent, I would have played 100 times for England.

CHAPTER ONE

Bloody noses, dirty knees

The simple, basic pleasures of life were as good as it got growing up in the 1950s on the Longacre council estate, Ash, just outside Aldershot.

Not that I ever complained; I just never knew any better.

Three days before the end of the Second World War and the conception of a lot of unplanned kids on VE Day, I was born on Friday, 7 September 1945, in Farnham Hospital to Edwin, a carpenter who later became a self-employed builder, and Nellie, who worked part-time in a small clothes shop. I was destined to be an only child.

My father's side of the family were tough, uncomplaining mining stock from Northumberland and the paternal grandfather I never knew died in a pit accident in the north-east.

Mum and Dad had met during the War when he moved south to join the Royal Artillery, training the searchlights on enemy aircraft. Nellie had an authentic military background. Hailing from Aldershot, it was no surprise to learn that the men on her side of the family were professional soldiers. Her father was a Grenadier Guardsman and spent part of the First World War imprisoned in France.

I was tickled to discover that I share my birthday with a couple of other decent defenders: Queen Elizabeth I of England, who had an impressive record tackling the Spanish; and the classy Marcel Desailly, a man I admire enormously, who played over 100 international matches for France, the country I have made my home and where I live quietly, reading, cooking and spending time with my wife.

As far as I'm aware, mine was a normal birth – although given the reputation I have acquired over the intervening years as Arsenal's notorious hatchet man, my four marriages, assorted courtroom appearances and time spent at Her Majesty's pleasure, I suppose you could be forgiven for thinking the midwife and nurses made the sign of the cross and blessed themselves when I appeared for the first time, before checking my body for the figures 666, the mark of the Beast, to the accompaniment of thunder and lightning in north Hampshire.

They would have been more likely to find me stamped with a two or a four, the numbers I was to wear with such pride, and I like to think even a little distinction, for Arsenal and England.

Mum and Dad couldn't afford a home to call their own when I was born and my first three years were spent lodging with them at my nan's in Wyke Avenue, Ash, in a house without electricity. It was gas-powered and I distinctly remember being led up the stairs by candlelight during a winter's night to bunk in with my teenage Uncle John, a fireman on the steam locomotives based at Guildford. It was common practice for family members in poor circles to share a bed in those days. Nan didn't have a bathroom and after tea on a Friday an ancient tin bath was filled with hot water and I'd receive my weekly scrub in front of the open kitchen fire.

I was later at home alone with Mum and Dad at 'Donibee' in Ashdene Road, but I knew no loneliness as a typically grubby urchin in short trousers with scarred legs and bruised knees, the legacy of endless games of football and cricket in the roads of the estate and on the local rec – not to mention the occasional punch-up.

Those fights could get a bit tasty, and I both dished out and suffered my fair share of bloody noses. I was well-built but just average height, I wasn't a bully and I never backed down in the face of a bigger boy. If trouble came looking for me, it wasn't in my nature to run.

Out of school, a rolling mob of us played in the fresh air until it got too dark to see the ball properly. The score might be ridiculous, something like 12-all, someone would suggest: 'Next goal wins', and then we'd all have a big ruck when the ball brushed a jumper, acting as a makeshift goalpost, arguing the toss over whether it counted as a legitimate in-off-the-post winner or whether the ball would have bounced out off a proper wooden upright. I would be fairly vocal, even then, because winning mattered to me, not that any of us would remember the result in the morning, of course. Whether or not the issue was resolved to general satisfaction, it was then a case of straight home, tea, bath and bed.

We lived in a plain, two-bedroomed upstairs flat with a combined sitting room-cum-kitchen and a bathroom. Rationing was still evident and Mum frequently entrusted me with the ration book to run down to the butcher's for a nice piece of liver or a bunch of sausages. I didn't have any favourite meals because there wasn't the variety to pick and choose. You simply ate what was put in front of you and were grateful for it, no nonsense.

I already attended Yeoman's Bridge Secondary School before Mum and Dad could afford to take a week off work and we enjoyed a family holiday for the first time in a caravan at Hayling Island, near Portsmouth. Before that, the highlight of summer was our communal trip from the estate by charabanc to the seaside on the south coast at Littlehampton, Bognor Regis or Southsea. Assorted families gathered early in the morning on the Longacre, chattering excitedly and clutching their rugs, Thermos flasks and sandwiches in brown paper bags. There must have been some Saturdays and Sundays when the weather was less than perfect and the parents glanced nervously skywards to grey clouds, but my only recollection is sunshine, lots and lots of lovely sunshine.

On arrival at our chosen destination, there would be a mad scramble among the kids to be first on the sand, staking territorial rights to a bit of beach for the day with a towel before wriggling into a pair of bathing trunks and hurtling into the sea.

After tea, tired but happy, despite the inevitable sunburn, our journey home would be broken by a stop at a roadside pub with an appropriate garden to shake the sand from our shoes. The thirsty men would disappear inside for a pint or two of Gale's Best Bitter, the mums would have a well-earned port and lemon, while the kids stayed outside – the fortunate among us with a bottle of pop and a bag of crisps. Everyone was in an even better mood after that and the singing on the coach commenced . . . 'Roll Out the Barrel' was a favourite as we rolled home.

If only I had succeeded in staying outside boozers in later life, particularly after I hung up my boots, I would have been spared considerable grief, financial meltdown and no little shame.

My formal education was a bit of a disaster and I was disorientated from the start. Due to some quirk in the system, having a 7 September birthday meant I didn't go to Heathcote Memorial Junior School until I was nearly six years old, along with a cousin who was eight months younger than me. I'm convinced that wouldn't have represented too much of an obstacle, given time, but then I was locked into this crazy pattern which continued at Yeoman's Bridge, where I seemed to spend two years in a higher class or two years at the same level. Nobody seemed to have a clue where I should be. As I wasn't academically inclined, it left me either floundering hopelessly out of my depth trying to play catch-up or bored stiff, praying for the bell to ring and signal morning break or lunchtime when I could leave everyone in no doubt about where my talents lay, with the ball at my feet on the unforgiving playground concrete following another successful thumping challenge.

At least I had the satisfaction of knowing I was in the same boat as two other boys. Little Graham Hanford's birthday was 6 September while Jimmy Smith, a great big chap, was born on 8 September. Inevitably, the three of us – unwise monkeys – sat hunched together and muddled through as best we could.

Still, I was lucky to attend Yeoman's Bridge because all the teachers seemed to be sports-mad and there was no pressure at all to do well in my studies.

Dad worked hard and always seemed to be busy; he was often out of the house by 7 a.m. and I never saw him again until six o'clock in the evening. Sometimes during the football season he would take me on the bus to go and watch Aldershot in the Fourth Division, against the likes of Bradford Park Avenue, Crystal Palace and Millwall, standing on the terraces underneath the iron roof behind the goal at the Recreation Ground.

But I was never happier than when playing football myself.

CHAPTER TWO

North Bank boy

My fledgling football career was soon up and running, and Mum and Dad proudly maintained a scrapbook of my progress from the representative schoolboy stuff through to my formative years as a professional. The cuttings have yellowed with age but they jog a few happy memories whenever I choose to revisit those muddy winters of dubbined boots, cork studs and heavy leather footballs of the late 1950s.

The competition came thick and fast from the day I made my debut as a wet-behind-the-ears Under-11 for the Aldershot and Farnborough Schools FA, where I had the great good fortune to be trained by the highly enthusiastic Charlie Mortimore, the former England Amateur international centre-forward who also played for Aldershot and Woking before becoming a games master at the local Cove Secondary School. Charlie became a local legend in 1950 when he scored five goals for the Shots in a 7–2 away win at Orient. His brother, John Mortimore, wore Chelsea's colours before going on to manage Portsmouth and later enjoyed tremendous success out in Portugal as the Benfica coach.

I soon established myself at right-back as a powerful tackler with a 'they-shall-not-pass' mentality when it came to opposing wingers. I became quite adept at penalty-taking much later in my career but chanced upon my first recorded miss in my parents' big blue book when we beat St Pancras 2–1 after extra-time to reach the third round of the London Schools Sun Shield.

The local reporter went under the pseudonym of 'Phoenix' and informed readers of the *Aldershot and Farnborough News*:

TRUE STOREY

The boys missed a penalty when the visiting goalkeeper Lyons, a giant 13 year old, made a save from Storey's spot-kick after Wolfenden had been guilty of handling the ball to stop a shot from Arnott.

I can't remember how impressionable we were back then in those simple days, but it's a good thing we weren't particularly sensitive because while he could be wonderfully biased in our favour, the mysterious 'Phoenix' didn't pull many punches when we failed to impress him. He had a love–hate relationship with our prolific centre-forward Ron Wilks, who scored over a hundred goals one season, and reported after another victory:

> Wilks, in the middle, although he scored both goals, was not up to his usual form, and he often shot weakly. He hit the framework of the goal on a couple of occasions too with shots that could have beaten the goalkeeper. The whole Aldershot and Farnborough side played well, and team manager Charles Mortimore had every reason to be proud of them. But he was still critical at the end. 'Disappointing' was his comment. He meant they should have scored more goals.

Fair-haired Ron's proudest moment came complete with the headline 'Young Ron Gets The Lot As Spurs Totter' after we beat Tottenham Schoolboys 5–1 to reach the semi-finals of the London Under-14s Charity Cup. My part in the proceedings merited this snippet: 'A second star of the match was centre-half Peter Storey. He played an exceptionally strong game and will fit like a glove into next year's Under-15 centre-half berth.'

Bashing Tottenham was just the sort of result I would come to relish, and we went on to beat East Ham in the final. That was a fantastic achievement because east London has always been a fertile breeding ground for hungry young footballers, right up with Merseyside, the north-east and Manchester. Mind you, my appetite for success was substantial.

The Mortimores, with their Chelsea connections, did their level best to steer me towards Stamford Bridge. John took some of us a couple of times to see First Division matches at Chelsea, where manager Ted Drake had won the First Division championship in 1955 with his team dubbed 'Drake's Ducklings'.

Now Jimmy Greaves, Terry Venables, Peter Bonetti, Bobby Tambling and Peter Brabrook were beginning to emerge as their new bright young things but Chelsea's best efforts to turn me into a Blue were in vain, because all I wanted to do was play for Arsenal from the moment I first set foot on the North Bank.

The morning of one of our visits had been spent in north London playing for Aldershot and Farnborough, and our treat after lunch was to visit Highbury to see the Gunners entertain a Wolves side featuring the legendary Billy Wright, later to be my boss, and Eddie Clamp. From the famous terraces, I could almost reach out and touch my boyhood hero, Jack Kelsey, the Arsenal and Wales goalkeeper.

The match on Saturday, 23 March 1957 was no classic, a 0–0 stalemate, but Wolves were still a big draw and I stood in a crowd of 51,021 as an impressionable 11 year old to see Arsenal take on the side which had won the First Division championship three years earlier. I was captivated from that day and fell in love with the club. Fortunately, it wasn't long before they took a shine to me too.

I was playing at centre-half for Aldershot schoolboys when Arsenal scout Alf Faulkner got to hear about me. He watched me several times, then came to see Mum and Dad one night. I was virtually 'on a promise' to the club from that evening, although it would be some time before I was asked to become an apprentice professional.

The following term 'Phoenix' penned the words beneath my first personal headline, and 'Busy week for Peter Storey' did scant justice to the excitement felt in our household as we read:

> It's been a busy week for Peter Storey, centre-half of the Aldershot and Farnborough Schools Under-15 team, who comes from Yeoman's Bridge School at Ash. He's fitted two big trials into one week.
>
> On Tuesday he went down to Portsmouth for one of the Hampshire Schools final trials, and yesterday he was off to Tottenham for the final trial before the London Schools FA side is picked.
>
> Peter was centre-half for the Hampshire trials and left-back for the London trial. If he is picked for London, it will be a terrific honour for the district, because the London boys are chosen from a district ranging from Aldershot, Colchester and Brighton, as well as the City itself.

TRUE STOREY

If he gets his place, he will be the first boy from the Association to play for London since Salesian College boy Rankine about ten years ago. London's first match will be against Manchester under floodlights at the Spurs' ground next month.

The London trial went well and I didn't feel the slightest inferiority complex coming in from 'the sticks' to compete for my place against boys who appeared to me to be slightly flash and certainly more streetwise. Of course, I had the confidence of knowing Arsenal already fancied me.

Even before I could shave, I was carving out a reputation as a solid, dependable player with a touch of versatility. I think the scouts liked the idea I could perform in either of the full-back shirts and also at centre-half.

The London schoolboys selectors had strange ideas about bringing the best out of us. They threw us straight in at the deep end with practice matches against Tottenham and Arsenal Juniors, where we were outclassed to the tune of 9–0 and 8–1.

Despite that hammering at Highbury, I obviously did enough to merit further attention. A letter duly arrived informing me I had been picked to play at left-back for London against Manchester in the autumn of 1960. It was an annual inter-city fixture for the Alf Clarke Cup, but I didn't get the opportunity then to shine under those promised floodlights at White Hart Lane.

The occasion was very special, as Mum and Dad joined a coachload of local supporters who travelled up to the match specifically to cheer me on. It was staged on a Saturday afternoon in the end, 22 October, rather than a midweek evening, because Spurs called off their First Division fixture against Cardiff City when it coincided with a Wales–Scotland full international.

'Phoenix' reported:

> Storey gave a stable display at left-back throughout and although London beat Manchester 6–1 and had the best of the play, Peter played capably and in typically unruffled manner. League secretary, Mr Walter Payne, who watched the game, said: 'Peter's heading and clearances were all constructive and he played well in this class of football.'

My schoolwork at Yeoman's Bridge might have been distinctly average, but I was gaining glowing reports by the week for the work I put in on the pitch. A pleasant careers officer asked me what I hoped to do when I left school. She was taken aback when I replied simply: 'I'm going to be a professional footballer with Arsenal', and went away to ask the teachers if they were aware of my grandiose plans.

I had a good engine and my sporting prowess extended to cross-country and middle-distance running, setting a record at the Guildford Schools' Athletic Association championships with a time of 58.2 seconds to win the boys' 440 yards for 13 to 15 year olds. After that, it didn't seem like two minutes before I was caught up in the process of trying to win a place in the England Schoolboys team, where I came into contact with several other likely lads who were to progress to the professional ranks with varying degrees of success.

Ilford was the scene of my first international trial on 11 February 1961, and now scouts from professional clubs other than Arsenal were beginning to take a serious interest. My local club, Aldershot, were too honest and above board for their own good, however.

Tapping up young players may be frowned upon, but it has always gone on, and always will. Here I was, right on their doorstep, and there were ample opportunities for the Shots to 'have a little word' with my dad, but nothing ever materialised. When Aldershot and Farnborough Under-15s beat Southampton 1–0, my citation in the report ran: 'Storey was the better of two commanding centre-halves. Cool, resourceful and with a shrewd footballing brain, he initiated attacks and moved forward to thrust them home at times.'

The reporter may briefly have sensed he was on to a scoop, but he was to be disappointed, informing readers: 'Watching the game was Mr Dave Smith, Aldershot Town manager, and Mr J Sirrell, the pros' trainer. Asked if he had any particular player in mind, Mr Smith said: "No, I'm just watching another football match."' If I had caught his eye, Smith was giving nothing away. His right-hand man became much better known as a manager in his own right – Jimmy Sirrell of Notts County.

Soon afterwards, the local paper revealed: 'Peter's prospects look bright because Arsenal have already approached him with the suggestion that he should join them when he leaves school,' before adding, rather pointedly, 'but he has not yet heard from Aldershot FC.'

That brought an immediate stinging rebuke from the Recreation Ground, and an apology under the headline: 'Peter Will Have To

TRUE STOREY

Wait Awhile', as Dave Smith argued his corner. Readers learned:

> Our article last week about Peter Storey's prospects as a professional footballer following his selection for an England international football trial has caused a bit of a rumpus. Mistaking genuine interest by Arsenal FC, Peter's family informed us that he had been 'approached' by the club, and our report asked why no similar approach had been made by Aldershot FC.
>
> Aldershot manager, Dave Smith, has been quick to point out that while Peter is at school no official approach can be made to him under FA rules by any club. He contacted Arsenal, who suggest that Peter's family may have been confused by the interest shown in the boy when he played in a London schoolboys' team in a private trial against the Arsenal Juniors at Highbury. It looks as if the story was a bit premature, but at least Peter can expect a call from the local club as soon as he leaves school.

I recall in the mid-'70s at Highbury when I was injured or suspended and training on my own, the chief scout Ernie Collett appeared with this tiny young chap and his father after giving them the grand tour of the ground. 'This,' Ernie told me proudly, 'is Kenny Sansom. He plays full-back and when he leaves school he will be joining us at Arsenal next season.' I greeted the kid, told him he could not be joining a better club and indulged in some light-hearted banter about kicking him all the way back to his home in Camberwell if he ever tried to nick my place in the team. A few days later I watched Kenny playing for England Schoolboys at Wembley, confident in the knowledge that Arsenal had recruited a right good 'un when, lo and behold, he turned up signing for Malcolm Allison at Crystal Palace. There was some money flying about at Palace and they boasted about becoming the team of the '80s, but it never materialised. Kenny did end up at Arsenal, but not until 1980, and by then he was worth £1 million.

Back on the England Schoolboys beat in 1961, I played for the South versus the North at the Bourneville Cadbury's ground in Birmingham in a trial match on 4 March and, finally, for England against The Rest at the Baseball Ground, Derby a fortnight later.

I was, frankly, left open-mouthed when I compared what I had to offer with the skills flaunted by John Sissons. The world-famous

England and West Ham United golden boy was, of course, Bobby Moore but I would happily have wagered my pocket money on Sissons becoming the ultimate hero at Upton Park. Here was a little left-winger with a great shot, incredible pace, the whole package. John, with his lovely blond hair, was born in the same month as me, not a million miles away in Hayes, and certainly looked the business for Middlesex whenever I came up against him at county level.

The London football scene in the early 1960s was buzzing with stories about 'The Boy' and how there was nothing he couldn't do. Consequently, there was fierce competition for his signature and the West Ham manager Ron Greenwood nearly got into serious trouble when the club pounced to get his name on a contract the moment John was old enough.

The Hammers' famous chief scout Wally St Pier had been tracking Sissons for ages, as had a good many other clubs, but this sort of 'homework' was strictly against Football Association rules, and when a newspaper tale of the coup leaked out, Ron had to pull off some nifty footwork to escape the hot water at Lancaster Gate.

It was no surprise when Sissons took his First Division bow in 1963 before making a little bit of football history the following year as the youngest scorer in an FA Cup final when West Ham beat Preston North End 3–2 at Wembley. Coincidentally, that afternoon Preston included Howard Kendall, the youngest player to appear in the final and a future opponent who tested me to the limit.

Mind you, the authorities wouldn't have been very impressed had they discovered what Sissons did with his allocation of 20 Cup final tickets. He once confided they found their way onto the black market via the notorious ticket tout Stan Flashman for something like £600, and John bought himself a Morris 1100 with the readies. He always worried Greenwood would rumble where the money for that car came from.

Fame didn't last, however, and Sissons simply seemed to fade away in a succession of moves to Sheffield Wednesday, Norwich and Chelsea, where he called it a day in 1975, aged just 30. The last I heard of him, he was living in South Africa. I once heard John explain, rather sadly I felt, that he didn't think he really fulfilled his enormous potential because he'd had too much, too young. By the time he was 18, he'd won the FA Youth Cup, the FA Cup and the European Cup Winners' Cup at Wembley with a 2–0 victory over TSV Munich 1860 in successive seasons. Lucky beggar. Wembley was a graveyard for my ambitions before my luck turned. Success may have come too early for him, but that was never going to be a problem for me.

I had covered myself with mud and sweat getting into the England reckoning but not much glory, and that's always been a tiny regret. There was nobody to blame but myself, though. Everything had progressed smoothly until the crunch came. In the South side, I partnered David Sadler, a nice lad from Maidstone on his way to Manchester United. Playing at centre-half, I got the better of the North's centre-forward Glyn Pardoe, who was destined to become a quality defender at Manchester City. In the final trial match at Derby, however, I had a poor match for England against The Rest, simple as that, and consequently wasn't selected to play in the opening international on 24 March 1961 against Wales at Vetch Field, where England won 7–3 for the Victory Shield.

Howard Kendall was my room-mate in Swansea and we talked long into the night about what the future might hold in store. It was common knowledge among the team that we were virtually all spoken for, we knew which clubs we were going to. Howard might not have slept so soundly then had he known how I would be obliged to try and snuff him out by fair means or foul after he left Preston North End and developed into a player I admired enormously at Everton.

Still, I punched the air with delight – and more than a little relief – the morning an embossed envelope dropped through our letterbox in Ash containing the news that I had been picked to represent England Schoolboys in their next match against the Republic of Ireland at Coventry on 8 April.

My abiding recollection of that afternoon at Highfield Road is being literally sick with nerves before the kick-off. I shouldn't have been feeling apprehensive at coming in to replace Barking's John Sainty because the Irish lads weren't very good and we beat them 8–0. It was still frightening stuff for a kid, pulling on that famous white shirt for the first time to represent your country, but I was to grow to love the feeling with a passion a decade later when Sir Alf Ramsey brought me in to play with the 'big boys'.

Afterwards, the Mayor of Coventry presented me with my England cap and our local paper reported: 'Peter was not over-taxed and played a cool and useful game.'

I was hugely excited in the days that followed as I looked forward to accompanying England on what was an extremely rare event in those days. In fact, I believe the plane trip for an away fixture in Germany was the maiden flight by an England Schoolboys team.

We were all naïve young lads flying out from London Airport (better known now as Heathrow), and there was fun and games in our dormitory on the first night in Düsseldorf, where we encountered duvets for the first time. To boys used to sleeping at home under traditional sheets and blankets, this newfangled continental bedding was head-scratching stuff. Just how were we supposed to deal with it? Eventually, the general consensus was that the duvets were simply Europe's answer to the sleeping bags several of us were familiar with as boy scouts, so we found a way of opening them up at one end and sleeping inside them.

I was changed and ready if needed to tackle the Germans 30 miles away from Düsseldorf in Hagen. But the call never came to remove my tracksuit. I hated that; I always wanted to play. But I couldn't complain because England pulled off an excellent 3–1 win.

Next up was a trip to Roker Park, Sunderland for a match with Scotland on 22 April, and more frustration as I was again held in reserve as England slipped up for once and lost 3–2, but then I sampled the delights of Wembley Stadium for the first time against Wales in a comfortable 8–1 win the following Saturday as a replacement for the England right-half, who was injured with a quarter of an hour to go. I would experience action beneath those Twin Towers on many occasions in the future, with more grief than glory.

On this occasion, 'Phoenix' faithfully recorded:

> Peter quickly blended with the side and gave a good display. When the final whistle sounded, he was making some shrewd forward passes and every one of the 350 boys from Aldershot and District schools who were in the vast Wembley crowd wished fervently that he had been playing for the whole match.

CHAPTER THREE

A proper shift

The best china came out, Mum baked a cake, my hair was neatly parted and I was grinning from ear to ear. The scenario meant only one thing: I was poised to be offered a job by Arsenal.

George Male arrived in time for afternoon tea, took off his hat and coat, ruffled my hair on his way into our lounge and plonked himself down in an armchair.

I only really knew him as one of the club's scouts, but Dad had regaled me with stories of his exploits as a Gunners legend of the 1930s and former club captain.

The grown-ups indulged in some general chit-chat before George turned to me and asked casually: 'You would still like to join us at the Arsenal, wouldn't you, Peter?'

I blushed, almost choked and spluttered out words to the effect: 'Of course,' and Mr Male, as he always was to me, told us when we might all be expected at Highbury to complete the formalities.

I left school, aged 15, at the start of the Easter holidays and went up to London with Mum and Dad by train the following day to sign. It wasn't the sort of thing the manager George Swindin concerned himself with, and after the official business was concluded in a matter of minutes, Mr Male took us to a nearby pub for lunch, nothing fancy. Just steak and chips all round, and a glass of Tizer in my case.

As an apprentice professional, I was to receive the standard £7 a week with bonuses. I liked the sound of that.

We travelled home, my parents as proud as punch, me with a big soppy grin on my face and a £20 signing-on fee which was heading straight into my newly opened bank account.

A PROPER SHIFT

'Storey Has Signed For Arsenal' reported the *Aldershot and Farnborough News*, which revealed:

> There need be no more speculation about the future of Peter Storey, the 15-year-old footballer from Ash, who last year captained Hampshire Schools and played for the England Schools side against Ireland at Coventry. He has signed professional forms for Arsenal. Among the other clubs keen to sign Peter were Tottenham, Chelsea, Southampton and Luton, but his father, Mr E Storey, a local builder, said: 'Arsenal had always been Peter's favourite team and I think he is doing the right thing. He has always wanted to be a professional footballer.'

I was soon being paid for nothing before a letter arrived informing me precisely when and where to report for my first taste of proper pre-season training in July.

The routine was simple: my alarm clock sounded at 6.30 a.m., breakfast consisted of tea and toast, then Dad drove me to the railway station in his old banger of an Austin Jowett in time for me to catch the train from Aldershot. Once at Waterloo, it was three stops on the Northern Line tube to Leicester Square followed by seven on the Piccadilly Line to the Arsenal Underground station and at 9 a.m. the bus left Highbury for London Colney to clock on for training at 10 a.m. Commuting would have been a costly business, but the club bought me a British Rail season ticket.

Cricket was all the rage in the summer of 1961 when I started work for Arsenal, running my nuts off on 10-mile pre-season training stints around the Hertfordshire countryside while Fred Trueman was running through the Australians during a gripping Ashes series. Despite his wicket-taking heroics, our national treasure couldn't prevent a 2–1 home defeat, while I couldn't avoid the odd blister or two. My discomfort was temporary, but Fiery Fred must have been severely pained at dismissing 11 Aussies in England's solitary victory on his familiar stomping ground at Leeds, only to be dropped for the final Test.

I was one of half-a-dozen new boys pushed straight into the deep end under Arsenal's two coaches, Ernie Collett and Alf Fields. The *News* reported: 'When the season starts Peter will only train in the morning. His afternoons will be spent learning the electrical trade

– one of the terms of his contract.' Someone had sold the reporter a dummy because when the season started nothing was further from the truth and nothing was further from my mind than becoming an electrician. To be fair, the notion in the game at the time was that professional clubs should offer their apprentices the chance to learn a trade or continue their education at college.

That prospect, certainly at Arsenal, was laughable. Deep down, I'm sure we all possessed a total belief that we were going to make it as professionals. The club weren't remotely interested in furthering our education; the coaches only wanted to see us developing our skills on the pitch. If any of us had gone to college in the afternoons or started to learn to become electricians, plumbers or bricklayers, it would have been taken as a huge sign of weakness, an indication that the individual did not have enough confidence in his ability to make it as a footballer.

Tales of apprentices cleaning the professionals' muddy boots, sweeping the dressing room, painting and decorating, and performing other menial tasks did not apply at Arsenal Football Club. I was pleasantly surprised to discover the club employed a kit manager whose job entailed laying out the day's requirements for each and every player at London Colney, from the superstar of his day, England international inside-forward George Eastham, to the lowest of the low – me.

The training was very hard at first. I was a fresh-faced kid straight from school and what struck me immediately was not the big-name first-team stars, but the youth-team lads who had already been at the club a couple of years: just how much better they were than me. I was a boy in stature, but they had already bulked up, filled out into men, and some of them looked very good players.

I had a momentary crisis of confidence before pulling myself together and reassuring myself that I wouldn't be here if Arsenal weren't confident I had potential.

I was swiftly branded 'Snouty', a nickname which stuck with me throughout my career. It had nothing whatsoever to do with tobacco or cigarettes, but everything to do with David Court, a talented, confident inside-forward who was a year older than me. Court was chatting to a couple of the other apprentices when I bowled up, enquiring: 'What's up, lads?' only to be told light-heartedly by Court to 'keep my snout out'. That was it, I turned up for work the next day to be greeted by Court loudly proclaiming: 'Here he is, old Snouty!' and that was me marked for life.

A PROPER SHIFT

George Swindin never interfered with the training routine and I seem to think we never saw a football until pre-season had been underway for a few weeks. Instead, those 10-mile runs seemed to be the preferred option of Ernie and Alf. About noon, after a warmdown, we'd shower before pouring into the canteen for meat and two veg, followed by what I'd describe as a 'proper pudding'. Forty years later, Arsène Wenger established a strict dietary regime at the club with mineral water, pasta, grilled chicken, steamed fish and lashings of salad, fruit and veg the preferred order of the day.

My favourite meal at London Colney comprised lamb chops, chips and peas with fruit crumble and custard, washed down with a big mug of strong tea. After lunch there was always time to let your meal digest, which was probably just as well in my case, and relax over a game of snooker, darts or table tennis. A few of the lads studied the racing pages but there weren't any card schools. That potential for a gambling vice didn't arrive on the scene until a few decades later, and was to impact very badly on several careers.

The afternoon training session at 2 p.m. consisted of the short stuff – sprinting and exercises – before Ernie and Alf called it a day at 3.30 p.m. The first team drove home to the suburbs in their smart cars, while the rest of us hauled our weary limbs onto the bus going back to Highbury.

Nobody much knew who I was, while I did my best not to appear too star-struck or gawp at the likes of a couple of Welsh World Cup players from the 1958 finals.

Mel Charles, a big signing from Swansea for £40,000, was brilliant in the air but suffered from dodgy knees and was not as good as his brother, the legendary John Charles. Mind you, who was?

My hero, Jack Kelsey, was still in goal and I was particularly pleased to discover he was a nice fella into the bargain. Sadly, Jack suffered a nasty back injury in November 1962 and never played again.

Terry Neill had got into the first team at a very young age and was holding down a place, while perhaps the biggest name of all was Eastham. Exceptional on the ball, yet very frail, his nickname was 'Corky' and he was aloof, rarely mixing with the younger players. Leeds United were about to impose their rough-house tactics on the First Division, the game was changing and Eastham's days at Arsenal were numbered.

Meanwhile, back on the train home to Aldershot, I closely followed the fortunes of Fred Trueman and England, picking up a discarded copy of the *London Evening News* or *Standard* to catch up on the latest sports news. I loved the way he knocked over batsmen like a force of nature, a destructive genius. I know a bit about stopping opponents and dumping them on their backsides but, hand on heart, I don't recall anyone ever sticking the label 'genius' on me.

I always wished I had Fiery Fred's flair, but even at 15 I sensed that if I were to make my living as a professional sportsman, I would have to make the most of other less eye-catching virtues I could bring to the party, such as reliability, versatility and being a first-class team player.

At close of play that summer, Trueman was probably relaxing with a smoke over a pint or two of bitter. I got home, had my tea and maybe watched a bit of *Dixon of Dock Green* on the telly, Honor Blackman in *The Avengers* – she was lovely – or a comedy series featuring Tony Hancock and Sid James, before collapsing into bed in a state of complete and utter exhaustion. I slept like a baby because I knew I'd done an honest day's work, put in a proper shift and I'd rather die than let myself down on the training pitch the following morning.

Saturday afternoons were to become the most important day in my life, but for now I was too tired to do much more than lounge on the sofa watching a bit of cricket and tennis. There was no question of me gadding out and about on the estate until all hours, flaunting myself as the 'Big I Am'. I wasn't one to use my status to impress the local girls.

Yes, I was an apprentice at Arsenal – the best club in the football world as far as I was concerned – but I'd only just started out in the game and, in any case, that sort of boasting and bragging wasn't in my nature.

CHAPTER FOUR

Real pukka job

The urgent talk among Arsenal's senior professionals as the start of the 1961–62 season drew closer revolved around how they had to try and close the gap on neighbours and traditional rivals Tottenham Hotspur. The 'enemy' were being fêted all around town, and throughout England for that matter, as the first club in the twentieth century to pull off the Football League and FA Cup Double.

Our traditional eve-of-season official team photograph must have consisted of 50-odd faces, the club's entire playing staff for the campaign. These days the biggest Premier League clubs seem to me to have a first-team squad alone pushing 50, and that's ridiculous. How on earth do the clubs justify such excess? How can the players all earn their money?

I discovered volleyball for the first time and enjoyed being a defender of a slightly different kind, jumping at the net to block opponents' attempts to smash a point. The physical movement may have been different from football, but the principle was the same – they shall not pass.

The five-a-sides were good fun too, then suddenly my energy was channelled into South East Counties League action on Saturday mornings, when I first played in the same youth team as Peter Simpson and Jon Sammels.

Peter became known to all of us simply as 'Stan' – a reference to the quieter member of Laurel and Hardy. The joke doing the rounds was that our Stan was so laidback he often needed waking up for the second half. In reality, he might have been a gentle soul from Norfolk, but he was always alert to any danger.

It was the start of a friendship which has lasted over forty years, and a partnership which saw the three of us feature in a few epic Arsenal achievements, but also several days of intense disappointment.

Jimmy Bloomfield's nephew Ray was another member of the youth team, although he never made the grade – and was to become the victim of a desperately harsh departure from the club which shocked everybody who witnessed it.

I settled in at full-back, carefully heeding the advice and little tips from Alf Fields to 'tuck in there' and 'get tighter' to forwards wearing the colours of such clubs as Tottenham, West Ham and Chelsea, where John Hollins was beginning to make a name for himself. I liked Alf; he knew what he was talking about. A nice fella from Canning Town, he didn't need to rant or rave to put his point across. I always respected that.

Keith Weller was with us too, playing a few games as an amateur, but he soon left for a tour of the capital in the colours of Tottenham, Millwall and Chelsea before enjoying his best times at Leicester City. Little did we know it then, but we were to have some rare old battles against each other.

The Hammers boasted my friend John Sissons in their ranks, but not for very long. He progressed very quickly. In fact, his rise to join the likes of Bobby Moore and Geoff Hurst in the first team at Upton Park was positively meteoric.

I found my feet fairly quickly and it wasn't long before I got a little taste of action in the reserves alongside goalkeeper Bob Wilson and Geordie Armstrong, two characters destined to become Highbury legends.

My £7 a week seemed to go a long way even after I had shelled out 30 bob to Mum and Dad for bed and board. The £1 for a win was literally a welcome bonus, and we never turned up our noses either at the 10 shillings on offer for a draw. All my travelling costs were met by the club and living at home meant I didn't exactly lead a riotous lifestyle.

Several of the other youngsters were in digs around Islington and found plenty of diversions to spend their money on, but I didn't really socialise and neither was I jealous when they related their tales of squiring young ladies around town, drinking, nightclubs and dance halls. Maybe they thought I was a bit boring, but I was driven and my focus was crystal clear: nothing was going to deflect me from a career in professional football – and anything else could wait. As for girlfriends, they might just well have been on a different planet, although I would later make up for lost time quite spectacularly.

REAL PUKKA JOB

I was much more interested in chasing up news of the first team. For the big boys, the 1961–62 season would end with Alf Ramsey's Ipswich Town as champions and Arsenal in tenth place.

I can recall that the team was in trouble if Alan Skirton, Mel Charles and Geoff Strong didn't score. In fact, that trio accounted for 46 goals, while the rest of the squad mustered only 23 between them.

There were problems at the other end of the pitch as well and the campaign was only two months old before Tottenham – in front of 59,371 supporters at White Hart Lane – West Bromwich Albion and Everton had plundered four winning goals apiece against Jack Kelsey and his defence, while Leicester City had piled in another four in a draw at Highbury.

High-scoring matches were commonplace, the fans invariably got their money's worth, and the defensive jitters returned with a vengeance in spring. Despite Skirton and Strong both scoring twice, Aston Villa went back to the Midlands celebrating a 5–4 win, and a fortnight later Fulham pulled off a stunning 5–2 win at Craven Cottage, a result which ultimately helped them narrowly avoid relegation. That misfortune fell to Cardiff City and, interestingly, the club I might have joined, Chelsea.

The high spot of the campaign was undoubtedly a handsome 5–1 trouncing of Manchester United in front of a home crowd of 54,099 in October, courtesy of goals from Skirton (2), George Eastham, John Barnwell and the 'famous' Gerry Ward.

I say famous; well at least he was to me as someone to look up to, because eight years earlier Gerry had set a record as Arsenal's youngest-ever player when he made his debut against Huddersfield Town at 16 years and 322 days.

I was a similar age in May 1962, yet felt as if I was a million miles down the pecking order.

Gerry never really pushed on from his early promise, however, and was quietly shipped off down the road to Leyton Orient.

Arsenal were not the sort of club to tolerate mid-table mediocrity and that tenth place had followed finishes of thirteenth and eleventh in Swindin's previous two campaigns. It was all too much for him. He took some terrible stick and resigned.

The Glory, Glory days for Tottenham under manager Bill Nicholson continued, to a familiar reaction of frustration and depression at our place. Tottenham's Double heroes succeeded in adding another FA Cup final victory, 3–1 over Burnley this time, to their collection of silverware after they had been narrowly squeezed out of the European Cup in the semi-finals by Benfica, the eventual winners.

Suddenly, I was off on a little foreign adventure myself to Switzerland, near Lake Lausanne and the Italian border. It was only the second time I had been abroad. The club arranged my passport, and it was an excited group of Arsenal reserves and youth-team players who boarded the boat train from Victoria to Dover for an overnight Channel crossing, followed by the long trek by rail across France to our eventual destination.

Most of the group were older than me; I didn't play a single minute in a tournament featuring a couple of Italian teams. Any frustration was offset by the fact I knew Arsenal felt the experience would prove beneficial to me. I considered myself lucky just to be there, certainly more fortunate than other 16 year olds on the books who were stuck at home. And the ice cream and pasta were a bit special, too.

There was no *Sky Sports News* back in the summer of 1962 and I only discovered that Arsenal's new manager was the legendary Billy Wright one morning at breakfast when Dad casually passed me the *Daily Mirror* over tea and toast, and said: 'You might be interested in seeing who you're going to be working for now, son.' Interested? I was gripped.

Wright had been virtually the David Beckham of his day, winning shedloads of honours as skipper of Wolves and England, and then marrying Joy Beverley, the eldest of the three Beverley Sisters – who were almost the Spice Girls of their era. The appointment was a surprise because Billy was considered to be firmly entrenched at the Football Association, looking after the England youth set-up.

When we got down to business, Wright brought in Les Shannon from Everton as chief coach, but the real eye-opener came on 16 July when the club paid Torino £70,000 to bring England centre-forward Joe Baker home from Italy. It was a fantastic bit of business because Joe went on to plunder ninety-three goals for the Gunners in just three and a half seasons.

Baker's signing caused great excitement when the 1962–63 season kicked off with me down the ranks, not in the reserves but playing at right-back for the A team. The third team, we did our stuff in the Metropolitan League against semi-professionals, the reserves of such clubs as Dartford, Gravesend and Maidstone. We were teenagers, largely 17 and 18 year olds up against fully-grown men, and, physically, it was strong, testing competition with a fair bit of travelling to away matches thrown in for good measure.

REAL PUKKA JOB

I signed professional terms at Highbury on 28 September 1962 – precisely three weeks after my seventeenth birthday. I didn't often splash out and treat myself, but I knew that most of my £20 signing-on fee was going immediately on a very smart dark blue Crombie overcoat I'd had my eye on in a shop down the Seven Sisters Road. That coat was a real pukka job and lasted me for years. The Crombie was a little touch of luxury I thought I'd earned.

None of the pitches were that great, in truth, most of the grass having disappeared by October or November, but sometimes we attracted quite decent gates. I remember one match at Crawley Town in particular being watched by a big crowd. I was stuck in that A team for three years and can't recollect playing more than about fifteen matches for the reserves before making the huge leap into the first team.

The problem, as I saw it, was that Arsenal had quite a few experienced players on their books whom Wright was unsure of – so they were in the 'stiffs' and that meant a logjam, stalemate for me. I was basically at the same level for three seasons.

My circumstances did change off the field when the commuting between north Hampshire and north London became too much of a grind and I decided to cut the apron strings at home with Mum and Dad.

Mr Male found me comfortable digs in East Barnet, just off Cat Hill, where I kept my head down for a couple of years as the only lodger. My landlady in that little terrace house was a widow, who made good wholesome food, and I knocked about a bit with her son. I wasn't at all homesick, popping back to Ash every couple of months or so to keep Mum and Dad sweet.

There was something to savour on the pitch too when West Ham came calling for a fourth round tie in the 1963–64 Youth Cup. They were the holders and included nine of the team which had turned over Tommy Smith's Liverpool in the final, including Harry Redknapp and first-teamer Sissons. I was at left-back and recall enjoying my night against Harry as we came from a goal down to win 2–1.

As my social skills and confidence grew, I fancied 'living it up' a bit more and moved in first with Jon Sammels for a year in Enfield before sharing the bills with Terry Neill in his bachelor bungalow in Cockfosters.

My abiding memory of life with Sammy is going down to the local launderette for the first time and the mistake I bet every single bloke can remember making at least once in his life. Lumping all the darks and lights into the washing machine together, I confidently turned the dial like a seasoned practitioner before sitting down to read the sports pages of the *Daily Mirror*. Easy, this launderette lark, I thought. But I was soon blushing like a right pillock in front of some women struggling to suppress their laughter when I fished out my gear and discovered my 'whites' were now a fetching shade of pink – and all because of a cheap pair of red socks which had caught my eye on a local market stall. Pink shirts might be quite fashionable for men this century but, believe me, they were considered extremely effeminate back in the '60s. I made my second big mistake when I tried to get away with wearing one of my favourite white-cum-pink shirts to training. I was ribbed unmercifully and became the butt of some cruel jokes about changing my name to Mrs Sammels.

My abiding memory of life with Terry is us waking up on a Sunday morning and searching the fridge in vain for something, anything, to eat. We weren't the most diligent of shoppers, our Saturdays being otherwise occupied, and we indulged in a lot of banter about whose turn it was to venture out and get the grub in. Invariably, Terry talked me into it. The club captain was three years older, full of smooth Belfast brogue – to such an extent that he was sometimes mistaken for Arsenal's manager long before he took the job in 1976 – and if all else failed, Terry threatened me with eviction. Back then, you had more chance of flying to the moon on a Sunday than finding an open supermarket, so I became a regular at a welcome little Kosher butchers in Hampton Square, Southgate where I found some very tasty steaks to fill a gap and keep Terry sweet.

I sensed I might start growing as a player in January 1965 when Arsenal, in a rich vein of goals, prepared for an FA Cup fourth round tie at minnows Peterborough, who had only been a League club for five years.

Baker and John Radford had both hit a purple patch, having scored four goals apiece in the previous three matches which saw Arsenal beat Wolves 4–1, Sunderland 2–0 and Leicester 4–3.

Substitutes were yet to be introduced at this level in England and I was immensely proud to travel to London Road as our official first reserve, just in case of illness or a freak late injury when the team were warming up.

The tight little ground was buzzing with over 30,000 packed inside, and I shivered, sensing the threat of a giant-killing in the air that cold, crisp winter's afternoon.

REAL PUKKA JOB

I relaxed when Raddy opened the scoring, but there was a sniff of danger when the equaliser came from that charismatic Irishman Derek Dougan, who tormented our Scottish centre-half Ian Ure for 90 minutes, and we eventually slumped to a 2–1 defeat.

'Oh! How The Mighty Fell' and 'Posh's Greatest Day' were two of the Sunday back-page headlines, recording an Arsenal humiliation to rank alongside the infamous 1933 defeat by Third Division South side Walsall. Travelling back from Peterborough in a very subdued party of Gunners, I stared out of the train window into the darkness with a mixture of disappointment at the result and relief that my services had not been called upon.

I played a dozen times for the reserves in the Football Combination that season and sensed I was close to making the big step up after going on a club tour to Italy and playing once, against Latina.

I desperately wanted to be a winner when I made my first-team debut . . . but I was going to be out of luck on that score, too.

CHAPTER FIVE

Elland Road nutter

Billy Wright had been in charge for three years and I'd watched from afar as things had gone from bad to worse, waiting and wondering when my time would come.

I never knew whether it was the management or the board of directors who came up with the bright idea of a six-match pre-season tour to the West Indies in the summer of 1965. I'm sure the intention was honest enough, and maybe Arsenal thought a fortnight in the Caribbean sunshine would be good for team-bonding and that the dramatic change in scenery from slogging our guts out at London Colney would work like magic and transform the team into potential First Division champions.

I was a surprise choice in the 14-man squad, and Billy told the press: 'Peter is a fine prospect who has progressed rapidly since joining us from school in 1961. We have watched Storey come through from our youth side to the reserves. This trip will show how near he is to being ready for League football in the coming season.'

As an exercise in preparing us for the rigours of an English winter and the customary testing trips to northern strongholds such as Liverpool, Manchester United, Everton and now Leeds, I felt the jaunt was worse than useless, a fiasco, a complete shambles.

It was just the sort of laidback trip you expected for an end-of-season jolly and, rather than team-bonding, the time away merely served to emphasise the splits in the camp. On one hand, you could see the experienced professionals – led by Joe Baker and George Eastham – were becoming increasingly disillusioned and, not to put too fine a point on it, pissed off with the management. They didn't have much respect for Billy, who was hitting the bottle at that stage. And on the other hand, there was me among the ambitious young thrusters, and little common ground between the two sides that I could determine.

I can't recall doing a single proper day's training in the Caribbean as we played the hosts and Trinidad among other island sides in the Jamaican Independence Anniversary tournament and, to make matters worse personally, when I did shake a leg, I pulled a muscle and only played in the final game.

Instead, we were letting our hair down, sunbathing around the hotel pool, going to parties, while some of the more enthusiastic drinkers in the squad were getting Planters Rum Punch down their necks like it was going out of fashion. Alan Skirton, for one, thought he'd died and gone to heaven. Our dashing winger's nickname, 'The Fish', was highly appropriate – because he drank like one.

There was some football too, but even that degenerated into farce against Jamaica when Baker was sent off and sparked a riot. It had been getting a bit rough when our big blond Scottish centre-half Ian Ure got kicked in the cobblers and Joe suddenly wheeled round and clocked their giant defender, who had been giving him some grief.

Bottles rained down on the pitch, forcing us to run and hide in the dressing room and summon a police escort to get us safely back to our hotel.

To outsiders, it must have looked as if the tour had been a success as we arrived back in London from the West Indies, via New York, four days before the start of the 1965–66 season, having won five and drawn one of the friendlies. And there was optimism when Baker scored both goals in a 2–1 home win over Stoke City on 21 August in the opening game of the campaign.

Three months and fourteen matches into the First Division fixture list and the lads had half-a-dozen victories under their belts, including a handsome 4–2 win over Manchester United. I remember being thrilled watching the United game on 23 September in a massive Highbury crowd of 56,757, which turned out to be the biggest gate anywhere in the First Division that season.

Matt Busby's team were champions, having clinched the title in 1964–65 on goal average from Leeds after winning their final match 3–1 at our place, and United could boast a team including George Best, Bobby Charlton, Denis Law, Nobby Stiles and Paddy Crerand.

Now revenge was in the air and after Charlton opened the scoring for United, Arsenal hit back strongly with goals from Baker, John Radford and Geordie Armstrong. United's hopes flickered briefly when John Aston pulled one back, but Eastham had the last word with the final goal of the afternoon.

Wright was a proud man that day, but things took a turn for the worse the next month following a hefty 5–3 beating at Blackpool, then a 2–2 home draw against a very poor Blackburn Rovers side, who were to haunt us all season.

I'd been playing sometimes at left-back, as well as on the right, and I had an inclination that I was going to make my first-team debut at Leicester on 30 October even before Wright took me to one side just before the teamsheet went up on the Friday morning, and said with a friendly smile: 'I hope you're ready son, because you're playing tomorrow on the left.'

I feared my first full appearance for Arsenal in the number three shirt wouldn't go down too well with Ulsterman Billy McCullough, a Northern Ireland international who had been first choice in that position at the club for six years and was the most experienced player on the books after two hundred and fifty appearances. Being dropped always leaves a sour taste and it must have looked to the fans as if Wright was holding McCullough largely responsible for an inconsistent start to the season.

He might have taken badly to losing his place to a novice, but he winked, offered me a warm handshake and wished me the very best of luck. Looking back now, maybe McCullough thought he was well off out of it. His career was drawing to a close and in July he would pack his bags and head south of the Thames to Millwall.

The record books show my debut at Filbert Street resulted in a 3–1 defeat, and Leicester's right-winger Jackie Sinclair proved an awkward opponent. There were worries, of course, little nagging fears that the manager might have seen something too raw and inexperienced in me, and that I might be tossed back into the reserve team pool to continue my professional education at a less demanding level.

That Sunday the local newsagent back home in Ash enjoyed a bonanza as Mum and Dad bought an armful of papers to read all about their son's exploits and Mum, bless her, told the *Aldershot and Farnborough News*: 'He is football-mad, it's his whole life. We are, of course, very proud of him.'

John Thicknesse's report in one of the nationals contained an accurate snapshot of the future:

Storey showed he had just as much determination as McCullough and a touch more finesse. But there was one incident in the first half that put one much in mind of his predecessor, when he coldly barged Sinclair into touch with the ball long departed. Storey suffered the referee's strictures with all the pointed inattention of an old hand.

Radford Barrett, on behalf of the *Daily Telegraph*, ventured: 'Storey's first game for Arsenal was doubly tough because his opponent was clever and his own passing faulty, yet it was promising in its determination.'

Another journalist claimed I 'left two Foxes players requiring lengthy treatment after a couple of bone-shuddering challenges', but only my pop at Sinclair springs to mind.

My next two matches left a marked impression and taught me that football can be a cruel, unforgiving business.

When the final whistle blew on a resounding 6–2 pounding of Sheffield United at Highbury the following Saturday, I had a big fat grin plastered all over my mug. Joe Baker, Skirts and Geordie had each scored two goals and I knew that in a minute or so the dressing room would be full of good cheer, jokes and ribbing along with the discarded kit, mud, bandages and the smell of liniment as our scorers competed with each other to claim man-of-the-match bragging rights and argue who would be getting in the first of many rounds at the White Hart in Southgate that evening. I couldn't wait.

My sense of anticipation burst like a balloon when I walked in to find Wright, a supreme defender in his glorious playing days, giving Eastham the mother and father of all bollockings.

Eastham couldn't comprehend why he was being monstered by Wright for the visitors' second goal – as if it mattered in the immediate aftermath of a handsome home win, which turned out to be our best of the entire campaign. Eastham quickly deflected the blame, pointed at me and casually informed the manager: 'It wasn't down to me, it was him.' I just thought: 'Thanks a bunch, George', as Wright tore a strip off me. I was an easy target, a wet-behind-the-ears twenty year old with all of two matches under his belt, and I suffered the indignity in silence, thinking just how unwarranted this criticism was and, even if I had been to blame for us winning 'only' 6–2 instead of 6–1, then the manager should have a quiet word with me in the privacy of his office on Monday morning.

That was typical of Wright. Sometimes if the first team had lost, he would come in after the weekend and take it all out on the lads who had come through the youth team – such as Geordie, 'Sammy' Sammels, Raddy and myself, run us into the ground on the track. I thought behaviour like that was bizarre, not to say extremely unfair. We were made scapegoats.

Trouble behind the scenes was commonplace, with Baker and Frank McLintock frequently engaging in huge arguments with Wright after matches. The manager had spent big money on that pair – £80,000 to bring in Frank from Leicester – and also recruited Don Howe and goalkeeper Jim Furnell. He was under pressure to get results but things were deteriorating.

I didn't feel much like a pint to celebrate my first win bonus in the first team, although it wasn't long before I was warmly welcomed into the post-match routine. Our motto was 'Win or lose, on the booze . . . get a draw, have some more', but it was by no means exclusive to Arsenal. There was a drinking culture at the club but, as far as I was aware, it was exactly the same at virtually every other professional club in England. Eastham was another highly social animal, while 'the enemy' in the shape of Tottenham's barrel-chested Dave Mackay and Alan Gilzean were always welcome additions to our school at the bar.

Skirton used to lead the lads into action in the afternoon in a snooker hall in Southgate from which they were frequently nipping out to run across the road and place bets at the bookies. I didn't mind a frame or two to while away the hours after training, but gambling on the horses has never been a particular vice of mine. It never interested me. A quid on the Grand National and the Derby was as much as I would wager.

After a home match, we popped into the players' tea-room to stock up on solids and usually either Skirts, Baker, David Court or 'Fingers' Furnell would give me a lift to the White Hart, where the drinking would kick off at 6.30 p.m. Most of the senior players brought along two or three friends and hangers-on. Others knew it was an Arsenal pub and the place would be rammed by seven o'clock – especially after a favourable result – until last orders and closing time.

Once I'd got the satisfaction of the Sheffield United win and the bollocking from Billy Wright out of my system, my mind turned towards the next match – Leeds United away. I knew it would be tough, but nothing could have prepared me for the violence I encountered.

ELLAND ROAD NUTTER

We were already heading for a 2–0 defeat, the first time we'd failed to score all season, when Jim Storrie left me staggering over on the far touchline from the dugouts with the referee's attention elsewhere.

I'd been getting stuck in, of course, because it was in my nature and Storrie must have taken exception to the treatment or thought I'd kicked him because, without warning, the Scot suddenly wheeled round and stuck the nut on me above my right eye. I found out 'Diamond Jim', as he was known, hailed from Kirkintilloch – just outside Glasgow – and this was a typical 'Glasgow kiss' meted out down Sauchiehall Street at chucking-out time every Saturday night.

I had faced hard men before during my apprenticeship, but Storrie's assault shocked me as I reeled backwards, struggling to stay on my feet. It was the first time I'd ever been 'done' on the pitch like that, and a despicable act to my mind.

Back in the dressing room at full-time, the lads could see a red mark and bump developing on my forehead and asked what had caused it. I thought I might get a bit of sympathy when I explained what Storrie had done, but my teammates just thought the incident was hilarious and the cry went up: 'Welcome to Leeds, pal!'

The incident was an eye-opener as much as a potential eye-closer, and sparked a personal love–hate relationship with Leeds which persisted throughout my playing career. It was mutual – we loved to hate each other. I knew after that winter Saturday in November 1965 that I would always have to stand up and be counted against them, be ready, willing and able to fight my corner. Any show of weakness was out of the question. 'So that's the way it's got to be,' I quietly told myself.

Don Revie's unlovely team had been promoted in 1964 and, after being pipped at the post by Manchester United in 1965, were on their way to finishing runners-up again, this time behind Liverpool.

I considered them a very good side, although they didn't need much encouragement to put the boot in. For all their ball players, they were bully boys, a fairly brutal outfit. Leeds already had a reputation for playing dirty and were responsible for other clubs following their example in order to compete. A lot of teams copied them and, hands up, I became Arsenal's main hardman while Ron 'Chopper' Harris fully merited his nickname at Chelsea. It took a very brave or foolish opponent to cross swords with Tommy Smith at Liverpool, while Nobby Stiles was as tough as they came at Old Trafford. If Norman Hunter didn't get you at Elland Road, there was a fair chance Billy Bremner would, and there was always Johnny Giles and Jack Charlton to mop up. The faint-hearted had nowhere to hide and British football was no place for shrinking violets or players of a nervous disposition.

John Spurling tells a good tale in his fine book, *Rebels for the Cause*, after I'd put Hunter on his arse one time:

> When the Leeds man hauled himself off the floor, he nodded at Giles and Bremner, then at Storey. The Arsenal player was 'targeted' for the rest of the game, but Leeds' contract killers failed to destroy the man and Storey gave as good as he got. Even the Leeds hatchet man must have been quietly impressed.

But it was unquestionably Leeds who started the cult of the hardman, enthusiastically encouraged by Revie.

The funny thing is, I always had a grudging respect and admiration for them and maintain they could have been just as successful, maybe even more so, playing fair and square. Instead, they developed a nasty habit of finishing runners-up in all manner of competitions far too often, falling at the final hurdle time and again. Maybe that was fate, justice, call it what you will, catching up with them for being masters of the game's dark arts.

That record of just falling short must have nagged away like a disease if you were a Leeds United supporter, but the rest of the country's fans lapped it up because Revie's mob were widely reviled outside Yorkshire. They frequently overstepped the mark, notably when Big Jack came up for corners and stood on the opposing goalkeeper.

Then there was their verbal abuse, the sledging – they started all that too. At least Leeds were predictable in one sense. I always knew what I was in for when fixtures against them rolled around. Some of the Arsenal lads looked forward to Leeds with as much enthusiasm as root canal work at the dentist without gas, but they never frightened me. Rather, I licked my lips in anticipation. If they wanted to dish it out again, then I could take it and repay them with interest and a few digs of my own. It was a matter of pride and personal honour with me that I never took a backward step physically against them after the Storrie dust-up.

My clash with 'Diamond Jim' was the first in a succession of ugly incidents I found myself involved in against Leeds, including one occasion when skipper Bremner could have blinded me when he decided to tattoo my face with his studs as I went down in a muddy goalmouth at Elland Road.

ELLAND ROAD NUTTER

The strangest thing is that years later, once I got to know Hunter, Giles and Bremner, we were capable of leaving all the aggro and hatred on the pitch after 90 minutes. I could perpetuate the myth that I could never stand the sight of the Leeds trio, but it would be a lie. When you get to know somebody, it does change things a bit. I mixed with Norman on England duty and found him to be a really nice character, so after that it was not unnatural for us to mingle in the players' bar following a Leeds–Arsenal fixture and enjoy a couple of beers together. It was similar with Giles once we had played in the same team for The Three against The Six in January 1973, a match at Wembley to celebrate the entry of the new Common Market countries, and we got on well with one another.

Jimmy Robertson was to be a teammate at Highbury until 1970, and when he returned in Ipswich colours we had a right ding-dong trying to kick each other up in the air but afterwards we ended up in the pub, finishing a long session with our arms round each other's shoulders.

CHAPTER SIX

Wright and wrong

Tony Hateley and I clashed on the halfway line at Highbury and a mini-brawl erupted. I squared up to him, fists were raised in anger, punches were thrown, although none landed with any great force or accuracy. The referee Maurice Fussey sprinted over and told us to cut it out, that we were behaving like children. Red cards would certainly have been brandished today, but we escaped without so much as a caution before shaking hands, glaring at each other and going our separate ways.

December had kicked off with us trailing 3–1 at home to Aston Villa when I got involved in that ugly stuff with Hateley, their big centre-forward. He was extremely powerful in the air, as he demonstrated by climbing way above poor Terry Neill to head in Villa's opener, and I was pig-sick at the prospect of losing after playing Arsenal's former right-winger Johnny MacLeod right out of the picture. I was delighted that my afternoon ended on a positive note, however, as Alan Skirton scored two late goals to salvage a point.

Afterwards, one of the lads gave me a friendly dig in the ribs in the dressing room, congratulated me on standing up to Hateley and said: 'Never take any shit from anyone, son.' I replied: 'Don't worry, I won't.' I had not gone out of my way to cultivate an image as a hardman. Blimey, I was barely 20, but I didn't feel anybody had the right to take any liberties with me on the pitch.

The previous Tuesday night we had entertained Moscow Dynamo at the start of the Russian club's tour to mark the twentieth anniversary of their exploits in Britain. They built a mighty reputation here in 1945 after arriving as complete mystery men from behind the Iron Curtain to draw 3–3 with Chelsea at Stamford Bridge, crush Cardiff City 10–1, beat Arsenal 4–3 before drawing 2–2 with Rangers in Glasgow. The seven-goal thriller in thick fog against the Gunners, played at White Hart Lane because Highbury had been unavailable for football during the Second World War, has gone down in history as an epic.

Now Dynamo had a bitterly cold evening in north London to contend with, but it was our performance which warmed the crowd because we won 3–0. I had a busy game, and more than a little good fortune, managing to score our third goal in the eighty-seventh minute with a cross which their giant goalkeeper Romaz Urushadze allowed to trickle through his fingers, while one reporter related: 'Left-back Peter Storey, besides scoring a goal, did not give 23-cap veteran Ivan Chislenko a kick – except one on the ankle which led to a 77th-minute penalty. Then inside-right Gusarov sent it yards wide.'

You often learn through your own mistakes and I was taught a harsh lesson against Dynamo when I made the cardinal sin of attempting to dribble the ball out of our penalty area on one occasion only to be robbed by a Russian. The bollocking I got from the rest of our defence and Billy Wright was wholly justified.

Christmas 1965 brought a double-header with Sheffield Wednesday and mixed fortunes – a crushing 4–0 defeat at Hillsborough on a dog of a rock-hard, uneven surface, which would never pass a referee's pitch inspection these days, followed by a 5–2 home win over the Owls 24 hours later on a lovely pitch, courtesy of Highbury's undersoil heating. We bottled it in Sheffield, where my indiscretions were deemed worthy of the headline 'Storey is booked', in a report which went on to relate: 'Storey, the only man who looked worthy of wearing an Arsenal shirt, completed the London side's day of gloom when he had his name taken by referee Ken Stokes for a foul on Eustace.'

We were anything but a united team and I feared Billy might be losing the plot after a 1–0 home defeat by Liverpool, when he chose to reveal:

> The atmosphere in defeat was so tense that half of my players could have burst into tears at the drop of a bootlace and the other half would have cut your throat if you'd said the wrong thing. This is what I want. Men unable to accept defeat without a fight within themselves. This to me was a victory to Arsenal . . . even though we'd lost the match.

TRUE STOREY

Bogey team Blackburn resurfaced with a vengeance as our season threatened to go into terminal decline. Although they were by far the worst team in the First Division, relegated rock-bottom beneath one-season wonders Northampton Town, and some 16 points away from salvation, Rovers beat us 2–1 at Ewood Park. That was a nasty surprise, but nothing compared to the shock in store for Arsenal the following Saturday when we returned to Blackburn for an FA Cup third round tie and somehow succeeded in losing 3–0.

To my mind, this was another humiliation to rank alongside the previous season's disaster at Peterborough.

We limped into February, drawing 1–1 at home against Burnley, and now the manager was under pressure after dropping his big guns, Joe Baker and George Eastham, and packing them off to play for the reserves at Northampton. The fans were less than amused by this turn of events and unfurled a banner reading: 'Sack Wright and Hill-Wood – we want Joe and George.'

Baker was a really good player, a terrific goalscorer, and his disillusionment was such a shame. To my mind, he deserved to play in a better Arsenal team. He was great in several respects, to my eyes. Although he stood only 5 ft 7 in., he might have been tempted to lord it over all of us after arriving for that club record outlay of £70,000 as Wright's first signing, following a season spent playing alongside Denis Law for Torino in Italy. He was a celebrity, the supporters idolised him, but for all his aura, he carried no baggage and treated us youngsters as equals. And for that, we respected Joe even more, as he frequently gave a few of us a lift home to Southgate after training at Highbury.

I never had a moment's hesitation when it came to jumping in Joe's car, although we all knew the story of how he nearly died in Italy after wrecking his brand new Alfa Romeo sports car. His injuries were nearly fatal and he spent six weeks on a drip. I once plucked up the courage to ask him directly what had happened, but Joe just smiled and said: 'Never live in the past, son. Anyway, I know which side of the road to drive on here.' And with that, laughing like a maniac, he swerved elaborately into the right-hand carriageway and safely back again before we hit a big red double-decker London bus.

Small, quick and nimble, he played with a certain dash and swagger, popping off little one-twos with his clever feet, and looking to finish. He was better than Jermain Defoe is today, more in the mould of Carlos Tevez, and as quick-witted off the pitch as he was on it, always laughing and joking.

Joe was a rare bird. Born in Liverpool, he cultivated a strong Scottish accent while growing up in Motherwell before going on to win eight senior England caps. As an out-and-out goalscorer for Arsenal, his record was outstanding – 100 goals in 156 competitive matches for a poor team. The great pity is that he wasn't at the club a few years later, then he might have had something tangible to show for his efforts in the iconic red and white shirt. Joe's gone now, the result of a heart attack at a charity golf event in Wishaw, Scotland in October 2003. He was just 63, and football doesn't make many like that any more, sadly.

Eastham was an enigma and always very much his own man. That much had been clear to everyone in football since 1959, when he'd refused to sign a new contract at Newcastle United. The Magpies were in no mood to let him walk away and retained his registration as a player. George took grave exception to this and argued the toss in the High Court, claiming unfair restraint of trade. The judge gave him the thumbs-up and our transfer system was never the same again. Decent enough to make England's World Cup squads in both 1962 and 1966, Eastham wasn't deemed good enough to play a single minute in either of the tournaments.

Wright was beginning to panic as the slump continued. In the second half of the 1965–66 season, he presided over just three wins, against Stoke City, Sunderland and Leicester, in twenty League matches.

He demanded 'hard work' and was pilloried in the press after a stalemate at Chelsea where we worked hard to nullify the menace of their new wonder-boy Peter Osgood, and I must admit we were sterile spoilers that afternoon at Stamford Bridge.

With me still on the left, our right-back Don Howe played all 29 League matches until 5 March when I saw him break his leg in a 0–0 home draw with Blackpool. It was a horrific injury, which made my stomach turn over, yet a complete accident. Don made a rare sortie into attack, racing through to try and score, but Blackpool's England goalkeeper Tony Waiters dived at his feet and Don fractured his shin. The bone was there for all to see, poking through the skin with all the blood.

That was effectively the end of Don's distinguished playing career; he always walked with a limp after that, although he did

TRUE STOREY

make one belated appearance at the start of the following season before hanging up his boots and turning to coaching.

At £45,000, Don hadn't been a brilliant signing in a playing sense. He was already past his prime when Wright went back to his native Black Country to buy the full-back from West Brom, hoping he'd be a great tactician and organiser. But I don't think Arsenal really saw those virtues blossom until Don became first-team coach in October 1967, and one of the very best in the business.

The end of the season couldn't come soon enough for Arsenal and Billy Wright. Sometimes he was found slumped on the treatment table, sleeping off a heavy drinking session, and that spring he was emotionally crippled.

Our Irish kitman Tony Donnelly told me the fans had turned against him to such an extent that Wright was too nervous to face them and instead stayed in the dressing room during entire matches. Donnelly's job was to keep Wright abreast of the score and pop his head around the door to relate messages such as: 'We're 1–0 down, boss.' That was indicative of the shambles the club had become.

Eastham was restored to the side but helpless to halt the decline which continued with a 3–1 home defeat by Newcastle, after which the fans were baying for Billy's blood outside the stadium. I peeked out of the dressing room window to see police had linked arms in front of the marble halls to keep the mob at bay, as they chanted: 'Wright must go, Wright must go', 'Bring back, bring back, bring back Joe Baker to us' and simply 'We want a manager.'

The bald facts were alarming because we had taken only six points from a possible twenty-two so far in 1966, scored only eight times in those eleven matches and had gone seven games without a win. Oh, and just to depress the directors still further, the gate against the Geordies was down to 13,979 to start with – and well under 10,000 by the final whistle.

Billy was as popular with some as Labour leader Harold Wilson, who had suffered the indignity of being struck in the face and bruised by a stink bomb thrown by a schoolboy at a rally earlier that March during his successful general election campaign. The manager was like King Canute in my view, as he said defiantly: 'I've got broad shoulders. I can take all that the fans dish out. If they can throw stink bombs at the prime minister, they won't hesitate to boo a football manager. I will dig my toes in to make them change their tune about Arsenal.'

WRIGHT AND WRONG

We couldn't even win when we had a match 'won'. The way we fouled things up sometimes was scarcely credible. West Brom on 11 April was a classic example when we were 4–1 up with 25 minutes to play. I will never forget that game, for all the wrong reasons. Two of the Albion goals were penalties and after they made it 4–4 in the eighty-fifth minute, we were even grateful to hang on for a point. How pathetic was that?

We were in the soft and smelly stuff, that's for sure. At one stage, it was so bad we looked in serious danger of going down with just six games to go following a 2–1 defeat at West Ham, and the atmosphere in the dressing room was really terrible.

Somehow we rallied, pulling ourselves together just in time, and a win and a draw against Sunderland over Easter eased the pressure. A 2–0 success at Roker Park was crucial and came courtesy of goals from Alan Skirton and 'Sammy' Sammels, and I could afford a laugh or two on the long trek home to London, despite missing a late penalty.

Yet, immediately after the Sunderland matches we lost 3–0 in succession to Sheffield United, Aston Villa and Leeds. Attendances plummeted to an all-time low from the high of 56,757 for the Manchester United match which had left Wright feeling so proud, to that 13,979 against Newcastle, 8,738 for a patchy draw with West Brom the following week, to the ultimate insult on 5 May when our friends from the north, Leeds, thrashed us in front of just 4,554 paying customers.

Nine months after Baker's double against Stoke, the Highbury crowds had dwindled to such an extent you could virtually count the individual spectators.

I don't recall there being anything brilliant on at the cinemas in north London that particular night – but the local punters had made it abundantly clear they were sick of the sight of us, and maybe they did prefer *Carry on Cowboy* or *Ship of Fools*.

Wright made wholesale changes for the final match of the season, against Leicester, and was bullish to the last, at least in public. He told the press: 'I expect the lads to give a first-rate show to prove that we mean business next season.' An own goal ended a home jinx which hadn't seen us win at Highbury since the turn of the year. I played alongside other youth products such as 'Stan' Simpson, John Radford and Geordie Armstrong but teenagers Gordon Neilson and Jimmy McGill were never to make the grade at the club.

TRUE STOREY

The curtain came down with Arsenal a mere five points clear of relegation in fourteenth place out of twenty-two in the First Division, and Wright claiming: 'We now have the foundation of a youth policy equal to Stan Cullis's at Wolves in my day and to Matt Busby's at Old Trafford before Munich.'

I was still on third-team money of £18 a week, despite having been ever-present for the last 29 League and cup games. To be honest, I suppose I must have been a little shy and intimidated by Wright, but it was my own fault; I was too scared to summon up the courage to knock on the manager's door and ask him for a wage rise.

I should have done, because I knew he rated me after telling the press corps:

> Peter keeps his head well in a tight situation. He is quite a dour character and very steady temperamentally. When he first went into the team we knew his tackling was good enough. He tackles hard. We wondered if his use of the ball would be up to first-team standard. That part of his game hasn't let him down. This lad may not become international class, but he will be one of the best full-backs in the League, a great club man. You never see any sign of temperament from Peter. He just gets on with the game. And he's as tough as nails. He's a good 'un. He's so tenacious in the tackle, always biting away. You've got to have that in a full-back.

Why was the campaign such a miserable failure? I think it was down to the manager, because the decline had been going on for a few years. Several of the older, senior professionals – notably Eastham and Baker – had been allowed to grow very disillusioned and fed up. They certainly weren't very enthusiastic on many away trips and that made it particularly difficult for the younger players, me included. We would have benefited from a little guidance and support, but it wasn't forthcoming.

When you consider this line-up: Furnell; Howe, Storey; McLintock, Neill, Court; Skirton, Radford, Baker, Eastham, Armstrong . . . then I think it demonstrates there was enough quality throughout that team to have achieved considerably more than leave our rapidly dwindling band of supporters chewing their fingernails, wondering when they'd see us win again.

WRIGHT AND WRONG

It wasn't a happy club, the dressing room needed sorting out, the team needed organising. And that was the manager's job.

My criticism of Wright might seem harsh to some. I haven't set out to rubbish his reputation. I'm just telling it the way it was when our paths crossed. Here, after all, was a living legend in English football, a man with one hundred and five international caps, ninety as captain, and a colossal character who had skippered Wolves to three League championships and the FA Cup. Maybe that was the root cause of Billy's problems. The original Captain Fantastic had known only success and adulation during his playing career. Maybe he thought life was always going to be that easy. When the boot was on the other foot as a manager, defeat followed defeat and he was a target for the hate mob. Billy's coping mechanism was to retreat into the bottle. Failure was alien to him, and a mixture of the pressure and booze warped his personality and changed him into a haunted, volatile, unpredictable character.

He didn't harm only himself; early in my career I witnessed him at London Colney, where he had turned up to watch the A team play one afternoon after he had clearly enjoyed a 'heavy' lunchtime. Ray Bloomfield was quietly going about his business, but evidently not to the manager's satisfaction, and Wright started abusing him. It wasn't the first time he had appeared to watch us in a distressed state, but Ray's reaction was a first – he simply turned around, looked at his verbal aggressor and walked off the pitch towards the dressing room. I felt desperately sorry for my young teammate and even worse the next day when he was summoned in and paid for what Wright must have considered 'insolence' by losing his job. He was simply sacked on the spot without ceremony.

The punishment was totally out of order. Ray had taken some terrible stick from Wright, who appeared to be cracking up – a man on the verge of a nervous breakdown. Today, in similar circumstances, Ray would undoubtedly be counselled by all manner of soothing voices at the club and the Professional Footballers' Association would have a field day jumping to his defence, with good cause.

In the early part of summer 1966, the nation was so absorbed with England's preparations for the World Cup on home soil that Wright was dismissed and almost slipped away unnoticed from Highbury.

I was pleased when he settled very successfully into a top sports job in TV back in the Midlands, and happier still to later meet the

TRUE STOREY

'real' Wright at several awards dinners when he was tremendous company and came across as a genuinely decent fella. He was as nice and relaxed as anything then.

Billy Wright was simply the wrong man at the wrong time for Arsenal. Quite a few people suffered as a result.

CHAPTER SEVEN

All about Mee

England deserved to reach the World Cup final in 1966, but nothing will convince me that the controversial third goal against West Germany should have stood.

Geoff Hurst's turn and shot, which bounced down off the underside of the bar, has been replayed thousands of times on television since that glorious July afternoon, and I maintain it has never been satisfactorily proved that the ball crossed the line. Even now, more than 40 years on, with all the available technology, the experts still can't prove beyond all reasonable doubt that the goal should have stood. I didn't think it was a goal then, watching on Mum and Dad's black and white telly in the front room at home in Ash, and nothing that has happened in the intervening years has emerged to change my mind. As far as I'm concerned, in those circumstances, you have to give the defending side the benefit of the doubt – like in a court of law.

Having earlier eliminated the spiteful yet talented Argentinians, however, and the magical Eusebio's Portugal, England were worthy champions, even if they did enjoy the significant advantage of playing exclusively at Wembley.

Arsenal's George Eastham was in Alf Ramsey's squad of twenty-two, but I don't think anyone was the least bit surprised he didn't feature in any of England's six matches and was unemployed in company with goalkeepers Ron Springett and Peter Bonetti, reserve full-backs Jimmy Armfield and Gerry Byrne, and central defenders Ron Flowers and Norman Hunter.

Eastham, in truth, hadn't done himself many favours during the preceding months and before August was out he was sold to Stoke City. To be fair, he enjoyed something of a renaissance in the Potteries, an Indian Summer to his career, and he featured in a couple of very high-profile matches against Arsenal.

I wasn't that fussed about getting an England ticket through Arsenal for any of the matches, preferring to watch on the telly – but I was more than interested to study Ray Wilson at left-back. Not many players beat him.

Here was a defender who could definitely teach me a trick or two. A seriously good player, Ray boasted lightning pace and used the ball intelligently. It is astonishing to think he spent most of his career in the Second Division with Huddersfield Town, and had already turned 30 by 1964 when he earned a long-overdue transfer to the big league with Everton. That sort of scenario is impossible to imagine today, as is Ray's profession as an undertaker when he hung up his boots. Maybe that would have suited me too, given the grim, even macabre, reputation I was to carve out in the game.

England were a touch lucky against West Germany, a very competent team, and fortunate earlier to emerge with all their limbs intact after a 1–0 victory in the quarter-finals over a nasty Argentina team with a strange inferiority complex – a side infamously labelled 'animals' by Ramsey.

Some of their tricks had my eyes popping out on stalks.

There were loads of crude challenges and spitting all over the shop. The aggro all came to a head when the skipper and chief culprit Antonio Rattin, who had led by example, was sent off and the match held up for ten minutes before he left the field of play, snapping, snarling and gesticulating. Ramsey physically refused to let England exchange shirts at the final whistle, justifiably in my opinion.

The Argies have always been like that, bitter and brutal whenever they're not getting their own way, for all their flair and brilliance. And nothing has changed to this day, to my mind.

Eusebio was fabulous, however, particularly inspiring Portugal single-handedly to come from 3–0 down to beat North Korea 5–3 at Goodison Park with four goals of his own, but, as an armchair viewer, I was very disappointed not to see more of Pelé for the defending champions. Brazil's most famous son was already a legend, but I don't think he was entirely fit coming into the tournament and got roughed up by Bulgaria in their opening match. Pelé sat out the next game and Brazil were torn apart by the Hungarians with Bene, Albert and Meszoly mesmerising in a 3–1 win.

Now there was no question that Brazil needed to raise their game to stay in the tournament and Pelé was brought back, only to be kicked to bits by the Portuguese. How the English ref George McCabe didn't send off any of Eusebio's mates was a complete mystery. It was cynical stuff, they knew Pelé was far from 100 per cent fit, and hacked and chopped him all match. Which is probably precisely what I would have done, under orders, given the circumstances.

I'd be pushing it a bit to claim we were all buzzing with a feelgood factor, basking in the afterglow of England becoming world champions for the first time when the 1966–67 season kicked off. Concern for the club and interest in the new manager took precedence over the World Cup, although the competition did have a lasting legacy. Before the tournament commenced, the style of play in English football could be a bit haphazard. Afterwards, I noticed teams in the First Division getting a lot more organised, much more professional.

That was most certainly the case at Highbury, where the new gaffer turned out to be an old familiar face in the shape of our physio Bertie Mee. Given what he was destined to achieve, it's odd to recall how Bertie was so unsure of his promotion that he made the directors promise, and had it written into his contract, that he could revert to tending calf strains and pulled groin muscles if everything went pear-shaped and he flopped as a manager in his first year.

I waited a fortnight for Bertie to settle into his new job before going in to tackle him over the subject of my wages, which had been nagging away at me throughout the summer.

I didn't beat about the bush, but pointed out that I'd been ever-present in the team since my debut at Leicester, making twenty-eight First Division appearances and one in the FA Cup, and felt I was worth a bit more than £18 a week.

Bertie was somewhat taken aback to learn what I was on, and said: 'Well, that won't do, will it, Peter? I think we could go to £30. How does that sound?' When you consider that there was £5 appearance money, £4 for a win and £2 for a draw, it sounded highly satisfactory to me – even though I knew it wasn't enough to put me on a par with the club's highest earners. I think Bertie was already fairly confident that I had the potential to be an integral part of his team-building.

He inherited a squad which was little short of a rabble and immediately instilled a lot of discipline. Bringing in Dave Sexton as first-team coach from Leyton Orient was a master-stroke, as he proved extremely popular with the players and got things organised on the pitch. Those Hungarians, who had acted so thuggishly against Pelé, had some really good players among them – and Sexton loved them to bits. He showed us film of them in action so many times, he drove us mad.

Sexton's expertise was vital because Bertie didn't have a clue when it came to tactics, not a clue!

Still, he did set about trimming the squad, which was beneficial for team morale. Under Billy Wright, there had been too many fringe players contributing next to nothing, yet adding to the general sense of disenchantment. In the new, tighter squad we felt we were all in it together, and that bred harmony.

Highbury was overdue for a spot of renovation itself – the spectacle of grandeur was badly in need of a polish. There were a few conspicuous cracks in the plasterwork of the grandstand, some of the red paintwork was badly faded and Bertie oversaw a £35,000 facelift for the offices and grimy outer walls of the main stand.

Bertie would have gathered from our most high-profile pre-season friendly that the team needed more than a lick of new paint. I had the dubious privilege of having to mark the Scottish genius 'Wee' Willie Henderson at Ibrox and I think the closest I got to Rangers' international right-winger all afternoon was five minutes before the interval when I fouled him to concede a penalty in a 2–0 defeat.

The new era did start on a positive note, however, when the serious stuff got underway, and we kicked off with three successive wins against Sunderland, West Ham and Aston Villa, but it wasn't long before I fell sick, the victim of mysterious insect bites which became infected and forced me into hospital and out of three matches. The finger of suspicion fell on bugs spotted at our training ground in London Colney and a few of the lads had a field day, teasing me about 'Hertfordshire malaria', but they had the smiles wiped off their faces when Frank McLintock was also admitted to hospital for treatment and wondered who would be next to succumb. Fortunately, that was as far as the 'plague' spread.

I was given a clean bill of health to return for the visit of Manchester City and a 1–0 win, more than eager to do my bit, and was rewarded with the headline: 'Stop the tough stuff Storey – it won't pay'. I suppose I had been living something of a charmed life. My rugged, no-nonsense approach was bound to catch up with me sooner rather than later and meet with critical disapproval.

I stopped Mike Summerbee dead in his tracks as early as the fifteenth minute and the City winger had to be carried off with a badly bruised ankle. Frank McLintock headed the winner, while I headed into the bad books of the *Daily Express*, which reported:

ALL ABOUT MEE

Peter Storey, Arsenal's left-back, is stepping dangerously close to a trap that has snared many more famous players. He is overdoing the tough guy act. Storey has enough potential to succeed in football without risking the wrath that will inevitably fall on him from referees – and surely Arsenal, too – if he persists in these unnecessary robust tactics. Ex-Arsenal captain Joe Mercer, City manager, describing a tackle by Storey on winger Summerbee, said: 'It was a bad foul. But a very effective foul because it cost us Summerbee for the last 75 minutes.' It was like losing your right arm. City never recovered.

Purists will shudder at this notion, but I think fouls such as the one I and other defenders put in on Summerbee did him a favour. Within a few years, Mike and Francis Lee, his big pal at City, had toughened up no end, and were even prepared to take it to defenders like me. 'Getting your retaliation in first,' we called it. Summerbee and Lee actually became better players due to the fact that they adopted a more physical approach.

And let's face it, Frannie got his own back time and again on defenders the way he collapsed dramatically in the area to con a penalty. It became a joke that City had signed a Chinese player called 'Lee Won Pen'.

Meanwhile, it seemed as if I was gaining a reputation, and it wasn't long before someone had a pop to test my mettle.

Three days after the City match, we let our standards drop and were held to a 1–1 draw at Highbury by Gillingham in the second round of the Football League Cup.

Our punishment was an awkward replay in Kent with the Third Division side fancying their chances, and not only because we had a disturbing injury list, which included Frank, Geordie Armstrong, 'Stan' Simpson and David Court.

We made very heavy weather of it with unseasonal September fog rolling in off the River Medway, and needed a late goal to spare our embarrassment.

The prospect of a giant-killing and the noisy backing of the large majority of a near-capacity 20,566 Priestfield crowd had stirred some of the Gillingham players to fever pitch.

I took great exception to a challenge from their dangerous forward Charlie Crickmore midway through the second half and snapped back at him. Cue mayhem, as a fan jumped over the low wall separating the terraces from the pitch and joined us in a punch-up which was broken up by police and ambulance men.

The feud continued back at Highbury in the second replay, when Charlie and I had another ding-dong and needed to be pulled apart from a pack of shoving, arguing players.

Gillingham started to try and bully and bash their way through and after we had gone 3–0 up with 20 minutes to play, they lost any semblance of composure and attempted to kick us to death. They failed on that score and were summarily dismissed from the competition 5–0.

I shed no tears for them, but the manager pulled me up short afterwards and told me: 'I like you, Peter. You and Jon Sammels are two of the most promising youngsters at this club, but watch your step. Manchester City and now this: you're of no use to me if you get sent off.'

Bertie ran a tight ship in several senses. Overnight away matches became a very different experience.

Under the previous regime, trips to the north had seen a few of the lads rubbing their hands in anticipation of a little slice of the life of Riley. After a comfortable train trip from Euston, travelling first class, we'd stay in a nice big luxury hotel – invariably the Midland in Manchester for Old Trafford and Maine Road, and the Adelphi in Liverpool for Anfield and Goodison Park – with the opportunity to take full advantage of a 24-hour cleaning service to have our shirts freshly laundered, suits smartly pressed and, of course, shoes cleaned. Everything was back with you, fresh as a daisy, first thing in the morning. All very nice. We never paid a penny for the privilege and also signed on the club's tab for all the tea, coffee and newspapers we could consume. The notion of putting our hands in our pockets for anything was totally alien. Several of the lads were happy to abuse the system and greedily grabbed what was on offer with both hands. They took liberties.

There was one amusing hotel incident concerning George Johnston, a little Scottish player who joined Arsenal in 1967 from Cardiff. We were over in Ireland to play a friendly which kicked off in the evening, so everyone was familiar with the routine – training in the morning before a modest lunch in the restaurant followed by an afternoon's rest or sleep in our rooms.

As always with Arsenal, the hotel was top notch, with a kitchen to match, and poor George got a little flummoxed when he studied the à la carte French menu as an immaculately dressed waiter hovered by his elbow, pen poised to take the order. 'I'll have that, please,' said George, stabbing his finger at the menu, and trying his best to look like a sophisticated man of the world.

We were all served quite quickly and started to tuck in when two waiters appeared with a trolley and bottle of brandy. Moments later flames leapt from the frying pan by the side of our table as George's brandy-flamed peppercorn sirloin steak, complete with butter, garlic and wine with a cream sauce was cooked in front of him. Bertie went ballistic, ranting and raving, while George blushed bright red, doing his level best to slide under the table to escape the embarrassing scene. As you might imagine, the rest of us lads offered our teammate tremendous moral support, almost pissing ourselves with laughter at his predicament.

But that was the end of à la carte dining, and we were told in no uncertain terms to stick to the set menu and choose plainly cooked chicken, beef or fish in future.

For years, my preferred option was steak before the match until, horror of horrors, some dietician somewhere claimed that a nice, juicy sirloin was the worst possible thing to digest before indulging in 90 minutes of high-energy sport. Virtually overnight, British beef was out and it seemed to be eggs on toast all round. I can't say the change had any effect whatsoever, beneficial or detrimental, on my performance.

Our travelling arrangements also changed after Bertie got his feet under the table. Previously, we'd let the train take the strain to the Midlands and the north but, sadly, hooliganism was beginning to become fashionable and our return journeys to Euston, St Pancras and King's Cross were interrupted too often for comfort. Some of our own younger fans from the North Bank and Clock End were no angels and had a nasty habit of pulling the emergency communication cord when we were in the middle of nowhere. It was bloody frustrating sitting there for ages, staring out of the window at the black nothingness of the English countryside or the twinkling lights of a faraway village when I was eager to get back to London for a good drink and a party.

England's motorway system was improving all the time, however, so it made sense to switch to coach travel, which also fitted in with Bertie's frugal ways.

So coaches became the order of the day and the favoured overnight accommodation was the functional Post House chain, where players were directly responsible for any little extras. Mutterings of resentment brought this terse response from the manager: 'One day you may appreciate what I'm doing for you.'

There was very little immediate appreciation for Bertie's hardline approach off the pitch. But I nodded in agreement. I knew what he meant. In later life, merely staying in a hotel might be a luxury – it most certainly would be for me – and instead of running up a bill for the club to collect, we would have to pay for everything ourselves, like normal people rather than spoiled little rich kids. I understood the manager's logic.

Bertie had a military background and was a stickler for punctuality and rules. I felt he took it too far at times when he would get carried away and go red in the face.

I recall one end-of-season tour in Cyprus when Frank McLintock, who was injured and not playing, sat down for our pre-match meal of scrambled eggs and instead casually helped himself to an apple from the bowl of fruit on the table. You would have thought it was a hanging offence the way Bertie exploded and went berserk at the skipper. I couldn't get it into my head how the manager could get so worked up over something so trivial as a piece of fruit.

My relationship with Bertie was uncomplicated. He could be a bit pompous, but I respected him to begin with. Fortunately, he delegated all the team stuff and tactics to Dave Sexton, and later Don Howe.

Bertie was no genius when it came to buying players and manipulating the transfer market. In fact, to be frank, the bulk of his later signings were mediocre. He wasn't solely to blame though, because he most certainly relied on the advice of his coaching staff before opening the club cheque book. Given his lack of tactical nous, he would never have bought a player of his own volition off the cuff.

The success we were to achieve was based on the players Billy Wright had introduced and youngsters, such as myself, who had come up through the youth-team ranks.

There were a couple of exceptions, however. Left-back Bob McNab arrived early in Bertie's reign from Huddersfield and proved to be arguably his best-ever signing. You certainly couldn't argue with the recruitment of George Graham, from Chelsea, either because 'Stroller', like 'Nabbers', was responsible for playing a part in a glorious chapter in the club's history.

Colin Addison, an inside-forward from Nottingham Forest, was less successful and found himself packed off to Sheffield United after 14 months.

ALL ABOUT MEE

Bertie's first campaign in the hot seat ended with Arsenal in seventh place in the First Division as Matt Busby led Manchester United to a second title triumph in three seasons.

The most notable feature of our record could be found in the goals-against column. We had conceded 75 goals in 1965–66 and that had been reduced to 47, but only 'Stroller' and Jon Sammels got into double figures at the other end of the park.

Tottenham, who beat us home and away, finished in third place but I felt there was a genuine sense of progress when we brought the curtain down on the season on 13 May with an unremarkable 1–1 draw at Sheffield Wednesday. What gave me hope for the future was that it meant we were unbeaten in our last dozen League matches, an encouraging run which had started when Sammy scored in a 1–1 draw with Busby's United in front of a crowd of 63,563 at Highbury on 3 March.

My personal contribution was thirty-four starts out of the forty-two League matches (the missing eight were down to those infected insect bites and a couple of injuries, rather than any dip in form) and one goal.

My strike-rate from open play was a constant source of amusement in the dressing room throughout my career, and after one rare collector's item, a teammate quipped: 'Snouty's scored . . . quick, check if it's a leap year!'

In any event, I registered my first Arsenal League goal against Nottingham Forest on 22 April 1967 in a 1–1 draw at Highbury witnessed by 36,196 paying customers. I wish it had been one to remember, a goal to savour, maybe a thunderous 25-yard rising drive, or perhaps a volley from a cross on the edge of the box. The truth is rather more prosaic. I simply found myself in unfamiliar territory, just outside the opposition penalty area, and when Frank McLintock slipped a free-kick sideways, I chanced my arm. I didn't hit a very good shot but it bounced and bobbled its way past the Forest goalkeeper, Peter Grummitt, into the corner of the net. They all count and my name was, at last, in the goal-scoring records.

CHAPTER EIGHT

You know what to do, Peter

I hated George Best with a passion whenever Arsenal met Manchester United, and I was deputed to 'do a job on him' out on the pitch.

I hated Bestie because he was just so bloody good. One time at Highbury, when I thought I'd been doing a fairly competent job of keeping him quiet, a United defender knocked the ball long and Bestie materialised out of thin air behind me, like a ghost.

Some who were there that day swear I suffered a blind panic attack, but I prefer to recall that it clicked my best bet would be to pass the ball back to Jim Furnell as swiftly as possible. And that's what I did. The only problem was that our otherwise diligent goalkeeper had momentarily switched off, totally unprepared for a pass, and was caught consequently out of position. I felt a right lemon, just standing there watching the ball sail into the net for an own goal.

Bestie's fans like to believe he had, in effect, scored without touching the ball, that his reputation had been enough. A few of the lads tried to console me afterwards with an arm round the shoulder in the dressing room, but I brushed them off. I wanted sympathy like a hole in the head.

I hated Bestie even more when he told Michael Parkinson what he felt about me: 'To my mind, that Peter Storey was a joke. How on earth did he get to play for England? I mean he couldn't even stop another player playing. My grandmother could do a better job. It's the easiest thing in the world to mark someone in a game. You can stop the best players if you stand in their boots. These close markers used to really piss me off at times.'

He was a brave little bastard, I'll give him that, and utterly determined never to be kicked out of the game at a time when flair players got next to nothing in terms of protection from the referees.

Bestie loved to try and make a fool out of defenders – me included, of course – by standing over the ball, beckoning opponents to lunge in with a challenge, before dropping his shoulder, whipping the ball upfield and leaving us flat on our embarrassed backsides. He gave me that treatment not once, but several times during the course of one match, and I read that: 'Lesser men would have desisted out of concern for their personal safety and future careers.' Although I recall we shook hands very briefly at the final whistle and exchanged knowing glances, inside I was seething. I felt so angry and humiliated that if I'd managed to get hold of Bestie properly in the tunnel, or down a dark alley, he might not have had a future career. Equally, I felt it was always a big mistake ever to show emotion or let opponents know what you were thinking. I wanted them to be concerned, to fret and do all the worrying, especially about what I might do to them. Revenge, or any form of physical violence come to that, is a dish best served cold.

The funny thing is I saw another side to Bestie much later in my career and although it would be an exaggeration to say we got on like a house on fire together briefly at Fulham, it was as if all the previous animosity and hostility had been a mirage. I didn't think it was the time or the place to tackle him over what he'd alleged in a book about me 'threatening to break his fucking legs'. It wasn't true; in any case, it wasn't me. I never talked much on the pitch and I'm sure a threat like that would have stuck in my mind. Arsenal versus Manchester United, me against him, had never been less than niggly and I knew how much I preyed on his nerves. But this was different, we were teammates and it was stuff such as Fulham versus Oldham and Orient – a bit lower-key all round.

It was the same with several players when you didn't really know them. For instance, I couldn't stand Alan Ball when he was at Everton but then he moved to Arsenal and it was immediately as if all the aggro we'd been through had been an illusion and never happened.

Once established, I wanted my reputation to count and work to my advantage. Here are a few choice words which have been used to describe me: assassin, bastards' bastard (courtesy of 'Chopper' Harris), boot boy, bully, calculating, 'cold eyes', destructive, dirty, hatchet man, merciless, pernicious, rogue, ruthless, thug, vicious. Bit strong, some of those, I think, although I'll hold my hands up and plead guilty to rogue. With my track record with women and the law,

TRUE STOREY

I've never exactly been Mr Goody Two-Shoes or a dead ringer for Little Lord Fauntleroy.

Being the uneducated fella that I am, I had to look up the definition of pernicious in a dictionary. It said: 'tending to cause death or great harm'. I'm surprised the government allowed me a number at Arsenal, rather than running out with a message on my back reading: 'This player can seriously damage your health'.

I've even heard it said dismissively that I 'couldn't play football'. Well, I never claimed to be another Johan Cruyff, but Sir Alf Ramsey did have sufficient faith in my ability to pick me for nineteen England matches between 1971 and 1973, when there was considerably more talent knocking around in English football than there is now, and international caps weren't two a penny. Then there was the little matter of 501 first-team appearances over a dozen years for Arsenal.

Part of my 'image problem' (a problem for others, I'd hasten to add, because I knew my role in the great scheme of things at Arsenal) is that I never pretended to be anything other than an out-and-out defender, yet I became deployed in midfield to negate opponents' creative players further up the park before they could get at our back four.

The purists hated that and I was an easy target for ridicule. Even Nick Hornby, an Arsenal fan, managed a dig in his book *Fever Pitch* when he claimed the '70s were over-rated 'and we overlook the fact that most First Division teams contained at least one player – Storey at Arsenal, Smith at Liverpool, Harris at Chelsea – who simply wasn't very good at football at all'.

That's total bollocks, an accusation I can't let pass without summoning my Arsenal skipper Frank McLintock as chief witness for the defence. In his autobiography, *True Grit*, he wrote:

> As a bloke 'Snouty' is quite enigmatic and of all my teammates he is probably the one I know least well. Despite his reputation as a hatchet man, he was an excellent footballer and would have been equally at home in any position in midfield or defence. The fact that he won more caps than any other member of our team speaks volumes for his ability but – in the same way as Nobby Stiles – he's been underrated because of his fearsome qualities in the tackle; indeed, again like Stiles, on the pitch he was not very nice at all and could be quite frightening.

YOU KNOW WHAT TO DO, PETER

> Cold and focused, Peter was great at sensing danger and was unflappable when we were under pressure. His gift for the simplest, the most vital tasks – winning the ball then giving it – gave a framework for the way we operated.

Any assertion that Tommy Smith 'simply wasn't very good at football at all' crumbles in the face of what he achieved in over 600 appearances for Liverpool over 17 years. He won four League championships, two FA Cups, two UEFA Cups, one European Cup (in which he scored a towering header against Borussia Mönchengladbach in Rome on his farewell appearance), one European Super Cup and three Charity Shields.

'Chopper' Harris could play a bit too, otherwise how do you explain him playing left-back for Chelsea in almost 800 matches for the best part of 20 years, winning the League Cup and then captaining the club to triumph in the FA Cup final and European Cup Winners' Cup?

Martin Peters, at West Ham, was a creative player I admired, and I thought he hit the nail on the head in his autobiography *The Ghost of '66*:

> Almost every team enjoyed one if not two players who were noted tough guys. Their principal function was to stop the opposition from playing. Today's defensive midfield players are angels alongside some of the hard men I faced, including Tommy Smith, Ron Yeats, Maurice Setters, Gerry Byrne, Ron Harris, Dave Mackay, Norman Hunter, Johnny Giles, Billy Bremner, Vic Mobley, John McGrath, George Curtis and Peter Storey. They could all play, but they all had a hard streak and were acknowledged experts in a tough battle.

Wide players had already started to disappear from the scene in the wake of England's World Cup success by Ramsey's wingless wonders, and the media were desperate for the glamour boys to thrive and entertain. They wanted swashbuckling players such as Rodney Marsh, Tony Currie, Stan Bowles and Alan Hudson to be granted the freedom of the pitch to express themselves all the time. There was a general demand for more cavalier players like that, but as a 100 per cent 'roundhead' I wasn't playing that game.

TRUE STOREY

I was never a conventional midfield player, just an extra defender in the middle of the park – more disgraceful than graceful, if the truth be told.

The lads used to joke that Don Howe was in danger of having a heart attack on those rare occasions I ventured over the halfway line into opposition territory. He would scramble to the touchline, bellowing: 'Get back, Peter, get back!' One–nil to the Arsenal was always good enough for Don, just as it was later when George Graham was manager between 1986 and 1995 in a reign responsible for the club winning two championships, one FA Cup, two League Cups and one European Cup Winners' Cup.

Going back to Bestie, I love that story about the football-supporting waiter employed on room service, knocking on his hotel door and entering with another magnum of champagne, discovering him in bed with a beautiful blonde Miss World, the floor awash with cash, and asking: 'Tell me, George, where did it all go wrong?'

Bestie got more than his fair share of the birds, while I got more than my fair share of the bird from rival fans. I can still sometimes close my eyes and see their angry, contorted faces, spitting hatred – and phlegm – at me from the terraces after I'd dumped their golden boy on his skinny, talented arse again. But don't run away with the notion I had a string of easy targets; that was far from the truth.

The Everton manager Harry Catterick, a great champion of playing the right way, once expressed his fears that the game was changing for the worse. It must have been the summer of 1967 when he said words to the effect: 'The First Division could become very robust, I noticed it creeping in last season', while the legendary Manchester United boss Sir Matt Busby lamented: 'Every team now has an acknowledged hard man. And some of them have two or more.'

Hippies were all the rage in 1967, the Summer of Love, and you could hardly go anywhere without hearing Scott McKenzie's number one hit 'San Francisco (Be Sure to Wear Flowers in Your Hair)' but the message to English footballers might just as well have been 'be sure to wear some double-strength shinpads down your socks!'

I had no way of assessing whether he was suitably appalled or impressed, when one journalist waxed lyrical and was moved to write: 'Storey tackles like a tiger, leaving a string of devastation in his wake.'

For all that, I was only ever sent off on three occasions; the first time for swearing, I think, alongside Frank McLintock at Burnley in

YOU KNOW WHAT TO DO, PETER

a 1–0 defeat in December 1967. The second offence which merited marching orders was pushing an opponent in a pre-season friendly in Norway, while the last came against Stoke, where I kicked John Mahoney, which was a surprise. If I was going to get the early bath against that lot, I'd have put money on it being for having a pop at Alan Hudson.

For me, it all started like this, a couple of months into the 1967–68 season, although I had already carved out a reputation by then as a robust competitor.

Dave Sexton departed in October to succeed Tommy Docherty as manager of Chelsea, and three weeks later Don Howe retired as a player, with Bertie Mee making him our new first-team coach.

Don wanted things to change, with Bob McNab starting to make the left-back spot his own and me pushed over to the right. Until now, I had always been a full-back, pure and simple – although a few wingers might argue the toss over the 'pure'. For certain games, however, I was given a specific man-marking job, the close, nitty gritty stuff. Up close and personal.

I was never told to kick opponents. Well, not in so many words, but the implication was always there. Whether it was Bertie or Don giving the urgent last-minute instructions before a big match in front of a packed crowd, there always seemed to be a little hush in the dressing room and a few of the lads' eyes would turn in my direction as I was told in a serious, deadpan voice: 'You know what to do, Peter.'

They didn't have to spell it out to me. I knew my orders translated into, 'Get stuck in and mark so-and-so, and put him out of the game.'

I will never attempt to even begin to make excuses for what I did in football, but I didn't really agree with what I was being told to do. No, I didn't like it. However, when that season kicked off I was still only 21 and desperate to keep my place in the team. If the manager had told me to swim under water and menace fish, I think I would have asked for a wetsuit, snorkel, harpoon and directions to the nearest beach. It's like when an imposing newspaper editor asks a junior reporter to do this and that, the kid isn't going to start asking moral questions and challenge the authority of his boss. If he's got an ounce of sense, he's just going to get on with the task to the very best of his ability. And that's precisely what I did.

Apart from Bestie, my early hitlist was to include Johnny Giles at Leeds, Everton's Alan Ball and Peter Osgood of Chelsea. No easy pickings there, that trio could all dish it out as well as take it. I knew I'd have to confront them at least twice a season, and there was always considerable feeling between us, none of it good-natured. It was all very well putting them down, but they would get up and kick you back. Ossie and I used to kick lumps out of each other, while lesser characters were intimidated.

Giles was a hard little sod, a talented playmaker with a vindictive streak to boot. In many ways I thought he was the one individual who summed up his club, Leeds, to a tee. With all that talent in his feet, quick wits and a razor-sharp brain to assess situations, you wondered why the dirty stuff surfaced so often – like scum on a glass of champagne.

There were never any easy matches against Giles, and the management were particularly keen for me to put him out of the game and cut off his supply of killer passes to Allan Clarke, Mick Jones and Peter Lorimer. He wasn't easily subdued and put off. In fact, Giles was just as likely to give me a kick as I was to 'do' him. I was amused to recall one particular encounter I had with the spiky Irishman, as related by Arsenal fan Ray Davies.

As any half-decent pop historian can tell you, Ray is better known as a fabulous musician and lead singer of *The Kinks*. He also spent a fair bit of his youth at Highbury and *The Times* recruited him to pen his own farewell tribute to the famous old ground when Arsenal moved to the Emirates Stadium. Ray wrote: 'I also witnessed epic encounters against Liverpool and particularly Leeds, when the superb Arsenal hatchet man Peter Storey managed to somehow foul Johnny Giles six times within a 15-yard run.' Only six? I must have had an off-day.

My violence was premeditated to the extent that I deliberately set out to intimidate opponents.

The trick was to get in as early as possible, hit them hard, give them a good wallop, make them feel as if they'd been in a car crash or hit a brick wall. The tackle from behind had yet to be outlawed and I got away with things which would get me locked up today. The referees weren't clued-up and guys like Hunter, 'Chopper' at Chelsea and myself knew full well that the worst we were likely to get for an early assault was the ref's admonishing finger wagging in our faces as a warning. Particularly if we could disguise the foul as simply a case of bad timing and go to ground ourselves, wearing a pained look of mock disappointment at being so clumsy. Ideally, you were looking for opponents to make a pass and then to go in, bang, a fraction late.

Refs always gave us bad lads the benefit of the doubt in the first few minutes and settled for a warning and a free-kick, rather than the yellow cards dished out like confetti today. Clumsy, my arse. We knew exactly what we were doing and pushed what we could get away with to the absolute limit.

I regarded my target for the afternoon as someone whose spirit had to be broken as quickly as possible. Once they started looking over their shoulder for me, wondering when the next bone-crunching tackle was coming their way, or began to get the needle and feel niggled, I knew I had them in my pocket.

It didn't matter to me particularly whether I put the frighteners on them and stopped them playing legitimately by means of a massive tackle, a massive tackle which took man and ball – or a massive foul, providing that didn't get me sent off, of course, or cost Arsenal a penalty or anything silly like that. In 90 minutes you learn that there's a time and a place for everything.

Brian Clough always liked to play the game the 'right way' but he could be the complete professional too. I had some intense battles with Derby's Archie Gemmill and had a wry laugh when the little Scot related how he'd got into hot water with his boss by retaliating instantly to provocation, and picked up bookings galore before Cloughie told him: 'Don't be a pillock and take a swing right in front of the referee's nose, Archie. Wait 20 minutes, and *then* do the bloke!'

I didn't feel any remorse or sympathy if I injured a rival; I wouldn't have been concentrating on my job if I'd let emotions get in the way. Equally, I don't recall doing any specific serious long-term damage to an opponent or ending anyone's career.

Sure, I literally went over the top a few times but I never broke anyone's leg. It was a dirty job but somebody had to do it. I did it and I did it well, closing opponents down, getting as tight as possible and generally making their lives a misery.

I took one hell of a lot of criticism on occasion for Arsenal's belt-and-braces approach to grinding out results, and I think the club were happy to let the spotlight fall on me because it deflected attention from others.

Inevitably, I had a few brushes with supporters at away matches when they gathered outside the players' entrance to shower me with abuse, spit, the odd coin or two and a rolled-up match programme. Then I could relax on the team coach heading back to London, secure in the knowledge that I'd had a successful afternoon.

The press loved to hate me too, none more so than Brian Glanville of the *Sunday Times*; he always seemed to be giving me stick. Most of the time it was water off a duck's back but once, before an Arsenal trip to Europe, I caught sight of him holding court before the charter plane left and something just snapped. Brian had written something, slagging me off again, and I cornered him in the airport and whispered in his ear: 'I'm going to fuckin' do you next!' Brian looked a bit shocked but, give him credit, it never prevented him from continuing to have a go at me in print. Fair play, he was entitled to his opinion and was paid to express it, even if I didn't agree with it. I think Brian was a bit braver than a few opponents I managed to subdue and leave cowering.

Jimmy Hill wasn't one of my greatest fans either. Before Jimmy became the face of *Match of the Day* he was head of sport at London Weekend Television and in the early '70s on one edition of *The Big Match*, fronted by Brian Moore, he really said his piece after Arsenal had dominated Crystal Palace physically, accusing us – and me in particular – of using bully-boy tactics and claiming that while we could certainly dish it out, we couldn't take it. I don't accept that at all because I was on the receiving end of plenty of rough stuff without a murmur of complaint. If you live by the sword, you've got to be prepared for the consequences. That was my unsophisticated take on the debate.

It was a tough, ruthless era which the *Daily Telegraph*'s Sue Mott, who watched with her dad from the Highbury terraces, summed up in one piece, entitled 'Heroes of the Seventies', which made me smile:

> It is hard to know which was worse, the morality or the haircuts. The depravity of some of the tackles circa 1970 would have made a Viking flinch. You wonder how we stood for it (no one who was anyone sat). Peter Storey of Arsenal would go into tackles peculiarly sideways, crablike, inflicting maximum damage on mortal bone and gristle in his way. Ron Harris of Chelsea was known as 'Chopper', like a gangland executioner. Leeds United had a team full of enforcers, of which Norman Hunter was merely the most notorious.

YOU KNOW WHAT TO DO, PETER

And then there was Cloughie, of course, who once paid me a compliment, of sorts, on TV when the discussion turned to the differing reactions of Norman Hunter and myself after we had 'done' an opponent. Clough was scathingly dismissive of Hunter's mock apologetic hands in the air routine, which suggested to the referee that his foul had been the sort of error which would never happen again. 'As for Storey,' said Clough, 'at least there's no pretence at being sorry on his part. He just hits the forward, gets up and walks away.'

CHAPTER NINE

Wembley woe, Fairs Cup fun

I started to develop a healthy interest in Frank Sinatra as a recording artist: 'I Get a Kick Out of You' has always been a particular favourite. I was also partial to the music of Jack Jones and Nat King Cole, as well as imported soul from America, which was beginning to take off in Britain in a big way. Tamla Motown, Stax and Atlantic were the major labels and my record collection grew most Friday lunchtimes.

Peter Simpson and I would hot-foot it down to the Finsbury Park branch of Barclays Bank, where our wages were paid in, to withdraw our spending money for the week. After a burger and a coffee, eyeing up the talent with their miniskirts, false eyelashes and white boots in the local Wimpy Bar, we'd hit the shops for clothes and records. I ended up with a very impressive collection of LPs, but they have all disappeared after so many moves over the years.

For shirts, I'd make a beeline to a little place in Shaftesbury Avenue which specialised in American gear – labels such as Ben Sherman were all the rage, with button-down collars. I always went for plain colours, rather than stripes. Lads who couldn't afford a 'Benny' had to settle for a cheaper Brutus, made from thinner cotton.

Quite apart from buying what we wanted off the peg, Peter and I could afford to have our suits made by Lou, a smashing little tailor.

We'd thumb our way through rolls of cloth in his place in Wood Green before choosing the precise material we fancied. Lou was the ultimate professional and insisted on two fittings before he'd stand back, survey his handiwork, cock his head to one side and announce: 'You'll do, my son.' I would happily pay £35 for one of Lou's three-piece suits, which we wore with braces. Lou was so good I eventually

WEMBLEY WOE, FAIRS CUP FUN

bought four of his distinctive suits – two in wool and a couple in mohair.

Arsenal suddenly found they couldn't cut their cloth accordingly, however.

The club had looked down their noses at the Football League Cup as something of an inferior competition, unworthy of their attention. Rotherham (1961) and Rochdale (1962) had reached the first two finals, but the big boys were soon obliged to take the competition seriously once the final changed from being a two-legged home and away affair, and was transferred to Wembley, where success meant an entry into Europe.

The second time we had entered the League Cup was in 1967–68, and I wouldn't knock it because the tournament sustained interest during a season which saw us slip back a couple of places in the League to ninth – fourteeen points (or seven wins) behind champions Manchester City.

The lads up front were firing on all cylinders as we plundered sixteen goals in seven matches to get past fellow First Division opponents Coventry City and Burnley, plus lesser lights Reading, Blackburn Rovers and Huddersfield Town, with George Graham in a rich vein of scoring form.

Unfortunately, the goals had started to dry up alarmingly in a run of eight League matches without a win when 2 March, the day of the League Cup final, dawned dull and overcast, an ominous portent of things to come.

Worse still, our opponents were Leeds, which meant a guaranteed war of attrition, one in which we would be second favourites – and rightly so. I make no bones about it, not many people outside north London expected us to win because Leeds were simply the better team.

I didn't have a good vibe from the moment I woke up, I felt a few things were stacked against us and that fate was not about to inscribe Arsenal's name under those of the seven previous winners – Aston Villa, Norwich, Birmingham City, Leicester, Chelsea, West Brom and QPR. It concerned me that since they had been promoted, Leeds had beaten us seven times in a row, and that they were overdue their first trophy under Don Revie. Three years earlier, I had seen Bill Shankly's Liverpool beat them 2–1 in the FA Cup final and I suspected Leeds were too good a side to keep falling just short; they weren't always going to be the bridesmaids. Cold logic told you as much.

TRUE STOREY

Billy Bremner was very bullish about Leeds' prospects, telling anyone who cared to listen how confident they were, to the extent that his only concern was over-confidence.

To nobody's surprise it developed into a largely drab, disappointing final, settled in the eighteenth minute by Leeds' marauding left-back Terry Cooper, who thumped in an angled volley. Almost inevitably, the goal was disputed.

I wasn't alone in arguing with the referee that Paul Madeley and Jack Charlton were illegally blocking off Jim Furnell when our goalkeeper came for an Eddie Gray corner. Jim's clearance was restricted to a flap to the edge of the penalty area where Cooper was lurking to send it back with interest.

The only other moment that stood out for me involved Frank McLintock, who was still upset at the manner of the goal. He adopted similar tactics and charged their keeper, Gary Sprake, at a corner shortly before half-time. That sparked a big bundle that included our Ian Ure, with plenty of pushing and pulling. Bremner and Big Jack were inevitably in the thick of it, defending Leeds' honour.

Frank was desperately keen to pull the game around because he had already suffered the acute disappointment of losing two Wembley finals – in 1961 and 1963, when Tottenham and Manchester United respectively beat his Leicester team in the FA Cup.

The Leeds mentality once they had sneaked in front was 'what we have, we hold', their sole objective to end all the Elland Road hard-luck stories, and they didn't much care how they achieved it.

Cooper's goal was 'job done' and they shut up shop. They had conceded just three goals in six games en route to the final in seeing off Luton Town, Bury, Sunderland, Stoke and Derby, and they were in no mood to risk another in the debit column.

There was, perhaps inevitably, a hangover from losing the League Cup final, in more ways than one. Losing in itself was a bitter pill, but the manner of our defeat in failing to put on a show, or fashion any decent chances worthy of the name, hurt too. We had a drinking session to drown our sorrows, but depression had set in.

Ten days later Second Division Birmingham City knocked us out of the FA Cup, 2–1 in a fifth-round replay at St Andrews before we lost five out of the next eight League matches without scoring. It was a wretched little run as Wolves, Everton and Sunderland all beat us 2–0, while Southampton must have thought they had won the pools, easing their relegation worries over Easter with a double, 2–0 at The

WEMBLEY WOE, FAIRS CUP FUN

Dell and 3–0 at Highbury, our worst defeat of the season as gates tumbled.

February 1968 had seen Bertie Mee pay £90,000 to bring in Bobby Gould, a bustling little striker, who had helped Coventry win the Second Division championship in 1966–67. He had played for the Sky Blues against us at Highbury and had a very good game against Terry Neill. I think the manager bought him on the strength of that.

Bobby was ineligible for our League Cup run but his goals at the end of the season played a large part in stopping the rot, along with some very sharp words from Bertie.

We signed off with five successive wins – including a very satisfying 4–3 victory over Leeds. For once, I couldn't give a toss about conceding three. It was just sweet to get one over them at long last and prove to everyone that there were goals in our team.

Losing to Leeds at Wembley was no disgrace – but going down 3–1 to Swindon Town, from the Third Division, 12 months later in our second successive League Cup final most certainly was.

I must shoulder some of the blame for 15 March 1969, a shameful day in Arsenal's history, because the player I was supposed to be marking out of the game, the Wiltshire club's mercurial left-winger Don Rogers, scored twice, although he never slaughtered me.

Nothing could have prepared us for the shocks to come, and there was no sense that we were taking Swindon lightly, despite our impressive run to Wembley which had taken us past Sunderland, Scunthorpe United, Liverpool, Blackpool and Tottenham, narrowly, after a couple of bitter exchanges in a two-legged semi-final.

Our fans in a crowd of 55,237 had gone home from White Hart Lane with a warm glow of satisfaction in late November when John Radford grabbed a last-minute winner over 'the old enemy', only for Jimmy Greaves to bring Spurs level overall a fortnight later in front of 55,923 at our place. But you can't keep a good man down and Raddy settled a niggly tie by heading the decisive goal.

I thought our League form was very encouraging, helped no end by Gould coming into the attack and hitting a purple patch. He scored seven goals in as many League games and in our last match before Wembley we warmed up with a thumping 5–0 win over Sheffield Wednesday at Hillsborough, where Raddy helped himself to a hat-trick.

With both finalists normally playing in red, the colour clash meant we both changed, Arsenal to yellow shirts and blue shorts, Swindon to an all-white kit, which made them resemble Leeds, ominously.

I'll get my excuses in, but the bald truth is that we under-performed extremely badly. If Swindon were underdogs, somebody forgot to tell them to stick to the script. One newspaper had Danny Williams' team tagged as small-town Cinderellas who would be swamped by a bucketload of goals.

The pantomime for us began, as I recall, when about eight of the lads went down ill leading up to the final and, as a suspected flu epidemic reared its ugly head, our League match on 8 March was postponed. I thought the lads were over-dramatising things and just had heavy colds, but that's maybe because I was unaffected.

However, nobody can argue with the fact that the pitch was in a diabolical condition after a spell of incessant rain. Three days earlier hundreds of gallons of water had been pumped off before England could take the field, and Geoff Hurst scored a hat-trick in a 5–0 battering of France. There was also plenty of speculation that the drains had been wrecked the week before the final when the famous turf was trampled underfoot during the Horse of the Year Show.

The surface soon deteriorated into a quagmire; it was in a terrible state, but, of course, it was the same for both teams.

I could happily have strangled Bob Wilson and Ian Ure when Swindon's first goal went in. It was an absolute joke, an almighty cock-up, with our goalkeeper and centre-half freezing over a back-pass, hesitating like tarts in a trance over who should take charge of the situation on the treacherous surface of mud and sand. When Ian did wake up, he hit the ball too hard, it bounced off Bob's leg and Roger Smart could hardly believe his good fortune in being offered an open goal to aim at ten minutes before half-time.

The Swindon goalkeeper Peter Downsborough was having a blinder down the other end as we bombarded him in an effort to equalise, and I had almost resigned myself to another 1–0 Wembley defeat when Gould played his 'get out of jail card' and popped up in the eighty-sixth minute with a headed goal after a rare error of judgement by Downsborough.

By rights, that should have shattered Swindon and given us a huge lift for extra-time but, if anything, the reverse was true.

Don Howe feared we had given our lot on a pitch which now seemed to be about a foot deep in mud in some places because he approached the referee Bill Handley in an effort to have proceedings abandoned after 90 minutes.

WEMBLEY WOE, FAIRS CUP FUN

With several of us slumped on the ground, socks rolled down, Don argued both sides were so knackered because of the boggy pitch that there was a genuine risk of serious injuries. He was right in one sense – our legs had gone, especially those belonging to the lads who had been sick in the week. Maybe it was a mistake to let Swindon see how tired we were.

We had been warned that Rogers was a dangerous player, easily capable of operating at a level higher than the Third Division, and he underlined the point now with two goals. Swindon regained the lead when Rogers pounced on a knock-down from a corner which should undoubtedly have been cleared into Row Z, and the Wiltshire mudlark wrapped up their victory when he skipped unopposed through our defence and took the ball round Wilson.

Rogers was 23 and being described as one of the most sought-after young players in the country. In today's game, the way agents work, he would have been packing his bags for the Premier League in an instant on the strength of what he achieved at Wembley. Swindon would have been powerless to resist a big-money offer, and he may well have gone on to play for England. I later discovered that the Manchester City coach Malcolm Allison came in for Don strongly, but that the Swindon board never even mentioned the fact to Rogers, let alone allowed him to listen to the Maine Road offer.

Everyone felt gutted in the losers' dressing room, none more so than Frank McLintock, who was so out of it following the final whistle he had to be reclaimed after wandering off in a daze with the army's band of musicians.

The mood was one of extreme disappointment. Bertie Mee was not very happy with the outcome, to put it mildly, and said he felt betrayed that we had let both him and ourselves down.

Certainly, there was a short period of doom and gloom at the club. I thought we had improved gradually over the previous two seasons, but losing to Swindon felt like sliding all the way down in a game of snakes and ladders and returning to square one.

As for poor Frank, a Wembley loser for the fourth time of asking, he wore such a pained expression you almost wondered if a poisonous snake had risen from the Wembley 'swamp' and bitten him on the bum.

Swindon went on to complete their 'Double' by winning promotion – although they were denied a place in Europe as League Cup winners because the Fairs Cup was then only open to top-flight clubs – while we regrouped, stopped feeling sorry for ourselves and managed a fourth-place finish in the First Division, 11 points behind champions Leeds. One significant reason for our rise was the goals against column, which registered a mere twenty-seven, compared with the previous campaign's extravagant fifty-six.

Now the 1969–70 season would see us heading into Europe, by virtue of our League position. I thought it was peculiar that the four English clubs when the tournament kicked off were Newcastle United, Liverpool, ourselves and Southampton. The Geordies were certainly there by right as holders, while no one could argue with Liverpool, who had finished runners-up to Leeds in the First Division. But because of the strict one-city, one-club nature of the competition, third-placed Everton were out in the cold, as were Chelsea (fifth) and Tottenham (sixth) because we were flying the flag for London. The final place bounced all the way down to Southampton, who had finished in seventh place – a dozen points behind unfortunate Everton.

Without boasting, the Fairs Cup never came alive for me until the semi-final draw pitted us with Ajax, which meant an introduction to Rudi Krol and Johan Cruyff, destined to become one of the greatest players of his generation – or any other, come to that.

The early rounds had been distinctly low-key, bringing us routine aggregate victories over Northern Ireland's Glentoran 3–1, Portugal's Sporting Lisbon 3–0 (when Geoff Barnett made a splendid penalty save in the away leg), French club Rouen 1–0 and then Romania's Dinamo Bacau 9–1.

I knew things were about to get deadly serious in the last four because Ajax represented a massive step up in class. Already one of the best teams in Europe, they boasted a large proportion of the Dutch international squad, and getting the better of them over two legs would be a magnificent achievement.

The previous season Ajax had been overwhelmed by AC Milan in the European Cup final, but there was not the slightest doubt of their pedigree and their brand of 'Total Football' saw them progress to become European champions three years running, beating Panathinaikos 2–0 at Wembley in 1971, Inter Milan 2–0 in Rotterdam in 1972 and Juventus 1–0 in Belgrade in 1973.

Quite why Cruyff, Krol, Gerrie Mühren, left-winger Piet Keizer and the other Ajax stars didn't come out to play at Highbury is a mystery, but they seemed apprehensive and tentative – two labels you could never stick on Charlie George in a million years.

WEMBLEY WOE, FAIRS CUP FUN

Maybe we deserved all the plaudits which came our way for once. I've noticed there's a tendency when exotic foreign teams come unstuck to question why they malfunction, rather than give British opponents due credit.

Anyway, Islington's finest was in his element that April evening, scoring twice and setting us up for a 3–0 victory.

Charlie announced himself to the Dutchmen with a long-range effort which deceived their keeper, Gert Bals, in the first half, and he rounded things off with a penalty when George Graham was felled after Jon Sammels had scored our second goal.

Cruyff had this really weird superstition where before kick-off he liked to give Bals a friendly punch in the stomach, then go and spit his chewing gum out into the opponents' half of the field. After the stopper's error of judgement for Charlie's opening goal, he risked another dig from Cruyff, who could be a bit of a perfectionist, although I had the utmost respect for him as a player.

The European season was compressed to give players going to the 1970 World Cup in Mexico sufficient time to prepare, so there was no time to soak up the plaudits for the job we saw out against Ajax in Amsterdam, losing 1–0 yet completing a comfortable aggregate victory, because the Fairs Cup final was scheduled for the following week.

Mühren, whose younger brother Arnold later made a huge impression at Ipswich Town, got the only goal of the game over in Amsterdam before half-time but our established back four of myself, Frank McLintock, 'Stan' Simpson and Bob McNab, in front of Bob Wilson, worked diligently to ensure that was the limit of their success.

Anderlecht, another club with an impressive European pedigree and boasting two players of the highest quality in midfielder Paul van Himst and striker Jan Mulder, lay in wait for us in Brussels on 22 April in one of the strangest matches I ever played in. It was the closest I've ever been to being passed to death. We were entrenched in the blood and thunder of the English League system, yet here was this bunch of crafty Belgians beating us with brainpower and the accuracy of their passing. They were unbelievably patient and we just let them weave their pretty patterns in front of us, then 'bang' they scored and we were 3–0 down after 70 minutes, with Mulder twice on target, before waking up to the fact we were on the wrong end of a very subtle, yet painful mugging. Had the first leg finished with that scoreline, it would have been all over and we would have been beaten finalists without a doubt.

Bertie and Don then pulled a master-stroke by hauling off Charlie, who had been in one of his miserable, hangdog moods, and brought on Ray Kennedy for only his fourth appearance. Young Ray started to put himself about in the air, rattled Anderlecht and suddenly scored a great header.

After the final whistle it was Frank's turn to play a blinder, in the dressing room. There was overall despondency at losing 3–1, but he emerged from the shower wearing nothing but a towel and his best *Braveheart* persona to rip the Belgians to pieces verbally. The tone of his rant was that there would be no 'fannying about' at our place and we'd just get stuck into them and duff them up.

Frank emphasised how Ray's goal meant we only needed to win 2–0 in the return leg to win the Cup on the away goals rule, and how he was supremely confident we had the physical muscle and finishing power to overturn the odds.

Frank told us: 'Get your heads up. I'll bet anyone we can win this because they can't defend crosses. We need to get our heads straight, really set our stall out to concentrate for 90 minutes and not concede. If we can get the ball out wide all the time and get crosses in, we will pulverise this team with our mental strength, physical power and heading ability.'

While the skipper was already fired up, I wasn't getting so carried away. All I knew was that if we scored an early goal, I fancied our chances.

The atmosphere at Highbury the following week was electric, a feeling matched only once in all the years I played for the club – the night we won the League at Tottenham.

Our fans must have sensed something special was in the air that spring night, because most of them turned up very early on 28 April and packed the terraces in a crowd of 51,612, singing their heads off to create a fantastic atmosphere. We knew Anderlecht were tasty going forward, but a little bit suspect defensively and their back four was soon breached when Eddie Kelly scored a cracker. The Belgians were pushed back by a wave of attacks before Raddy exposed their weakness in the air and levelled matters on aggregate with a thumping second-half header.

I knew we were home and dry if it stayed that way, because of Ray's precious away goal, and Anderlecht knew it too as they came at us with

WEMBLEY WOE, FAIRS CUP FUN

increased urgency. Mulder fired a warning shot which rebounded off a post, but we were an irresistible force that evening. Jon Sammels hammered in a glorious effort with 15 minutes to go, Frank got his hands on a winners' trophy at last and that was the cue for a massive pitch invasion as supporters scrambled off the North Bank and the Clock End to mob myself and the other lads.

Winning the Fairs Cup meant shrugging the monkey off Arsenal's back because it was the club's first trophy for 17 years, since winning the Football League in 1953 when dear old Joe Mercer was playing for Tom Whittaker's Gunners.

It was a nice bit of silverware and recognition, but in no sense did we think we'd cracked the secret of success.

The Fairs Cup run saved our season because I thought we were rubbish in the League. Back down in twelfth place with 42 points from 42 matches, 'average' summed us up perfectly, with 12 wins and 12 defeats.

As far as I was concerned, what we had achieved in beating Glentoran, Sporting Lisbon, Rouen, Dinamo Bacau, Ajax and Anderlecht was a world away from the holy grail of proving ourselves the best team in England over nine months.

CHAPTER TEN

When love breaks down

Professionally, my life was fine; privately, it turned ugly six months after I married Susan, a lovely brunette, in the golden summer of 1969. My Tamla Motown collection increased when Stevie Wonder released 'My Cherie Amour' and I thought of it as 'our' record.

The exact date of the wedding escapes me, but it must have been June or July because most of the Arsenal lads were away on their holidays. What I am sure about is what a special time it was, with a bit of indefinable magic in the air – and on the sports fields of England. Golfer Tony Jacklin shot 280 at Royal Lytham to win the Open, Ann Jones recovered to beat Billie Jean King 3–6, 6–3, 6–2 in the women's singles final at Wimbledon and Ray Illingworth skippered England's cricketers to a 2–0 series triumph over the great Gary Sobers' West Indies side.

It might have been near the end of the decade, but I recall the '60s were still in full swing. Yeah, I know it sounds a bit soppy now, but with youth on your side, you did feel like reaching for the stars, that anything was possible, and we were all captivated when Apollo 11 went into orbit and Neil Armstrong became the first man to set foot on the moon.

As if to celebrate, David Bowie and Zager & Evans provided the soundtrack to the sunshine in London with their massive hits 'Space Oddity' and 'In the Year 2525'.

Several 'happenings' occurred in America, massive rock concerts featuring artists such as Jimi Hendrix, Led Zeppelin and Janis Joplin, culminating in the daddy of them all, Woodstock, while over here the Rolling Stones played a free concert in Hyde Park.

John Lennon and Yoko Ono released 'Give Peace a Chance' and

WHEN LOVE BREAKS DOWN

it must have struck a chord with Richard Nixon. The US president promised that troop withdrawal from Vietnam would begin, and he wasn't lying for once.

London had not witnessed a sunnier June for 40 years and in the middle of July a mate of mine in Hertfordshire rang complaining the thermometer in his garden was nudging 91°F.

I couldn't have been happier, honestly.

It had been a long, steady courtship for Susan and me, lasting four years, and all began when my good pal 'Stan' Simpson's girlfriend, Anne, thought I needed cheering up and fixed up a blind date for me with a friend of hers whose parents owned a hairdressers. I took Susan to a cosy club I knew in Regent Street, near Carnaby Street in the West End, for a drink and to listen to a singer. We hit it off straight away, got engaged 12 months later and eventually had a church wedding near her home in Cockfosters. I didn't have a stag night, but I enjoyed a few glasses of champagne with my best man and landlord, Terry Neill, and Stan at the reception in a big hotel near Hadley Wood – it was quite a posh do – before Susan and I jetted off to Tunisia, our honeymoon destination.

I thought it was going to be sunshine and roses all the way, but she cleared off after six months before returning for a while to try and make a go of it and investigate whether I had mended my boozy, carefree ways. But a leopard can't change his spots, and my first wife packed her bags for good and kissed goodbye to our strained life together at Hilltop Close, Cheshunt on Monday, 1 February 1971.

I can be so specific about the date because although that night was spent, like so many others, celebrating over a few jars in the White Hart at Southgate, this time I was flavour of the month and everyone seemed to want to buy me a drink. I was fresh from holding my nerve to score the last-minute penalty winner which had edged us past Portsmouth 3–2 in an FA Cup fourth-round replay at Highbury earlier that bitterly cold evening.

I didn't get home at some ridiculous hour, for a change, because we knew when enough was enough, and I didn't need reminding that I had Colin Bell and Francis Lee coming my way in a talented Manchester City team on the Saturday.

This was the season when everything was coming together on the pitch and we all sensed something rather special might be in the air.

Still, it must have been a bit after midnight when I turned the key in the front door and immediately sensed something was amiss. Our three-bedroom detached house suddenly felt very empty and I knew I wasn't going to find Susan upstairs in bed reading a magazine. It dawned on me that she had left again – this time for good – when I checked various cupboards and wardrobes to discover all her possessions were missing.

There was no explanation, no farewell note. If there were any tears goodbye, they weren't shed by me. I know that sounds callous, but it's the truth.

Like a great many sportsmen of my vintage, I suspect I got married too young, and it didn't take long for us both to realise, with mounting regret and resentment, that we were simply 'wrong' for each other. I was certainly not cut out to be married so young; there were too many distractions, although our relationship was fine before the marriage and there was no reason to suspect it wouldn't work out.

It wasn't that I didn't love Susan when we exchanged our wedding vows, it was just that I also loved the freedom life as a professional footballer in London granted me – the access to the girls, the glamour, the booze and the parties with a tight-knit set of teammates set to achieve great things. So yeah, I very probably did love that more than her, and I'll also admit to being selfish and immature, young and stupid. She must have felt she was living with a lunatic.

I was having a good time, living the typical – or at least what I took to be typical – life of a footballer whose results were good and whose team were playing well. I didn't need a wife; I would have been better off with a mum in the kitchen and a tart in the bedroom. That's the truth of the matter. Everything was rosy at Arsenal and I just got carried along in the general swing of things, on a high with happy teammates.

Susan still worked as a hairdresser in the family business, and I feel sure she would have appreciated a nice, clean-shaven executive working in the City. I don't mean this to sound condescending, and I'm not trying to score points this late in the day, but she could have kissed him goodbye on the front step as he strode off in his pinstripe suit, bowler hat, with an umbrella and briefcase to catch the morning train into town. She could have been there for him when he came home in the evening, ready with his tea and a pair of slippers.

I couldn't give her that, or anything approaching it, never in a million years. A footballer doesn't lead a normal, conventional nine-to-five life. Instead, I think I must have given her a dog's life in our brief time together as man and wife. I was young, red-blooded, not

WHEN LOVE BREAKS DOWN

the worst-looking bloke in London, and as soon as the match had finished, I wanted to know what the score was off the pitch as the cry went up in the dressing room: 'Where are we going tonight, lads?'

Most of the team were social animals, and always up for a good time – especially Frank McLintock, George Graham, Bob McNab, John Radford and 'Stan' Simpson.

Frank and George were nicknamed 'The Krays' by some of the lads – although not to their faces, for obvious reasons – on account of how close they were, almost like twins. They always seemed to go everywhere together, tall, dark-haired, imposing characters with a sense of their own importance.

This is what Frank, our skipper, wrote in *True Grit*:

> At parties, if you glanced in Snouty's direction all you could see was his tonsils as he threw back his head and roared with laughter. But the rest of the time he would be monosyllabic and even grunted those solitary words, working on his image as Arsenal's own Clint Eastwood.

It just seemed like the most natural thing in the world to me, particularly after a good win, to go out on the town with the lads and, inevitably, that meant girls and plenty to drink. It was a glamorous, pop star kind of life.

Some wives expect their husbands to go home after work, but I got too involved and, looking back now, I can see I must have made Susan lonely and miserable. But that's hindsight for you, a bloody wonderful gift – and totally useless.

The first time Susan left me, saying simply: 'I've had enough, I'm going', it was a bit of a shock and I was disappointed. The second time I wasn't really that bothered because by then I knew there was very little chance of us growing old and grey together.

I never really spoke to her parents, while my mum and dad would never have dreamed of interfering. Susan and I lost touch completely and I was told she remarried. That's as much as I know. We weren't together long enough to discuss starting a family. There were no immediate divorce proceedings; that came several years later, when I separated from Susan in an uncontested action.

I didn't jump straight into another steady relationship – there were too many alternative temptations, too many groupies, I suppose, among the girls in our regular set at the White Hart boozer, and I needed no encouragement to play the field.

I reacted in typical fashion to living on my own and the house became Party Central. Bertie Mee and Don Howe learned that Susan had left me for good but had no inclination to get involved. I wasn't a child, after all, but a well-paid professional, and I'm sure they would only have become concerned had my form deteriorated. On the field, I started to perform even better, so the management were prepared to indulge my lifestyle.

I was quite happy in my own company at home and self-sufficient, although several small local restaurants, dry cleaners and launderettes suddenly benefited from my regular patronage. I wasn't helpless by any means in the kitchen, though, and quite adept at knocking up a meal after successfully picking my way around Sainsbury's.

It wasn't long before the lads got wind of Susan's disappearing act, however, and my home inevitably became an open-house, a magnet for noisy, late-night parties which went on until four or five in the morning, complete with music, singing and shouting – much to the annoyance and aggravation of my prim and proper neighbours in the cul-de-sac, invaded by the marauding White Hart crowd. I would sometimes wake up to discover a few girls lying about the place in various states of undress.

Sunday mornings could get embarrassing, sneaking all the empty bottles into the dustbin before trying to smuggle two or three giggling females out of the house past honest, upright citizens returning from church, washing their cars and trimming their lawns. It was like a scene from a Carry On film or the 'Confessions of' series.

The neighbours became so fed up with my behaviour, particularly when it caused them to lose sleep, that they organised a petition in protest and brought it round to my front door early one evening as I was preparing to go out on the razzle, requesting that I tone things down.

That put a real damper on my night. In fact, I was so ashamed that I went to an estate agent the following morning and put the house I'd barely owned for a year on the market, instructing him: 'I paid £8,750 for it and I'll sell to the first offer matching that. I'm not interested in making a profit.'

It's peculiar and a touch ironic to reflect that while I was fronting up to the toughest footballers in the First Division on a regular basis and trading lumps and bumps, a piece of paper signed by the

WHEN LOVE BREAKS DOWN

local community could have embarrassed me so much. It must have touched a nerve . . . who said I never had a sensitive side? It wasn't as if they were actually forcing me out of my home, merely pointing out that my behaviour was a bit antisocial and causing them grief. Guilty, as charged.

Within a matter of weeks I had moved into a flat at Cockfosters, above a row of shops and near the tube station, with a big Arsenal fan called Jimmy Curran I'd met through the White Hart boozing school.

CHAPTER ELEVEN

Double delight, double despair

How can you be at the heart of such a frenzied night, becoming champions of England, beating your deadliest rivals in their own backyard with a last-gasp goal in your last League match of the season in front of a capacity crowd of 51,992 and another 50,000 estimated fans locked outside . . . and still feel so alone?

I haven't got a clue – but I know I did.

And that's just the half of it, because with the First Division title safely in the bag, I suffered a shocking experience at the hands of Bertie Mee, who attempted to ensure I missed the FA Cup final against Liverpool.

I couldn't have done any more to help Arsenal to the momentous Double in 1970–71, a season which saw my first marriage collapse, yet ended with me proudly making my England debut, despite Bertie doing his best to sabotage my international chances.

But I wasn't on the pitch when the final whistle sounded to acknowledge the Gunners as champions or FA Cup winners.

It was as if I had spent ages making love to the most beautiful woman in the world, only to be kicked out of bed five minutes before the climax.

Few punters marked us down for glory after we won only two of our first six matches, and it dawned on us we would be missing three major players with injuries for a substantial period. Jon Sammels fractured an ankle bone in Denmark during pre-season, 'Stan' Simpson was out of the game for over three months, recovering from a cartilage operation, and when we kicked off on Saturday, 15 August, against the defending champions Everton at Goodison Park, Charlie George wrecked his ankle, colliding with their keeper Gordon West in scoring an equaliser.

DOUBLE DELIGHT, DOUBLE DESPAIR

Mind you, we were extremely grateful for Stan's replacement, John Roberts, who provided a pass for George Graham to chip a very late goal to clinch a 2–2 draw.

The following Monday night brought another point from a stalemate at West Ham, but once we got cracking properly, I started to appreciate what a potent partnership we might have in attack where Ray Kennedy, a strapping 19 year old from Northumberland, had replaced Charlie and proved a perfect foil for John Radford as they feasted on a diet of quality crosses from George Armstrong.

Raddy soon scored a hat-trick in a 4–0 win over Manchester United, while Ray got the only goal of the game to see off Huddersfield Town in a somewhat less emphatic home success three days later.

I particularly enjoyed tracking one figure in United's blue change shirt and making his life a misery. It was not that long after George Best had ambitiously signed an eight-year contract at Old Trafford, guaranteeing him at least ten grand a year. Keeping Bestie sweet was wishful thinking, while United were in decline now and not a patch on the team which had won the European Cup in 1968.

We lost for the first time at Chelsea, 2–1, before steeling ourselves for what we knew would be a really tasty affair three nights later – Leeds United at home. It was the usual horrible match where you had to grit your teeth and trade kick for kick. Billy Bremner succeeded in winding up young Eddie Kelly, who lashed out in retaliation and got himself sent off inside half an hour; I recall the referee needed an eight-man police escort to see him safely back to his dressing room.

Although it was the first point Leeds had dropped following five straight wins, I sensed they were perfectly satisfied with the outcome. In time, that 0–0 draw was to have huge implications.

I honestly don't think it dawned on us that the Double was on until the last few weeks of the season. Certainly, we had been well behind Leeds in the race for the title at one stage – seven points adrift, in fact. Don Revie's side had set a furious pace and been beaten only once, 3–0 by Stoke in the Potteries, before the turn of the year.

Well before then, a fight of an altogether more literal nature had proved significant. We were already a close-knit set of lads, but the events of a balmy September night in Rome bonded us further together. The defence of our Fairs Cup crown started with Raddy scoring twice in a 2–2 draw against Lazio, where we were greeted by fireworks, flares and missiles before being confronted by a team who dedicated 90 minutes to the dark arts of kicking, spitting, gouging, elbowing and pulling our hair – and that was when they weren't obviously cheating in front of the referee!

It was a warm, sticky night and the atmosphere was even closer when both sides turned up with bad feelings simmering for the post-match banquet in a restaurant without air conditioning.

The game had been downright nasty and despite a decent result, I was feeling very pissed off. My image might have been Mr Cool, but I've always sweated a great deal; in my favourite book about Arsenal at this time, David Tossell's *Seventy-One Guns*, Frank McLintock remarks: 'Peter could hold a newspaper and it would dissolve, he was sweating so much. But in that restaurant he was simply growling at the Italians, who were seated only about ten yards away.'

Both sets of players were eyeing each other warily as we sat down for some pasta and red wine, and the Lazio mob were seething when a couple of our lads began mincing about with the continental leather men's purses we'd been given. It was a culture clash and maybe we were out of order. In any event, it soon became a little bit more than a case of 'handbags'. I understand the flashpoint came when Ray and Peter Marinello went for a pee and encountered four or five Lazio players preening themselves in the gents' mirror. Words were exchanged, Ray and our gentle Scottish winger were bundled out of the front door and into the street; punches were exchanged and Marinello was hurled over the bonnet of a taxi. The first I learned of any trouble was when Bob Wilson returned to our table and announced: 'There's a fight outside.' Suddenly, the restaurant was left looking like the *Mary Celeste* as we made for the street, to be greeted by mayhem.

The skirmish was very confusing, with lots of pushing and shoving. Frank summed it up for me when he said: 'For a while it was like the Wild West, we all piled in.' I singled out a Lazio player who had been guilty of some of the worst excesses earlier that evening, drew back my right fist and gave him an enormous smile. He was a pretty boy and reacted by spreading his hands wide across his face, imploring me not to stick one on him. A sitting duck, it was all too tempting, but with the police turning up, blue lights flashing and toting guns, and club officials rushing around trying to break things up, the anger within me subsided.

Stranger still, both sets of players returned to the banquet and carried on with the food. However, the clash prompted predictable 'Battle of Rome' newspaper headlines, although Bertie did himself no end of good within our dressing room by declaring: 'I am proud to

DOUBLE DELIGHT, DOUBLE DESPAIR

be the manager of these players. They withstood terrible provocation during the match. I cannot condone fighting but the players all have my sympathy.' John Roberts made me chuckle some time later when he confided: 'That bag of mine, Snouty. It was lovely.'

Lazio, predictably, bottled it at Highbury – they were there in body but not in spirit for the return leg, which we won 2–0, and I had the satisfaction of providing the passes from which Raddy and Geordie Armstrong scored our goals.

It developed into a decent competition for me because in November I slotted home the decisive penalty against Sturm Graz as we overcame a 1–0 deficit from the first leg in Austria. There was genuine pressure when I ran up to take that kick deep into injury-time at the end of the match, but my nerve held and within the hour the lager was flowing at the White Hart as we toasted a 2–1 aggregate victory. It was one night when I was guaranteed not to have to put my hand in my pocket, as most of the pub seemed to want to buy me a drink.

The Belgians, Beveren-Waas, were brushed aside in the third round before the European tournaments went into hibernation until spring. I should have provided us with the comfort of an early lead in the first leg at Highbury, but suffered a rare error of judgement from the penalty spot this time. Ray bailed me out of the dog-house with a couple of goals, and a 4–0 win meant my mistake was virtually forgotten by the end of the evening. It was all over for the Beveren-Waas part-timers bar the shouting, but there wasn't much evidence of that in Belgium and we played out a stalemate in front of a subdued crowd.

Meanwhile, back in the First Division, our friends from Tottenham squeezed out a 2–1 win at Elland Road on 9 January and then Liverpool won there 1–0 a month later. The inspirational Billy Bremner was injured and, significantly, missed both defeats, but still Leeds were ominously well-placed to press for the Double themselves on 13 February when they travelled as League leaders to complete the formality of knocking out Fourth Division minnows Colchester United in the FA Cup and claiming their place in the last eight. What followed was one of the greatest upsets in the history of the grand old competition as the pride of Yorkshire were turned over 3–2 by a collection of rejects and has-beens labelled 'Grandad's Army', led by two-goal Ray Crawford, a veteran rescued from the non-League scrapheap who had been the First Division's top scorer ten years previously with Ipswich.

Leeds reacted just as I expected and claimed 11 of the next 12 available points just as we hit a nasty wobble which threatened to derail our pursuit of them.

A useful test of a good team is how you respond in adversity, and we let ourselves down badly at Derby in late February. I remember one report said we were bustled out of our stride, outwitted, rarely looked like championship calibre and were lucky, in the end, to restrict the margin of defeat to 2–0. It was a typically awkward uneven Baseball Ground surface, but you'd never have guessed it from the performance of Roy McFarland. Derby's England centre-half had been taken to the cleaners once or twice before by Raddy, but not this time. He not only found time to score the opening goal but totally dominated too for good measure.

The other goal came from Kevin Hector. He frequently haunted Frank McLintock, who was never quite sure which side the Derby striker would try and pass him.

Travelling back down the M1, I said to one of the lads through gritted teeth, with no great wit or imagination: 'This is bollocks', and made a mental note to concentrate harder, tackle more fiercely and generally compete with everything I had left in the tank. Fortunately, I was far from alone in my determination. Coming on the back of defeats in our two previous away matches (2–1 at Huddersfield and 1–0 at Liverpool), Derby was a significant turning point in our season.

Given the manner in which we competed and our enthusiastic deployment of the offside trap, nobody in their right mind could accuse Arsenal of being 'southern softies' – but those three successive defeats in the north and the Midlands did have critics claiming we lacked the consistency to overhaul the Leeds machine, which still held a six-point advantage, worth three victories, over us on 20 March.

We didn't officially win the League title until a momentous evening in May, of course, but we certainly did the spadework in our following nine matches after Brian Clough's side beat us. Nine games and nine victories, scoring sixteen goals and conceding just one, scored by Saints skipper Terry Paine at The Dell. This was the winning run that put the heat on Leeds between 2 March and 20 April: Wolves (away) 3–0; Crystal Palace (away) 2–0; Blackpool (home) 1–0; Chelsea (home) 2–0; Coventry (home) 1–0; Southampton (away) 2–1; Nottingham Forest (away) 3–0; Newcastle (home) 1–0 and Burnley (home) 1–0. To be honest, it wasn't the most demanding set of fixtures you could

DOUBLE DELIGHT, DOUBLE DESPAIR

have asked for, but you can only beat what's put in front of you. And remember, there was no margin for error.

While our League form was taking care of itself and we answered that question of consistency in emphatic fashion, our progress in the FA Cup was less assured.

First up came Yeovil away, a banana skin if ever there was one. The clamour to see this potential giant-killing was immense and with the non-League club sensing a heaven-sent opportunity to clear their overdraft, they bumped up the price of tickets from 22p to 75p on the terraces, and from 32p to £1.50 for seats, making them the most expensive in the country for a third-round match.

Arsenal had suffered a number of embarrassing defeats by rank underdogs in the Cup, and there was the sniff of another shock on Yeovil's infamous sloping pitch. Taking everything into account, we were apprehensive travelling down to Somerset, especially as snow during the week might turn things into a lottery.

Come 2 January, the day of the big match, the Huish was still covered in the white stuff and Yeovil were furious with the referee for giving the pitch the thumbs down, but we weren't complaining.

All midweek evening football was temporarily banned because of emergency power restrictions, so we returned on Wednesday for a 2 p.m. kick-off and soon plunged the Southern League club into gloom. We set about them from the start and did the business 3–0, thanks to a couple of goals from Raddy and one from Ray.

We squeezed past a very game Second Division Portsmouth outfit in the fourth round when I equalised at Fratton Park with a penalty, and also scored the winner in the replay with another successful spot-kick that memorable early February night when my marriage went up the spout.

It was a filthy wet Saturday down on the south coast and Pompey were in a desperate state in the bottom half of the Second Division. The previous month, Carlisle had done them 6–0 and they were on an awful run, but that didn't deter a bumper crowd of 39,659 from turning out in the rain. There was a massive bust-up when their left-back George Ley tipped a shot from Raddy round the post ten minutes before half-time and the referee awarded a corner. Frank McLintock was straight in his face and, after being persuaded to consult a linesman, the ref changed his mind. I picked the ball up, stuck it down on the penalty spot, dried my hands on the front of my shirt and struck the kick to the left of John Milkins' dive. That should have been enough, but Portsmouth equalised in the last minute through Mike Trebilcock, obliging us to play another match we could well have done without.

The replay did, however, enable us to welcome back Charlie George for the first time since the opening match of the season and he marked the occasion by racing away to score a brilliant equaliser in the thirteenth minute after an early wake-up call from Norman Piper. All credit to Pompey, they flatly refused to go quietly after 'Stan' Simpson gave us a 2–1 lead and Ley levelled the score just before the hour. Then, with the prospect of extra-time looming, Eoin Hand tripped Raddy and it fell to me to take another penalty. This time, I decided to change tactics and had the satisfaction of tucking the penalty well up inside Milkins' right-hand post as he dived in the opposite direction.

Manchester City, our fifth-round opponents, provided serious food for thought, and now Charlie was firing on all cylinders. He had played in a home League win over City the previous week and this time Charlie's two goals proved too much at Maine Road for Joe Mercer and Malcolm Allison's men, who had only a goal from Colin Bell to show for their efforts that Wednesday.

The tie had been rained off on the Saturday, much like the original fixture at Yeovil, which had fallen victim to snow, but we were in good heart and the party really went with a swing on the trip back to London with a few toasts to Colchester for their weekend exploits which had stunned Leeds – and Charlie, of course.

Charlie's ability was never in question. Some of the things he did in training and matches for Arsenal, and later Derby in the European Cup, took your breath away. I felt he lacked consistency, however, and because of his suspect temperament and mood swings he was sometimes in danger of letting the team down. Charlie's biggest crime is under the section in the record books which lists his England caps . . . all one of them, gained against the Republic of Ireland in 1976. And even then Charlie only managed just over an hour before a lacklustre performance saw Don Revie haul him off in favour of Gordon Hill. With discipline and focus, Charlie should have played at least 50 times for England. And Dave Mackay should never have been allowed to steal him away to Derby for £90,000 in July 1975. As it is, he'll just have to be content with being a legend at Arsenal to this day – and knowing Charlie as I do, I'm sure he'd happily settle for that.

Leicester were obdurate opponents in the sixth round of the FA Cup, a competitive team on their way to being crowned Second Division champions. Boasting players of the quality of Peter Shilton

DOUBLE DELIGHT, DOUBLE DESPAIR

in goal and David Nish at left-back, they were difficult to break down. We drew 0–0 at Filbert Street before Charlie, darling of the North Bank, enhanced his reputation with the only goal of the replay in front of a huge Highbury crowd of 57,443.

Cup football of the European variety returned in March when I was on target to clinch a 2–1 home victory over Cologne in the last eight. I was never renowned for my goal-scoring exploits, but this one has always stuck in my memory as it was an especially good one. We were on the attack with 20 minutes remaining when the ball was half-cleared to the edge of the area and I connected sweetly with a left-foot half-volley which found the target nice and low.

That wasn't enough though, and our grasp on the Fairs Cup was wrenched away when the Germans replied with a penalty in a 1–0 victory which sent them through by virtue of away goals. It was a sickener because Cologne conned a very dodgy early spot-kick out of the referee and spent the rest of the match rolling on the floor as if they'd been shot whenever we tackled them.

We had a few beers to numb the sense of disappointment at going out of Europe, but we couldn't afford a hangover because four days later Stoke City were waiting for us in the FA Cup semi-final at Hillsborough.

CHAPTER TWELVE

I'll always have Sheffield

Romantics go misty-eyed at the mention of venues where great players enjoyed defining moments in their careers. Think of Gordon Banks, and his Save of the Century plunge in Guadalajara to divert Pelé's certain headed 'goal' up and over the bar in the 1970 Mexico World Cup, or the arrival of 19-year-old George Best, superstar, in 1966 with his magnificent 'El Beatle' performance in Manchester United's 5–1 European Cup thrashing of Benfica in Lisbon, where he scored twice.

Me? I'll always have Sheffield.

A little 'history', a bit of 'previous' was beginning to develop between Arsenal and Stoke City as we prepared to meet at Hillsborough with a place in the FA Cup final at stake on a sunny afternoon in late March. They never made it easy for us and six months earlier we had come badly unstuck at the Victoria Ground, suffering a complete systems failure as wily Tony Waddington's team took us apart 5–0.

When Dennis Smith and John Ritchie sent the Potters into a 2–0 half-time lead, I feared the worst; we all did.

The mood in our dressing room during the interval was serious, rather than sombre. We didn't need reminding that the next goal would be critical. If we scored it, and quickly, we were right back in with a shout. If Stoke made it 3–0, it really was game over.

I won't sing my praises, however, but rely on the *Daily Telegraph Football Chronicle* to get in a few rare good words on my behalf under the headline 'From spoiler to scorer: it's another Storey': 'Peter Storey's reputation has been built up as a midfield spoiler, a ruthless destroyer, the "iron man" of Arsenal's defence. But every dog has his day, and Storey's came at Hillsborough in the FA Cup semi-final against Stoke.'

It didn't start out that way. Harry Burrows whipped in a corner from the right with his left foot and I got a sick feeling in the pit of my stomach when big Smithy, their centre-half, blocked my attempted clearance on the angle of the six-yard box and the ball rebounded freakishly high into our net.

Our misfortune continued. 'Stan' Simpson headed the ball away and Charlie George, after trapping it perfectly on his chest, played a poor, misguided back-pass which was gratefully gobbled up by Ritchie to put Stoke two up, and deservedly so, at the interval.

But soon after half-time, I replied with probably the finest goal of my career.

Geordie Armstrong's throw-in from deep on the left was hoisted high into the air over his own head by Ray Kennedy; John Radford and George Graham both went for the ball, but it broke to me on the edge of the area. I wasn't renowned for my shooting ability but I took off and hit the sweetest of right-foot volleys past Gordon Banks.

We kept pressing and pressing for the equaliser, but it looked as if it would never come and our hopes of the Double would be dashed. The match was deep into injury-time when Mike Pejic fouled Graham, Geordie floated in the free-kick and there was an almighty scramble before the ball bounced behind for a corner off Gordon Banks.

Over came Geordie's flag-kick, up went Frank McLintock and Banks was nowhere as John Mahoney dived full length on the line to keep Frank's header out with his hand.

I'll let that *Chronicle* report give an unbiased account of what happened next:

> George had gone off injured, so Storey – the other penalty-taker, not because of any dead-ball ability, but for his ice-cool temperament – strode up to take the spot-kick against the world's best keeper. It was not a particularly good kick, but he sent Banks the wrong way, and had kept Arsenal in the Cup.

I don't reckon I ever scored a more important goal than that volley which brought us back from the dead, closely followed by the penalty, of course. My stomach tightened when the referee, Pat Partridge, one of the best, blew his whistle and pointed dramatically to the spot. He'd enjoyed a perfect view of Mahoney's desperate handling offence and I can vividly recall McLintock, our skipper, celebrating with the rest of the lads, hugging one another as if the whistle had already sounded for a 2–2 draw.

Instinctively, I wished I was anywhere else in the world but here at Hillsborough, being followed by 53,000 pairs of eyes.

I thought the TV commentator, Brian Moore, captured the mood perfectly when he said: 'Storey is the man with the terrible responsibility, and there are Arsenal players who daren't watch.'

It was one of those defining moments I sensed would live with me forever. Score and the goal would be taken for granted; miss and Arsenal were out of the FA Cup, it would all be my fault and I'd never hear the end of it. It can be all too convenient to claim you win as a team and lose as a team. That way of thinking can soften the blow for a player who has cocked things up. Yes, it is a team game, but sometimes individuals must show bottle.

George Graham could read me better than the rest of the team and summed up the intensity of the moment in *Seventy-One Guns* when he said: 'Peter must have lost half a stone taking that penalty. He was very quiet, but he was just sweating without saying anything. He was soaked.'

I placed the ball on the spot at the Leppings Lane end of the stadium in front of all the Stoke supporters, walked back nine or ten paces, betrayed my nerves with a little skip and ran in to make contact and shoot.

The article was correct in that it wasn't one of my most cleanly-struck penalties, but Banks made the mistake of committing himself to going to his right a fraction before I hit the ball, and I had a split-second in which to slip the ball past him the other way.

I bow to no one in my admiration of Banks, but I thought the occasion of that FA Cup semi-final got to him, and that the Stoke captaincy was a burden. He had been far from his customary calm and composed self.

Gordon was distraught and related: 'I thought Storey might hit it to my right and all my body weight went to my right. It wasn't even a good penalty. It wasn't far from my left but I couldn't react and get down.'

I've cringed watching England make a complete and utter balls-up of so many penalty shoot-outs to bow out of assorted World Cups and European Championships with their tails between their legs. Penalties are not a nice way to decide tournament football matches, but until someone comes up with a better idea, players must accept the pressure, show a bit more bloody-minded professionalism and get on with it. The body language of some £100,000-a-week England superstars in penalty shoot-outs has been wretched. Devoid of confidence, it seems to me they are half-expecting to miss, rather than score.

I practised every now and then at London Colney against Bob Wilson and Geoff Barnett, and scored time after time. The goal looked as big as anything, but it was a very different story in a match with 40–50,000 fans praying for you to be a hero or a villain. Suddenly, the goal shrinks, the opposing keeper resembles a giant and behind him there might very well be thousands of faces twisted in hatred, willing you to cock up.

I got the job of taking penalties for Arsenal by default. Mind you, I always got the nasty jobs. When Charlie wasn't around, nobody else fancied touching them with a bargepole. My technique was classically simple and invariably the same. I would settle the ball on the spot, brush my hands down my shirt or shorts, avoid eye contact with the keeper, turn back and run up as if I meant business, concentrating with all my might, before deciding at the last moment to shoot low to the left or right close to the inside of the post.

I'd never call it fun; at times it was real pressure, and I was very lucky that the handful of penalties I missed in my career didn't count for much in the final analysis and weren't in crucial games. As I have already mentioned, I failed from the spot at Sunderland, for example, in 1966 when Arsenal were on their way to a 2–0 win, and I also missed one against Beveren-Waas in the Fairs Cup earlier in the season before we belted in four goals.

Maybe I wasn't lucky; maybe I made my own luck.

In any event, back at Hillsborough, Stoke's confidence was shattered. They knew they had blown their big chance, the momentum was with us and when the teams reconvened at Villa Park the following Wednesday evening we were pretty sure we would emerge victorious. Arsenal swarmed all over the Potters in Birmingham; it wasn't much of a contest and the only surprise was that we didn't have more to show for our dominance than a 2–0 win.

There were no dramas this time, although Stoke's Mike Bernard had tried to stir things up by boasting how he had easily coped with Charlie George in Sheffield. The response was a typical Charlie piss-take, an extravagant back-pass to Bob Wilson at the first opportunity to let everyone know his nerves were still very much intact.

George Graham left his would-be marker for dead in the thirteenth minute to climb high and thump a clinical header past Banks from a Geordie Armstrong corner, and the second half was only two minutes old when John Radford simply escaped down the left and crossed low to give Ray Kennedy a goal on a plate.

Our place in the FA Cup final assured at last, it was time to continue hunting down Leeds, and 17 April was the pivotal Saturday when we went top for the first time, beating Newcastle United at Highbury thanks to a fabulous shot from Charlie, while Leeds were controversially beaten 2–1 at home by West Brom in the match infamous for the 'miles offside' goal.

I still chuckle at the memory of Albion, playing in a yellow and blue away strip identical to ours, taking a 1–0 lead after Tony 'Bomber' Brown intercepted a sloppy Norman Hunter pass 15 yards inside his own half. The linesman was waving his flag for offside against Colin Suggett, but he was nowhere near interfering with play. Brown almost stopped to have a look around before carrying on into acres of space before slipping a pass across Gary Sprake for Jeff Astle to run in and score at the far post. There was even a hint of another offside in the final ball and suddenly all hell broke loose. Several Leeds fans invaded the pitch, on came the police to frogmarch them off, while the other linesman was struck on the head, felled by an object from the terraces. Revie came on to remonstrate with the officials, all to no avail. When the dust settled and referee Ray Tinkler consulted his linesman, the goal was allowed to stand but the repercussions were immense – and the following season Leeds were fined £750 and ordered to play their first four home matches elsewhere, ending up with two fixtures at Huddersfield and one apiece at Hull and Hillsborough. They drew two of those 'home' matches, as well, 0–0 against Wolves then 1–1 against Tottenham, and lost the title to Derby by a single point.

I missed my first match of the season three days later when Arsenal edged past Burnley 1–0 at Highbury on a tense Tuesday night.

I wasn't injured, suspended or out of form. Far from it, in fact. Sir Alf Ramsey had called me up for my England debut the following evening against Greece in a European Nations tie. Bob McNab was also on international duty, which did not impress Bertie Mee one little bit, as he was obliged to shuffle his defence, bringing in John Roberts for Bob at left-back while Eddie Kelly filled my midfield role. Charlie scored the only goal of the game against the Clarets from the penalty spot, and we could all relax for a few days.

I'LL ALWAYS HAVE SHEFFIELD

I returned as an England player on the Saturday when our nine-match winning streak came to a disappointing end at West Brom, where 'Bomber' Brown equalised four minutes from the final whistle. We could hardly complain too vigorously about that dropped point at the Hawthorns, though, because Albion, who had not previously won an away match for 16 months, had of course done us an almighty favour the previous week at Leeds.

All eyes were focused on Elland Road for our visit on 25 April, a Monday night. It was always going to be a titanic clash because there was no love lost between the clubs at the best of times, and the stakes had been raised dramatically by West Brom's highly debatable goal, which had left Revie and his lot whining like stuck pigs.

So it was that we ventured into Yorkshire for a potential championship decider. With 61 points from 39 matches, we knew the title would be ours if we beat a brooding Leeds outfit, who had 60 points from 40 games and were nursing a massive sense of injustice. It was a tough, tough game and the occasion Billy Bremner chose to stamp on my face. It was always no holds barred between me and Billy, whether the occasion was Arsenal versus Leeds or England versus Scotland.

Bob McNab once told me he felt our rivalry seemed not so much a question of sport as a war of attrition, and that in certain games the ball could have been removed from the pitch and the two of us wouldn't have noticed. Bob reckoned that there was one match when the two of us were just waiting to 'do' the other, and neither of us dared put a foot in because the other would have steamed in and ripped it off.

I just recall going down in our area during a goalmouth melee and shutting my eyes as Billy's studs came down on my nose and cheek. Heat of the battle stuff, I'm sure. Not even Billy would have been that callous in his manner of assault. I suffered a few little cuts, more nicks than anything, but nothing major. Fortunately I didn't need any stitches but I moaned like hell about the injury-time winner from Jack Charlton, which seemed to be yards offside. Now it was our turn to go crazy at the referee, Norman Burtenshaw. Bob Wilson and Frank McLintock led our outraged complaints, but later on television we noticed that 'Nabbers' had been slow to get out. Even a 0–0 draw would have meant we could have clinched the League title at home to Stoke at the weekend, but there was no sense of depression travelling home. We were still fairly optimistic and secure in the knowledge that the destiny of the First Division championship was in our own hands.

TRUE STOREY

Given the outcome of the FA Cup semi-final, Stoke, understandably, were in no mood whatsoever to do us any favours in our penultimate League match. In fact, the Potters were intent on making life as uncomfortable for us as possible by packing their midfield and operating with one up front. There were over 55,000 punters inside Highbury when they came calling on Saturday, 1 May for a must-win fixture, and it was frustrating stuff, deadlocked at 0–0 going into the second half. I don't imagine the tension on the terraces eased any when I started making my own Mayday distress signals after taking a heavy knock on an ankle when I went into a tackle. I found I couldn't get up without assistance and knew immediately the injury was nothing innocuous. Eddie Kelly, a Scottish teenager with attitude and a swagger, came on to replace me and grabbed the headlines by scoring the winning goal. Suddenly, I found myself on crutches with no chance of playing 48 hours later.

Meanwhile, Leeds were completing their fixtures with a routine 2–0 home victory over Nottingham Forest, which meant we either needed to beat Tottenham two days later or emerge with a goalless draw.

My next outing was in a taxi to see a medical consultant in Park Street in the West End, where my fears were realised and the injury was diagnosed as damaged ligaments. 'Time and rest should do the trick,' the doctor said cheerily. 'It could have been worse.' I think the poor chap was a bit unnerved by the way I glared back at him. I was thinking to myself, worse? What could be worse than missing Arsenal's most important night for years – and very probably the FA Cup final too?

Any draw at White Hart Lane other than 0–0 and the championship would be on its way to Elland Road because of the vagaries of goal average.

The build-up to this titanic derby was crazy, with Don Revie demonstrating a warped grasp of our local rivalry by claiming Spurs would prefer Arsenal to win the championship, and let us have it, because that would be a feather in the capital's hat, a victory for the south over the north.

I could hardly think of a tougher fixture than a trip to Tottenham, an exceptionally gifted team poised to finish third in the table and who already had the Football League Cup trophy on their sideboard following a 2–0 victory over Aston Villa at Wembley courtesy of two goals from Martin Chivers, whose tally for the season stood at thirty all told.

I'LL ALWAYS HAVE SHEFFIELD

Tottenham were the only club that century who had done the Double, and they were desperate to keep it that way. Their manager Bill Nicholson always insisted the two most important matches every season were against us, while their skipper Alan Mullery, who had missed the previous match with a touch of lumbago, was so fired up for our visit that he would probably have needed to have had one leg amputated to prevent him taking the field against us.

If you couldn't be at Tottenham that Monday night, then tough. A satellite beam back to Highbury was as unlikely as live television coverage. There would be no TV highlights either, so I was not in the slightest bit surprised to hear of Arsenal fans exchanging their FA Cup final tickets for a guaranteed seat at Spurs.

I hobbled into the South Herts Golf Club in Totteridge after lunch and we set off in good time on a coach journey down through Palmers Green and Edmonton, which should have taken no more than 30 minutes. It took an hour and a half. The congestion in Tottenham High Road was unbelievable, a human tide of bodies and vehicles that was scarcely moving. Our driver switched off the engine at one point because he feared it would overheat, but the coach still moved forward due to the pressure of the crowd, and Frank McLintock played a blinder by spotting Geordie Armstrong's wife and daughter, Barbara and Marje, in the crush and dragging them on board to safety. Bertie Mee started to protest that it was in breach of club rules to have a player's family on board and was rewarded with a few choice expletives from the club skipper. Eighty yards from the main entrance, we decided to make a run for it – a limp in my case – and fought our way into the ground. One bonus of the lengthy delay was that the lads had no time to worry about the match. There was barely time to get stripped and prepare for action.

Mullery and the normally placid Alan Gilzean were soon getting stuck in as if their lives depended on it, the atmosphere crackling on and off the pitch. I was out of my seat in the dugout when Frank had a chance to win it from 12 yards in the seventy-fifth minute, only for the referee Kevin Howley to collide with him in pure Keystone Kops fashion. How costly would that be? I wondered, as the sweat started to trickle down my back.

Arsenal were four minutes away from gaining the 0–0 draw which would be sufficient when Tottenham's Jimmy Neighbour and Cyril Knowles combined to lose possession. Charlie delivered a low cross, Joe Kinnear prevented Raddy getting a clear sight of goal and Pat

Jennings dived to push the deflection away on the left. Geordie was first to react, looked up and floated over a wonderful cross. Six yards out, Ray Kennedy connected with a powerful header which soared above Knowles on the line and grazed the underside of the bar on the way in.

This may sound bizarre, but that goal served only to make our task *harder* in the last few minutes and another four of injury-time. Although there might have been disappointment, it would have been no disgrace for Spurs to draw at home to us. But losing, that was another matter.

Suddenly, it was like the Alamo as the white shirts poured forward intent on the equaliser which would have claimed the League on behalf of Leeds United.

I feared for the safety of Bob Wilson as first Martin Peters, then Mullery, went in dangerously hard on him. I nearly lost it too, shouting: 'Blow the fucking thing, for fuck's sake, ref!' not that Mr Howley, officiating in his last match, could have heard me in the bedlam. Eventually, the whistle went and the red and white hordes swarmed onto the pitch from all four corners of the ground.

Yet I must have been the loneliest Arsenal player or fan in the cauldron at Spurs that Monday night. I felt totally out of it after Ray decided an epic encounter with that dramatic late header and Bob prevented an equaliser which would have proved catastrophic.

I had played in 40 of our 42 matches and, of course, I was desperate for Arsenal to win and take the title, yet I still felt something of a stranger in our dressing room amid the champagne, back-slapping, well-wishers, singing, wet towels and discarded kit. I felt out of it at the White Hart too, when our party arrived shortly before midnight for a marathon five-hour session that had the tacit approval of our management. And regardless of what had just been achieved, to my mind, the job was only half-done.

It wasn't just me; a lot of players feel that strange sense of exclusion when they aren't directly involved.

Suddenly, I think I knew a little of the emotional pain and bitter disappointment Jimmy Greaves experienced when he was injured during the World Cup and watched as his replacement Geoff Hurst became a national hero. Jimmy spoke about feeling like a total outcast because England didn't need him for the big push to become world champions, although he played in the first three matches against Uruguay, Mexico and France before a deep gash on his ankle meant he lost his place to Geoff. Jimmy missed the quarter-final against Argentina and the semi-final with Portugal, but was fit to face the West Germans – and Alf Ramsey, plain Alf as he was then, simply looked the other way and kept faith in Geoff.

Missing the title-decider at Tottenham was gut-wrenching, and made me all the more determined to play in the FA Cup final five days later.

Imagine my conflicting emotions, then, when Bertie put me through a fitness test so stringent it can only have been designed to make me break down and miss the showpiece Wembley event against Liverpool.

I have thought long and hard about what happened between the manager and myself, and the conclusion I've reached is definite: he didn't want me to play.

The Wembley build-up began after training at London Colney on the Wednesday, when Bertie and Don Howe held a meeting to discuss Saturday's arrangements. I felt affronted as Bertie turned to me and said: 'You're going to be sitting with us, Peter.' Sure, I was carrying an injury, and still in a lot of pain, but it was only midweek and I felt the manager was being unnecessarily hasty in dismissing my chances of playing in the biggest match of the season.

Not for the first time, Don came to my assistance and said: 'Hang on, he might be fit. You never know, Bert.' I appreciated his sentiments, although I feared the worst. Deep down, I knew it was a long shot that I'd be wearing Arsenal's yellow number four shirt at Wembley. My hopes had hardly improved when I went to bed on Thursday evening, despite a mixture of physiotherapy and rest, and I thought morosely: 'The gaffer's right, I am bloody well going to be stuck on the bench with him and Don.'

I'm not a great believer in miracles, but someone must have been looking out for me, because when Friday dawned my ankle felt almost 100 per cent; all the pain had disappeared.

I turned up at Highbury for a little spot of light training with the team, wearing a broad grin. I told the manager about the overnight transformation and that I was fit to play. He appeared perplexed and said, with a sense of irritation: 'I don't know, we'll see,' before taking me out alone on the pitch for an unbelievably gruelling fitness test. Bertie had been a brilliant physiotherapist before becoming manager and knew exactly what he was doing. Several other members of staff could have supervised a routine fitness test, particularly George

Wright, the first-team trainer, but Bertie took me alone, which was strange.

He tried to make me break down, I'm absolutely convinced of it, because Eddie Kelly had done so well against Stoke and Tottenham, and he wanted the confident young Glaswegian to face Liverpool instead of me. I would have been gutted if Bertie had told me honestly to my face that because Eddie was looking so sharp, he was going to take my place in the final – but I would have had more respect for the manager.

I felt physically sick because of the sudden, unexpected exertion and I wasn't quite right in the head either. The manager had just done my brains in. I could recall occasions when Bertie was, not to put too fine a point on it, up shit creek without a paddle and asked, pleaded sometimes, with me to do him a favour and play when he was fully aware I was carrying an injury and some way less than fully fit. I never ever kicked up a fuss. I was always happy and proud to go to work on behalf of Arsenal Football Club. I'd be out there on my knees if they wanted me. Other players might feel a twinge and start looking for a weekend off, but it needed to be a proper injury before I was unfit. Fred Street became our physio the following season and had it right when he toured the dressing room, asking: 'Right lads – any aches, pains, strains or bruises? Peter? Any broken bones?'

There was anger and a little confusion too. I was 25 years old, approaching my prime in my sixth season as a first-choice player. Surely I wasn't about to become surplus to requirements?

My body was screaming for mercy by the end of that session, which concluded with Bertie saying tersely: 'You'll do, then,' before turning smartly on his heels. I had half a mind to reply: 'Thanks a lot, boss!' but thought the better of it. Anyway, I had more to worry about now than the prospect of marking Steve Heighway – that bloody ankle had flared up again, surprise, surprise.

Come Saturday morning, the injury was nagging away like my ex-missus with a bee in her bonnet and I was very apprehensive about whether I could last 90 minutes of an FA Cup final which, according to the weather forecast for that fine May, was about to be staged in scorching conditions. But sure as hell, I wasn't about to share my misgivings with the manager, because he was to blame for my untimely relapse.

I was pumped up from the first whistle and it took me less than 20 seconds to make my mark with a late challenge which stuck Heighway on his educated backside just outside our area. I pinged a few useful passes around and was quick to get up and down the right touchline in support of our attacks, too eager midway through the first half when Ray Clemence gathered a centre and immediately found me clattering into his chest. Clem went down with a pained expression and Tommy Smith looked daggers in my direction. A few choice words were exchanged, 'off' being prominent among them.

By the second half, I had my socks rolled down around my ankles and was limping noticeably. That gave Bertie the opportunity to do what he had always wanted and employ Eddie, who replaced me shortly after the hour. I took a reluctant place on the Arsenal bench for the rest of the afternoon while players went down like ninepins with cramp as the furnace-like heat inside Wembley touched 90°F. The atmosphere was cranked up another few notches in the first minute of extra-time when Heighway hurtled in from the left and, with everyone anticipating a low cross, succeeded in beating Bob inside his near post. Ten minutes later, we equalised when Raddy hooked an overhead kick into the heart of the Liverpool defence. Nine times out of ten, the danger would have been snuffed out by any one of Emlyn Hughes, Smith or Clemence, but they simply froze and Eddie forced the ball on, with George Graham claiming the final touch, although that's never been satisfactorily proved, and the goal is now generally accepted to be Eddie's – the first scored by a substitute in a Wembley Cup final.

Arsenal's recovery was in no doubt, however, and was completed in stunning fashion when Charlie accepted a little square pass inside from Raddy and fired an explosive winner chest-high inside Clemence's right-hand post with that hammer of a short back-lift he possessed. It was classic Charlie, a one-off, and so was his goal celebration as he collapsed in jubilation on his back, arms stretched above his head in an iconic pose.

The Double was in the bag, Bertie capered around hugging everyone he could find in a yellow shirt – apart from me – and Frank had just enough stamina remaining to climb the thirty-nine steps to the Royal Box and lift the Cup at Wembley after losing on his previous four visits as a finalist. I went up, too, at the end of the line with just Pat Rice and 'Stan' Simpson behind me.

I felt numb. The match had been 0–0 when I'd departed, all the relevant action had taken part without me and suddenly it was almost as if I'd played no part in the final whatsoever. I've seen photographs of myself on the pitch afterwards, one arm around Eddie with Frank on someone's shoulders and cheeky Charlie wearing the lid on his head. I'm the one player in the frame without a broad grin on his face. Strange, I know, but perfectly true.

In time, I became immensely proud of what Arsenal achieved in 1970–71, constantly defying the odds and coming from behind. Only special teams do the Double. One word summed us up – remorseless. We never knew when we were beaten; our powers of recovery during 90 minutes, and sometimes beyond, were immense. From the opening fixture of the season at Everton, where we twice fell behind before salvaging a point, to the last – the Wembley epic with Liverpool – we came out fighting with our backs to the wall.

Leeds, meanwhile, deserved something for their efforts over the previous ten months and eventually lifted some silverware in the shape of the Fairs Cup, their reward for beating Juventus in June.

I knew what I had contributed to Arsenal's epic season and confirmation arrived when I was named as substitute in this Rothmans Golden Boots XI (4–2–4 formation): Gordon Banks (Stoke and England); Chris Lawler (Liverpool and England), Frank McLintock (Arsenal and Scotland), Bobby Moore (West Ham and England), Terry Cooper (Leeds and England); Billy Bremner (Leeds and Scotland), Martin Peters (West Ham and England); George Best (Manchester United and Northern Ireland), Martin Chivers (Tottenham and England), Ron Davies (Southampton and Wales), Francis Lee (Manchester City and England).

A press panel of Fleet Street's finest football reporters plus TV front men David Coleman and Jimmy Hill undertook to vote for the top 11 players in Great Britain, and my citation read: 'The versatile Storey, at home equally in defence or midfield, was an integral part of Arsenal's triumph in the 1970–71 season and, perhaps slightly to his surprise, virtue was rewarded when he gained his first cap against Greece. Here he played at right-back although he is established in midfield at Highbury. Strong, quietly efficient, he can expect further calls from England in the coming seasons.'

CHAPTER THIRTEEN

Alf's kind of animal

I played international football for England for a little over two years – nineteen caps under Sir Alf Ramsey, which began with a 3–0 victory over Greece in a European Championship qualifier at Wembley on 21 April 1971 and ended with a 2–0 friendly defeat by Italy in Turin on 14 June 1973.

Played 19, won 11, drawn 5, lost 3, goals for 20, against 12 – and I enjoyed every minute of it because my England career was so unexpected, right out of the blue, such a bonus.

George Eastham was certainly surprised by my elevation to the ranks of a defence boasting World Cup winners Gordon Banks and Bobby Moore. Ernie Collett, Arsenal's third-team trainer, told me how he had always had faith in my ability but when he ventured an early opinion in company that I would play for England one day, Eastham jumped on him and insisted: 'Oh no, he won't. Ramsey thinks Storey's a bloody animal!'

Ernie was undeterred by Eastham's strident 'animal' revelation and put his money where his mouth was by striking a cash bet. I hope the wager was settled in full.

I was extremely proud to play for England alongside Banks, Moore and other remaining heroes of the 4–2 victory over West Germany, such as Alan Ball, Geoff Hurst and Martin Peters.

There was never an inkling at my end that Alf was measuring me for a cap in the spring of 1971. My concentration was focused on Arsenal's Double bid when the phone rang the day after we'd beaten Coventry City 1–0 at home, and I picked up the receiver to hear Jeff Powell of the *Daily Mail* informing me that I'd been called up for the forthcoming game against Greece in a fortnight. I thanked Jeff and

TRUE STOREY

gave him his story, telling him I was genuinely shocked and playing for England had never crossed my mind, and also that I would be doing my level best to justify Alf's faith in me if I were fortunate enough to play.

Alf had scores of players to choose from and competition to make the squad, let alone pull on the famous white shirt, was intense. The Premier League today is capable of providing fantasy football but, unfortunately from the perspective of the England manager, too much of it comes courtesy of foreign players he can only sit and admire.

The morning after Jeff's phone call there was an official letter from the Football Association awaiting me at Highbury, confirming my England appointment to join the party assembling at the Hendon Hall Hotel. I was very apprehensive, having never met Alf before and never represented England at either youth or Under-23 level. The summons to international football was a major surprise, and in fact it crossed my mind: 'Am I good enough, or am I going to make a complete prat of myself?'

Bob McNab, the only other Arsenal player in the squad, sensed I was a bit uneasy and tried to reassure me, saying: 'You'll be fine, son. Alf's got defenders coming out of his ears and if he didn't rate you, you'd never have got the nod.'

There was such competition for the England number two shirt that the identity of the defender in possession was to change five times in six internationals, with this running order: Keith Newton, Emlyn Hughes, Paul Reaney, myself, Chris Lawler and Paul Madeley.

If you thought Bertie Mee was pleased for me, you couldn't be more wrong. Had he known how to spit feathers in disgust, believe me, they would have showered out of his mouth upon hearing that 'national service' meant Bob and I would miss a rearranged League fixture against Burnley at Highbury on 20 April – the evening before the Greece game.

The Turf Moor side were a particularly sorry sight, well on their way to losing the First Division status they had proudly held since just after the Second World War. Yet it was perfectly understandable that Bertie didn't want to leave anything to chance and he felt sorely inconvenienced. There was no margin for error now in our championship race with Leeds, and he wanted his strongest team out on the pitch to tackle the Clarets.

Bob and I were called into the manager's office to discuss the clash of interests with him and Don Howe, and Bertie didn't beat about the

HOT SHOTS: Success as captain of the Aldershot and Farnborough Schools Under-13 team. (Courtesy of the author)

WRIGHT GENERATION: Arsenal manager Billy Wright shows off his squad before the 1965–66 season. Back row (from left): Billy McCullough, Don Howe, Peter Simpson, Ian Ure, Bob Wilson, Jim Furnell, Tony Burns, Alan Skirton, John Radford, Terry Neill, Frank McLintock. Front row: Peter Storey, Jimmy McGill, Geordie Armstrong, Brian Tawse, Jon Sammels, Tommy Baldwin, Joe Baker, David Court, George Eastham.
(© *Daily Mirror*)

EYES DOWN: Peter Osgood ranked among my most formidable opponents, and he came out on top when Chelsea beat Arsenal 3–0 at Stamford Bridge in September 1969. (© *Daily Mirror*)

LOOKING DAGGERS: Emlyn Hughes gets a sharp reaction to tugging my shirt in this battle against Liverpool at Highbury in November 1970. (© *Daily Mirror*)

DANCING WITH WOLVES: Caught at full stretch against Jim McCalliog as the ball falls to Hugh Curran during our home win over Wolves in December 1970.
(© *Daily Mirror*)

BROOKING, NO ARGUMENT: The elegant West Ham playmaker Trevor Brooking had to go in this challenge as Arsenal won their London derby 2–0 at Highbury in January 1971.
(© *Daily Mirror*)

NIGHT TO REMEMBER: This late penalty knocked Portsmouth out of the FA Cup on 1 February 1971. Hours later, I went home to discover my first wife, Susan, had left me. (© *Daily Mirror*)

GENTLE TOUCH: Congratulations from a young Gunners fan at Hillsborough after my two goals against Stoke City forced an FA Cup semi-final replay in March 1971. (© *Daily Mirror*)

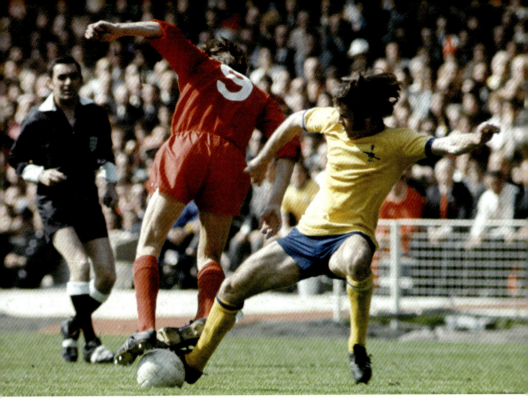

HEIGHWAY ROBBERY: There is no way that Liverpool winger Steve Heighway is coming past me in the 1971 FA Cup final. (© *Daily Mirror*)

ODD MAN OUT: Bertie Mee's treatment of me meant I was the only Arsenal player who could not force a smile after our FA Cup final triumph at Wembley to clinch the Double. (© *Daily Mirror*)

BAHAMAS BEACH BUNCH: Time to relax with a well-earned drink in Nassau at the end of the 1971–72 season. Back row (from left): John Roberts, Peter Storey. Centre: brewery representative, Steve Burtenshaw, Alan Ball, John Ritchie, Geoff Barnett, Peter Simpson, Sammy Nelson, Pat Rice. Front: Ray Kennedy, Frank McLintock, Bob McNab, Bertie Mee (standing), Geordie Armstrong, Bob Wilson. (Courtesy of the author)

THE EYES HAVE IT: Totally focused on helping England beat Scotland 1–0 at Wembley to win the Home International Championship in May 1973. (© www.sporting-heroes.net)

POLEAXED: The England squad on duty for the fateful World Cup qualifier against Poland at Wembley in October 1973. Back row (from left): Trevor Brooking, Dave Watson, Emlyn Hughes, Tony Currie, Paul Madeley, Norman Hunter, Colin Bell, Ray Clemence, Phil Parkes, Martin Chivers, Peter Storey, Bobby Moore, Martin Peters, Harold Shepherdson (trainer). Front: Kevin Keegan, Kevin Hector, Colin Todd, David Nish, Peter Shilton, Allan Clarke, Mike Channon, Roy McFarland. (© *Daily Mirror*)

SHOCK, HORROR: The tabloids had a field day when my crimes came to court. (© *Daily Mirror*)

BADGE OF HONOUR: The Emirates Stadium holds no memories for me, but I was extremely proud to be a Gunner. (© *Daily Mirror*)

ALF'S KIND OF ANIMAL

bush. He stated boldly: 'It's no good, Peter, we've got a game against Burnley. I want you to contact the Football Association and pull out. And as for you, Bob, you're definitely playing for us!'

I was dumbfounded and began to take an uncommon interest in the state of my footwear – but I was sure of one thing. If I'd obeyed Bertie's orders it would have spelled international suicide. Alf was not noted for his tolerance in club versus country matters, and he would have taken a very dim view of the affair. Why should he bother selecting me again if I hadn't been keen enough for England, yet managed to play for my club 24 hours earlier? Don Howe had won 23 England caps with West Brom, so he knew precisely what it meant to represent your country. Bob and I were extremely grateful when Don came to our rescue, telling the manager: 'You can't ask them to pull out.'

Under pressure from the man he relied upon so heavily, Bertie relented and plotted ahead to face Burnley with a reshuffled defence.

My thoughts turned to England after Arsenal had beaten Newcastle 1-0, and I was grateful for my roommate Bob's presence. His was one friendly face I could count on absolutely at Hendon Hall – I couldn't guarantee the reception I'd get from Francis Lee, Martin Chivers and Allan Clarke, forwards I routinely tried to subdue by any means possible in the First Division. I knew it would be like the first day at school and I didn't want to look like a wet-behind-the-ears kid.

All the apprehension and tightness in my stomach disappeared as I was welcomed into the fold and Alf was fantastic, such a warm character. I soon understood why his players, Bobby Moore especially, loved him and would never have a bad word said against him. On television and in public, Alf came across as cold, distant, aloof and stilted. But that persona was false and forced. He had taken elocution lessons, his basic Dagenham roots were always lurking in the background and Alf was happiest surrounded by the England team, just being himself. In the flesh he was a different person, such a thoroughly nice man.

I never could square Eastham's insistence that Alf thought I was a 'bloody animal' with the man who took me quietly to one side after a training session early in the week at Roehampton and asked: 'How do you feel about playing right-back?' Given that I'd spent the season in Arsenal's midfield, I was taken aback, but pleasantly surprised all the same. 'I don't mind,' I replied and Alf continued: 'You're playing, then,' before swearing me to secrecy. He was at pains to ensure his plans didn't leak out. All very cloak and dagger, I thought. Greece were hardly going to adapt their tactics because

TRUE STOREY

I was wearing number two rather than number four on my back, were they?

Imagine my surprise then that evening in our hotel room when boisterous Bob, who always had plenty to say for himself, came bouncing through the door to announce: 'I'm playing right-back and you, Snouty, you'll be on the bench. But don't tell a soul – it's supposed to be a secret.' Bob's previous England appearance had been way back in 1969 against Romania and I felt confused, yet happy that my pal was going to win another cap. Alf was in no danger of losing his marbles and taking on the Greeks with two right-backs, so he must just have changed his mind and forgotten to tell Bob that he wasn't playing after all.

I thoroughly enjoyed my first England experience, although Greece weren't the greatest team. To be honest, I even felt a little sorry for them because this wasn't a meaningless friendly but a Euro qualifier, yet they arrived in London without any of their Panathinaikos stars who were being saved for a European Cup semi-final against Red Star Belgrade. Mum didn't go to Wembley; she was too nervous and couldn't bear to ever watch me play, so Dad and a pal used the two complimentary tickets I was given by the FA.

They saw me deliver a centre from which Lee completed the scoring with a spectacular diving header following goals from Chivers and Hurst.

England lined up like this that evening: Banks, Storey, Hughes, Mullery, McFarland, Moore, Lee, Ball, Chivers, Hurst and Peters.

Veteran England reporter Norman Giller noted on the England Football Online website:

> Peter 'Cold Eyes' Storey got his first England call-up as reward for his consistent performances for an Arsenal team on the way to a League and FA Cup Double. A hard-tackling midfield ball winner for the Gunners, he went back to his original position of right-back for his first taste of international football.

After the Greeks had been sent packing, England had four more games before the curtain fell on the season. I was fit enough for the following international against Malta at Wembley in another Euro qualifier on 12 May – four days after I'd limped out of the FA Cup final, but I didn't feel upset at being left out. Rather, I was just pleased to be part of the squad. As I mentioned, Alf had an embarrassment

ALF'S KIND OF ANIMAL

of riches in the right-back department, and in any case there was no disappointment, no envy as I watched Lawler in the number two shirt stroll through a 5–0 win which was so one-sided I don't think Banks had a save to make in 90 minutes.

Alf gave me the nod for an important mission in Belfast on 15 May, the start of the Home Championship campaign, although he might easily have had my head on a plate for the bad publicity the violent climax to this bittersweet day would have brought to the England team, had it become public knowledge at the time.

My orders from Alf were succinct: 'Mark George Best.' So that's what I did, wearing the number four shirt in midfield.

I know it narked Bestie no end that I did a job on him against Northern Ireland at Windsor Park that Saturday and he failed to score. That was one–nil to me, as was the result in England's favour, thanks to Allan Clarke's late winner. Bestie was even more irritated that his controversial 'goal' never stood that afternoon. It was one of the most skilful, impudent acts I ever witnessed on a football pitch. He merely waited until Banks was in the process of throwing the ball up to hoof downfield, and promptly nipped in to whip it off the toes of England's greatest goalkeeper. Bestie knocked it over Banks and, in the race to reach the bouncing ball, got there first to head home. However, the Scottish referee, Alistair Mackenzie, ruled George had been guilty of ungentlemanly conduct, and awarded England a free-kick instead, much to the annoyance of Bestie and the Belfast crowd.

I could hardly have been happier or more satisfied on the charter plane flight home to Heathrow, downing a few bottles of lager and enjoying a laugh and a joke with the rest of the England team and the press lads. When we landed, the *Daily Star*'s larger-than-life Peter Batt and the *Mail*'s Jeff Powell suggested we might carry on to the Astor Club in Berkeley Square for a meal, cabaret and a spot more liquid refreshment, as guests of Peter's brother Jim, a hardman, and his pal Les Burman, a diehard Arsenal fanatic who also worked as a minder providing security.

I needed no persuading and a gregarious gang of us enjoyed a thoroughly entertaining evening. We were in a little world of our own and a few bottles of champagne came our way – as well as a spot of glamorous female company.

Unknown to us, however, there was another group of red-blooded men in the Astor whose mood could only have been totally at odds to our euphoria.

TRUE STOREY

That afternoon the Leeds rugby league team, loaded with internationals in a side reputed to be on a £5,000-a-man bonus to win, had kicked off the 1971 Challenge Cup final against Leigh as 5–1 on favourites. Eighty minutes later, Leigh's player-coach Alex Murphy had inspired a shock 24–7 win by his boys and Leeds had repaired to the Astor to lick their wounds and drown their sorrows.

Given the circumstances, I can well imagine that our boisterous table might have acted like a red rag to a bull, especially with Batty in full flow. He could never be described as a shrinking violet, while I was already a hate figure among the northern city's sporting fraternity.

But to be fair, we never had a moment's trouble from the Leeds lads until the time arrived to leave – and then it all kicked off big-time.

A massive rugby league player appeared to be sleeping it off on a chair in the foyer when I tried to squeeze past him. I couldn't avoid his tree-trunk legs and politely asked: 'Excuse me, mate, do us a favour and shift your legs, will you?' I was taken aback by his response and backed off a few yards as he spat back: 'Fuck off, you piece of shit. You'll have to crawl under my legs if you want to go home.'

Mayhem broke out, and within minutes the foyer of the posh Astor Club was full of brawling Leeds players scrapping with Les and Jim, who had sensed the blood like a shark. It was an unequal battle as a succession of rugby league lads met their match and ended up poleaxed while Batty, Jeff and I stood there wide-eyed.

Alf Ramsey would have been far from impressed.

My stop-start international career continued when I sat out a 0–0 draw with Wales at Wembley before returning for a very satisfying 3–1 win over Scotland on 22 May. England, with five points, were Home International champions. We played really well and were much the better side. Scotland included Frank McLintock and I remember my Arsenal skipper was totally gutted to be back at Wembley a loser, just a fortnight after lifting the FA Cup. We exchanged glances at the final whistle – no more. 'Bad luck' from me would have sounded patronising.

The play-one, miss-one routine saw me out of the England team at the start of the 1971–72 season. This time I was cursing my misfortune after taking a bang on the ankle during Arsenal's 3–0 home win over Leicester in late September. The injury kept me out for five weeks and ensured I was at home the following month with my feet up, watching on TV as England squeezed a 3–2 victory over Switzerland in Basle to go top of our Euro qualifying group.

ALF'S KIND OF ANIMAL

The Swiss were back at Wembley in November – and so was I, but we were sloppy and careless in our passing after Mike Summerbee scored inside the opening ten minutes, Switzerland equalised and we couldn't raise our game sufficiently to deny them a point in a 1-1 draw. The press weren't too happy, but we weren't complaining because the bottom line now meant that only defeat by four goals or more in Athens could deny England a place in the European Championship quarter-finals.

Northern Ireland legend Billy Bingham had taken over the Greek national team, but he was powerless to prevent us qualifying for the last eight in style with a comfortable 2-0 win in December. Alf wanted a positive response after the Switzerland game and he got it by going 4-3-3 with Alan Ball, Colin Bell and Martin Peters in midfield providing plenty of ammunition for a front three of Lee, Chivers and Hurst. I could only applaud Alf's tactics from my seat on the substitutes' bench.

England were installed as one of the favourites, with West Germany and Italy, to become European champions in 1972. The other five quarter-finalists were Belgium, Hungary, Romania, Russia and Yugoslavia, and there was feverish speculation for weeks about who we might pull out of the hat before the draw was eventually made in mid-January, then a sharp intake of breath as we were paired with the Germans.

England had beaten them in the 1966 World Cup, of course, and they had taken their revenge in cruel fashion in the heat of Mexico four years later. Alf put his faith in the team which had polished off the Greeks to tackle West Germany at Wembley in the first leg on Saturday, 29 April, but his best-laid plans were sabotaged at the eleventh hour when Derby manager Brian Clough suddenly withdrew centre-half Roy McFarland with a mysterious injury. Two days later, Derby were due to entertain Liverpool on a Monday night in their final match of the season, which they had to win to stand any chance of becoming First Division champions. If the stakes were high for Alf, they were perhaps even higher for Clough. Alf lost it completely with Clough, who had been very vocal in his criticism of the England manager on TV panels, and mocked the Derby boss for claiming to be a patriot. A quick, mobile centre-half, McFarland was a tremendous player and a big loss.

Norman Hunter came in to partner Bobby Moore at the back amid fears England might lack pace. I was on the bench again and watched as England were destroyed 3–1 by an exceptional German side featuring Berti Vogts, Franz Beckenbauer, Günter Netzer, in particular, and Gerd Müller at the very top of their form. It made for painful viewing as Netzer exploited the space in front of Moore and Hunter.

Poor Alf was torn apart in the media and then slaughtered again because he decided to drop Lee and Peters for the return leg in Berlin the following month and play Norman and myself in midfield. Alf was ridiculed and accused of trying to save face when England needed goals in Germany. It finished 0–0 in the pouring rain, but many critics forget how close McFarland and Chivers came to scoring. Norman and I really got stuck in, and afterwards the German coach Helmut Schön complained we'd been brutal, accusing us of employing 'jungle tactics'. I think I did well to make Netzer think twice before trying his tricks near our goal, although he did manage to rattle our bar with an outrageous free-kick from 35 yards.

In his book *50 People Who Fouled Up Football*, Michael Henderson cites Sir Alf, complaining:

> For the return leg in West Berlin, Ramsey packed his team with defenders. Peter Storey, the Arsenal defender, who should never have been let anywhere near an England team, was selected alongside Norman Hunter, Emlyn Hughes, Roy McFarland and Paul Madeley, and England duly secured a goalless draw. Afterwards Netzer joked that every England player had autographed his leg. England lost dignity that day, and it was Ramsey's doing.

I have always been an easy, convenient target, of course, but that criticism of Alf overlooks the fact that, years after the event, Schön freely admitted that he had *wanted* England to come and attack because then he felt his side might have scored six goals!

Alf's gameplan had been correct but in the two games against us, the Germans really had been the better side and deserved to go on and be crowned champions of Europe, beating Belgium 2–1 in the semi-finals before thumping Russia 3–0 in the final in Brussels in June.

We were despondent in the immediate aftermath of Berlin, but I felt Alf's trust in me was total, a matter which I think is best demonstrated by the fact that the stalemate with the Germans began my run of 15 successive England appearances.

ALF'S KIND OF ANIMAL

The European Championship was not a concentrated established summer tournament as it is now, nor such a significant prize, and it wasn't long before all eyes were trained on the road to the 1974 World Cup finals.

Before qualifying began, there was the little matter of domestic pride at stake again in the Home Championship, which I started against Wales at Ninian Park by having a running feud with Terry Yorath in a 3–0 win. Three days later the Northern Ireland player-manager Terry Neill, my old Arsenal teammate, almost ran out of people to buy drinks for and talk to death after he scored the only goal at Wembley. It was a magnificent way for Terry to mark his fiftieth international appearance and, despite defeat, I was happy to join him in a lager or two and tease Terry about the luck of the Irish.

There wasn't any back-slapping or much laughter at the end of the week when England ventured up to Hampden Park for the centenary international against Scotland. It was nasty, bitter stuff – right up my street as Norman Hunter and I went to war against Billy Bremner, Denis Law and Bobby Moncur. We won 1–0 with an Alan Ball goal, but the critics had a field day complaining that football was the loser.

My memories of that Saturday in May are all positive, however.

I knew I would settle down again one day with the right woman and, although it had been great fun going through the 'selection process', the seeds were sown that evening.

Ironically, I had to fly back to London to discover the next great love of my life, Cathy McDonald, a very attractive, petite brunette who hailed from Glasgow, of all places – a city where my name was something considerably worse than mud following the bitter kicking match Norman and I had just indulged in.

As Arsenal players were few and far between in the England ranks, I became quite friendly with Martin Harcourt Chivers, to give him his full name. He was a brilliant centre-forward and hard as nails. I had been obliged to kick him more than once in Arsenal–Tottenham derby matches, but it never seemed to have the slightest effect or slow him down. I had great admiration for Chiv and he accepted that whatever the score was between us as deadly rivals over 90 minutes on club duty, we could still be mates at the end of the day and share a drink, or preferably a few.

We roomed together on away trips and, on the plane, we were sitting together when he said: 'I think we've earned ourselves a big night out, Snouty. I fancy giving the Playboy some stick, are you coming?'

High on England's win and fancying a few sherbets to dull the pain from all the bumps and bruises I had collected that afternoon, I needed no encouragement to accompany Chiv to the VIP room of the Playboy Club in Park Lane, and that's where I met Cathy – a bona fide Bunny Girl. She was very taken with my mutton-chop sideburns, which were all the rage with hairy blokes at the time. We got chatting and I asked her if she fancied joining me after work in the basement disco, which she did. We had a great laugh dancing to T. Rex's 'Metal Guru' and had a lovely smooch at the end of the night when the DJ played that slow ballad 'Without You', Harry Nilsson's version of the Badfinger original. Out of the corner of my eye I clocked that Chiv was well away with the tasty-looking bird he'd pulled.

Eventually, it was time to say our goodnights to the ladies, but not before Cathy and I had exchanged phone numbers, and it must have been four or five that spring Sunday morning when Chiv casually announced: 'Come back to my place, Peter, and I'll get the missus to cook us some breakfast.'

I was dubious, sensing that the long-suffering Mrs Chivers might not be overjoyed at being greeted by her somewhat worse-for-wear husband and his drinking partner with a request to start cooking bacon and eggs. I warned Chiv that if the frying pan came out, we might have to duck – but he was having none of it.

Then I pointed out that at 6 a.m., she had every right to be still tucked up in bed fast asleep, but Chiv was insistent: 'Don't worry, I'll wake her up. I'm hungry.'

It was well-known that Martin was a bit of a lad and that the couple's relationship was on the rocks. As you can imagine, Mrs Chivers gave us short shrift and slung us both out of the house, and the rollicking she gave Martin was fearsome to behold. I was, frankly, impressed.

He was brave as a lion on the pitch, but looked a little sheepish turning to me to admit defeat and saying: 'Come on, I think we'd better find a café instead, Snouty.'

Unsurprisingly, I didn't see much of Mrs Chivers after that little episode – but I was soon a welcome visitor at Cathy's flat off Cromwell Road in South Kensington.

When the landlord decided to sell the building, Cathy had to move out sharpish. Fortunately, I knew a character working for a property company and he steered us towards a fantastic penthouse flat on a

ALF'S KIND OF ANIMAL

100-year lease in St John's Wood, a stone's throw from the recording studios in Abbey Road made famous by The Beatles.

I more or less moved in straight away. Certainly, I spent more time there than in my own place in Hadley Wood. Eventually, Cathy and I did start living together, but it was 1975 before we decided to make things permanent – well, as permanent as things ever could be with me – by getting married.

Back on the international scene in 1972, I had a lot of sympathy for Mick Mills when he made his England debut at right-back in an October friendly against Yugoslavia at Wembley. We could only draw 1–1 and it was another four years before poor Mick, run ragged by a very tricky winger called Dragan Dzajic, played again at that level.

Alf switched me from midfield to right-back the following month for our opening World Cup qualifier against Wales in Cardiff – and I rubbed my hands in anticipation, because my opponent was Leighton James. I was never keen on doing a man-to-man marking job but was happy to make an exception in his case. James was just a little too mouthy for my liking and, for all his talent and pace, I was confident of dominating him physically and mentally. Alf was especially keen to win because it was his hundredth match as England manager, and Alan Ball scored the only goal of the game to give him the present he craved most of all – victory.

James had his revenge in January 1973 in the return tie by laying on a goal for John Toshack. With creative minds such as Kevin Keegan, Rodney Marsh, Ball, Bell and Chivers in the team, we should not have needed to rely on an equaliser from Norman Hunter for a point from a draw which felt more like a defeat in the circumstances. Certainly, it was regarded as something of a moral victory by the Welsh.

The World Cup qualifier in Poland in June loomed large on the horizon and there was little in England's preparations for that extremely important match to suggest we would fail.

I took great satisfaction in winning two more caps in victories over Scotland, the first in a 5–0 romp in the snow at Hampden in a friendly to celebrate the Scottish FA's centenary; the second in a 1–0 win at Wembley which completed a clean sweep in the Home Championship, following a 2–1 win over Northern Ireland at Goodison Park and a 3–0 thumping of Wales at Wembley.

We weren't great against Northern Ireland in a strange game. It should have been their home fixture at Windsor Park, but was transferred to Merseyside because of the Troubles in Belfast. I gave away a penalty which enabled Dave Clements to equalise, and the Everton crowd gave us the bird.

Confidence should have been high following four successive wins and only one goal against, courtesy of my rash challenge, but Alf was agitated in May after our last warm-up match because we looked toothless in attack against Czechoslovakia in Prague. I was shunted over to left-back and we needed a goal from Allan Clarke in the final minute to salvage a draw.

Poland in Chorzów in June was a disaster. They had Wlodek Lubanski at the top of his form, scoring twice and giving Bobby Moore a torrid time – we had Bally sent off and I was moved again, into midfield. Many people have conveniently chosen to forget what a good side Poland were. Even without Lubanski, who subsequently suffered a broken leg, they were destined to finish third in the 1974 World Cup in West Germany – beating Brazil 1–0 in a play-off. They qualified from a Group of Death in Munich and Stuttgart with maximum points, beating Argentina and Italy, and were only eliminated 1–0 by a German side, who were on their way to becoming world champions.

The Poles had a good team ethic and several outstanding individuals. The goalkeeper, Jan Tomaszewski, was never the 'clown' Brian Clough unsuccessfully attempted to portray him as; Kazimierz Deyna, who later played for Manchester City, Andrzej Szarmach and Robert Gadocha were quality players, and Grzegorz Lato ended up as the leading scorer at the 1974 World Cup, with seven goals.

Still, Poland were somehow seen as 'unfashionable', which led to the knives being sharpened for Alf back home. Four days after the 2–0 defeat in Chorzów, we beat Russia 2–1 in Moscow. The heat was almost unbearable inside the Lenin Stadium, the conditions stifling and humid, but I was in considerably more danger of coming to personal harm after the match, a mug who got mugged.

We had a little reception with the Russian team before moving on to the British Embassy, the only place it was really safe to have a drink, and we were gagging to quench our thirst. My pal, Big Chiv, had scored our opening goal, and the embassy staff were delighted to help him celebrate by shovelling great big beakers of brandy and port in his direction. Martin was terribly ill after making it back to the hotel in one piece, which is more than can be said for me.

I am told I left the embassy in a taxi and the next positive sighting of me was made by Martin at six in the morning, banging on the window of our ground-floor room. To this day, I have no recollection whatsoever of the missing hours. Chiv is certain 'I must have been off on a promise with some bird', while all I'm certain of is that when he opened that window to let me climb in, I was missing my wallet and my nice expensive watch. All things considered, I rated that a narrow escape.

The summer tour was destined to end in further disappointment thanks to a 2–0 defeat by Italy in Turin where some chap called Fabio Capello scored one of the goals to give his country their first victory over England in forty years. Capello, whatever became of him, I wonder?

While we were in Italy, Martin's wife blew it to the press that he had left her and run off with a Playboy Bunny Girl, and I had to take the receiver off the phone in our room to stop all the reporters badgering him for his reaction.

Travelling back from Heathrow to the FA's headquarters, Alf came down the coach and warned Chiv to expect a 'welcome party' of photographers.

I was seething. Martin was a good mate of mine. We had always looked out for each other and I felt I wanted to do something, anything to help him. So as the coach came to a halt in Lancaster Gate, I was the first man off and I came out swinging. Swearing and cursing, I actually succeeded in chasing away a handful of snappers, creating a diversion for Chiv to make good his escape from the press pack. The two of us met up later for a good laugh and a bottle of wine over supper.

Although I didn't know it at the time, the Italy match was to prove the last of my 19 caps.

I was on the bench at Wembley on that fateful October evening in 1973 when England's world – and Alf's – fell apart. Nothing less than victory would take us to the World Cup tournament and, in that context, I could accept why Colin Bell was selected in front of me in midfield, while Paul Madeley and Emlyn Hughes had become the established pairing at full-back.

England pounded the Polish goal without success and the tension rose noticeably when Norman Hunter unaccountably lost possession out on the left wing and the ball was transferred inside to Domarski, whose low shot went under Peter Shilton's dive. Clarke soon equalised with a penalty.

TRUE STOREY

There was farce on the sidelines with five minutes to go when Alf half-turned and said over his shoulder: 'Get changed, Kevin', and two substitutes, Kevin Hector and Kevin Keegan, both started pulling off their tracksuit bottoms. Keegan's time as an England hero was yet to come; this was Hector's big moment, and he came so close to changing the course of history, with a header which was blocked on the line.

The Poles withstood the England cavalry charge and the final whistle signified the end of an era.

The Derby player only made one other appearance in an England shirt, for the last quarter of an hour of a friendly against Italy, and I was interested to see that football had left him far from financially secure and that when he hung up his boots he had to go back to work as a postman. Maybe I too should have followed a different path than the pub when I called it a day; then I wouldn't have been responsible for so much grief.

Now it became a matter of when, not if, Alf departed. My services were not required for the following match, another defeat by Italy with another goal from Capello, yet I was all set to earn my twentieth cap against Portugal in Lisbon the following April. FA Cup commitments and withdrawals bit deeply into the squad, but I was fit and raring to go the morning before the game, only to pick up an injury in training. I went into a tackle with Martin Chivers and his knee went into my thigh. I had been picked to play, but never recovered in time, and was forced to watch and suffer a 0–0 draw in silence.

Three weeks later, Alf was sacked and it was, finally, the end of a terrific run by the most successful manager England have employed.

The emergence of Colin Todd at Derby meant my time in international football was also over. I was overlooked when Joe Mercer became caretaker England manager for a handful of matches, although there was no chance of being ignored immediately when Alf's permanent successor was unveiled.

Don Revie could be accused of many things, but a lack of thoroughness and attention to detail was not among them. He began by naming an initial 81-strong England squad, so it was standing room only when most of us piled into a hotel lounge in Manchester in September 1974 for Don to introduce himself and expound his theories on how he would make England a team of world-beaters once more. My abiding memory of that meeting was Don banging on about money and how he had got our appearance money raised from £100 to £300. Emlyn Hughes was among the lads who looked at each other with an expression of shock and distaste. That was so cheap; playing for England was never about the money, it was all about honour and pride. Revie was a strange character, a bit suspect, with a dark side to him. I wasn't surprised when a bribery scandal from his days at Elland Road caught up with him.

It always seemed to revolve around money with Revie. The manner of his eventual departure from the FA was in keeping with the man, as he accepted a fortune in oil money in 1977 and did a runner to coach the United Arab Emirates. Not for nothing was he known in the game as Don 'Readies'.

Don didn't fancy me as an England player, but I don't think my international status would have been extended had Brian Clough got the England job either, as I feel the Derby manager deserved, because, to be frank, he didn't like me.

I played with over thirty England colleagues in my two-year stint of national service and can state, quite categorically, that this 4–4–2 combination with a midfield diamond (myself at the back, Martin Peters to the front) would have been the most effective: Banks; Madeley, McFarland, Moore, Cooper; Storey, Bell, Ball, Peters; Lee, Chivers.

CHAPTER FOURTEEN

Three Lions on my shirt

Here's my full England record, plus the Common Market celebration match and a couple of other representative fixtures in which I played (with times for goals and substitutions where available):

●

**21 April 1971: European Championship qualifier –
England 3 Greece 0 (Wembley).**
England: Gordon Banks (Stoke), Peter Storey (Arsenal), Emlyn Hughes (Liverpool), Alan Mullery (Tottenham), Roy McFarland (Derby), Bobby Moore (West Ham, capt), Francis Lee (Manchester City), Alan Ball (Everton), Martin Chivers (Tottenham), Geoff Hurst (West Ham), Martin Peters (Tottenham).
Scorers: Chivers (22 mins), Hurst (70 mins), Lee (86 mins).
Substitute: Ralph Coates (Burnley) for Ball (78 mins).

Greece: Hristidis, Gaitatzis, Toskas, Stathopoulos, Spiridon, Kambas, Kudas, Sinetopoulos, Dedes, Papaioannou, Kritikopoulos.
Substitutes: Chaitas for Kambas (75 mins), Delikaris for Dedes (88 mins).
Attendance: 55,123

●

**15 May 1971: Home International Championship –
Northern Ireland 0 England 1 (Windsor Park, Belfast).**
Northern Ireland: Pat Jennings (Tottenham), Pat Rice (Arsenal),

Sammy Nelson (Arsenal), Liam O'Kane (Nottingham Forest), Allan Hunter (Blackburn), Jimmy Nicholson (Huddersfield), Bryan Hamilton (Linfield), Eric McMordie (Middlesbrough), Derek Dougan (Wolves, capt), Dave Clements (Coventry), George Best (Manchester Utd).
Substitute: Tommy Cassidy (Newcastle) for McMordie (60 mins).

England: Banks, Paul Madeley (Leeds), Terry Cooper (Leeds), Storey, McFarland, Moore (capt), Lee, Ball, Chivers, Allan Clarke (Leeds), Peters.
Scorer: Clarke (80 mins).
Attendance: 33,000.

●

22 May 1971: Home International Championship – England 3 Scotland 1 (Wembley).
England: Banks, Chris Lawler (Liverpool), Cooper, Storey, McFarland, Moore (capt), Lee, Ball, Chivers, Hurst, Peters.
Scorers: Peters (9 mins), Chivers 2 (30 mins, 40 mins).
Substitute: Clarke for Lee (73 mins).

Scotland: Bobby Clark (Aberdeen), John Greig (Rangers), Jim Brogan (Celtic), Billy Bremner (Leeds), Frank McLintock (Arsenal), Bobby Moncur (Newcastle, capt), Jimmy Johnstone (Celtic), David Robb (Aberdeen), Hugh Curran (Wolves), Tony Green (Blackpool), Peter Cormack (Nottingham Forest).
Scorer: Curran (11 mins).
Substitutes: Francis Munro (Wolves) for Curran (46 mins), Drew Jarvie (Airdrie) for Green (82 mins).
Attendance: 91,469.

●

22 September 1971: League of Ireland 1 Football League 2 (Dublin).
League of Ireland: Thomas, Bacuzzi, Finucane, McConville, Herrick, Kearin, O'Neill, McGough, Leech, Bradley, Matthews.
Scorer: Matthews pen.
Substitutes: Marsden for McGough, Hale for Bradley.

Football League: Banks, Lawler, David Nish (Leicester), Storey, McFarland, David Sadler (Manchester Utd), Alan Woodward (Sheffield Utd), Kevin Hector (Derby), John Radford (Arsenal), Peter Osgood (Chelsea), Hughes.
Scorers: Osgood pen, Radford.
Substitute: Colin Todd (Sunderland) for Lawler.

●

10 November 1971: European Championship qualifier – England 1 Switzerland 1 (Wembley).
England: Peter Shilton (Leicester), Madeley, Cooper, Storey, Larry Lloyd (Liverpool), Moore (capt), Mike Summerbee (Manchester City), Ball, Hurst, Lee, Hughes.
Scorer: Summerbee (9 mins).
Substitutes: Chivers for Summerbee (83 mins), Rodney Marsh (QPR) for Lee (83 mins).

Switzerland: Prosperi, Ramseier, Chapuisat, Perroud, Stierli, Odermatt, Blättler, Kuhn, Balmer, Künzli, Jeandupeux.
Scorer: Odermatt (26 mins).
Substitute: Meier for Jeandupeux (63 mins).
Attendance: 90,423.

●

13 May 1972: European Championship qualifier, quarter-final second leg – West Germany 0 England 0 (Berlin).
West Germany: Maier, Hottges, Breitner, Schwarzenbeck, Beckenbauer (capt), Wimmer, Hoeness, Flore, Müller, Netzer, Held.
Substitute: Heynckes for Hoeness (51 mins).

England: Banks, Madeley, Hughes, Storey, McFarland, Moore (capt), Ball (Arsenal), Colin Bell (Manchester City), Chivers, Marsh, Norman Hunter (Leeds).
Substitutes: Summerbee for Marsh (20 mins), Peters for Hunter (57 mins).
Attendance: 76,200.

●

**20 May 1972: Home International Championship –
Wales 0 England 3 (Ninian Park, Cardiff).**
Wales: Gary Sprake (Leeds), Peter Rodrigues (Sheffield Wed), Rod Thomas (Swindon), Terry Hennessey (Derby), Mike England (Tottenham), John Roberts (Arsenal), Terry Yorath (Leeds), Ron Davies (Southampton), Wyn Davies (Manchester City), John Toshack (Liverpool), Alan Durban (Derby).
Substitute: Gil Reece (Sheffield Utd) for Roberts.

England: Banks, Madeley, Hughes, Storey, McFarland, Moore (capt), Summerbee, Bell, Malcolm Macdonald (Newcastle), Marsh (Manchester City), Hunter.
Scorers: Hughes (25 mins), Marsh (60 mins), Bell (61 mins).
Attendance: 34,000.

**23 May 1972: Home International Championship –
England 0 Northern Ireland 1 (Wembley).**
England: Shilton, Colin Todd (Derby), Hughes, Storey, Lloyd, N Hunter, Summerbee, Bell (capt), Macdonald, Marsh, Currie (Sheffield Utd).
Substitutes: Peters for Currie (58 mins), Chivers for Macdonald (69 mins).

Northern Ireland: Jennings, Rice, Nelson, Terry Neill (Hull, capt), A Hunter, Clements (Sheffield Wed), Danny Hegan (Wolves), McMordie, Dougan, Willie Irvine (Brighton), Tommy Jackson (Nottingham Forest).
Scorer: Neill (33 mins).
Attendance: 64,000.

**27 May 1972: Home International Championship –
Scotland 0 England 1 (Hampden Park, Glasgow).**
Scotland: Clark, John Brownlie (Hibs), Willie Donachie (Manchester City), Bremner, McNeill, Moncur, Archie Gemmill (Derby), Asa Hartford (West Brom), Peter Lorimer (Leeds), Lou Macari (Celtic), Denis Law (Manchester Utd).
Substitutes: Jimmy Johnstone for Gemmill (50 mins), Green (Newcastle) for Donachie (74 mins).

England: Banks, Madeley, Hughes, Storey, McFarland, Moore (capt), Ball, Bell, Chivers, Marsh, Hunter.
Scorer: Ball (28 mins).
Substitute: Macdonald for Marsh (84 mins).
Attendance: 119,325.

11 October 1972: Friendly – England 1 Yugoslavia 1 (Wembley).

England: Shilton, Mick Mills (Ipswich), Frank Lampard sr (West Ham), Storey, Jeff Blockley (Arsenal), Moore (capt), Ball, Mick Channon (Southampton), Joe Royle (Everton), Bell, Marsh.
Scorer: Royle (40 mins).

Yugoslavia: Maric, Krivokuca, Stepanovic, Pavlovic, Katalinski, Paunovic, Petkovic, Vladic, Bajevic, Acimovic, Dzajic.
Scorer: Vladic (50 mins).
Substitutes: Rajkovic for Pavlovic (10 mins), Holcer for Katalinski (46 mins).
Attendance: 50,000.

15 November 1972: World Cup qualifier – Wales 0 England 1 (Ninian Park, Cardiff).

Wales: Sprake, Rodrigues, Thomas, Hennessey, England, Trevor Hockey (Sheffield Utd), Leighton Phillips (Cardiff), John Mahoney (Stoke), Wyn Davies, Toshack, Leighton James (Burnley).
Substitute: Reece for Rodrigues (60 mins).

England: Ray Clemence (Liverpool), Storey, Hughes, Hunter, McFarland, Moore (capt), Kevin Keegan (Liverpool), Chivers, Marsh, Bell, Ball.
Scorer: Bell (35 mins).
Attendance: 36,384.

3 January 1973: Common Market celebration match – New ECM (The Three) 2 Old ECM (The Six) 0 (Wembley).

The Three: Jennings (Northern Ireland), Storey (England), Hughes (England), Bell (England), A Hunter (Northern Ireland), Moore (England, capt), Lorimer (Scotland), Johnny Giles (Republic of Ireland), Colin Stein (Scotland), Bobby Charlton (England), Henning Jensen (Denmark).
Scorers: Jensen (47 mins), Stein (69 mins).
Substitutes: John Steen Olsen (Denmark) for Bell (74 mins), Ball (England) for Jensen (60 mins).

The Six: Christian Piot (Belgium), Marius Tresor (France), Berti Vogts (West Germany), Horst Blankenburg (West Germany), Franz Beckenbauer (West Germany), Johan Neeskens (Holland), Jürgen Grabowski (West Germany), Wim van Hanegem (Holland), Gerhard Müller (West Germany), Günter Netzer (West Germany, capt), Georges Bereta (France).
Substitutes: Dino Zoff (Italy) for Piot (46 mins), Wim Suurbier (Holland) for Tresor (46 mins), Ruud Krol (Holland) for Beckenbauer (46 mins), Herbert Wimmer (West Germany) for Van Hanegem (46 mins).

●

24 January 1973: World Cup qualifier – England 1 Wales 1 (Wembley).
England: Ray Clemence (Liverpool), Storey, Hughes, Hunter, McFarland, Moore, Keegan, Bell, Chivers, Marsh, Ball.
Scorer: Hunter (42 mins).

Wales: Sprake, Rodrigues, Thomas, Hockey, England, J Roberts (Birmingham), Brian Evans (Swansea), Mahoney, Toshack, Yorath, James.
Substitute: Malcolm Page (Birmingham) for Rodrigues (60 mins).
Attendance: 62,273.

●

14 February 1973: Friendly – Scotland 0 England 5 (Hampden Park, Glasgow).
Scotland: Clark, Alex Forsyth (Manchester Utd), Donachie, Bremner (capt), Eddie Colquhoun (Sheffield Utd), Martin Buchan (Manchester Utd), Peter Lorimer, Kenny Dalglish (Celtic), Macari, George Graham (Manchester Utd), Willie Morgan (Manchester Utd).

Substitute: Colin Stein (Coventry) for Morgan (18 mins).

England: Shilton, Storey, Hughes, Bell, Madeley, Moore (capt), Ball, Channon, Chivers, Clarke, Peters.
Scorers: Lorimer own goal (6 mins), Clarke 2 (14 mins, 85 mins), Channon (15 mins), Chivers (75 mins).
Attendance: 48,470.

12 May 1973: Home International Championship – Northern Ireland 1 England 2 (Goodison Park).

Northern Ireland: Jennings, Rice, David Craig (Newcastle), Neill, Hunter, Clements, Hamilton, Jackson, Sammy Morgan (Port Vale), Martin O'Neill (Nottingham Forest), Trevor Anderson (Manchester Utd).
Scorer: Clements pen (22 mins).

England: Shilton, Storey, Nish (Derby), Bell, McFarland, Moore (capt), Ball, Channon, Chivers, John Richards (Wolves), Peters.
Scorers: Chivers 2 (9 mins and 81 mins).
Attendance: 29,865.

15 May 1973: Home International Championship – England 3 Wales 0 (Wembley).

England: Shilton, Storey, Hughes, Bell, McFarland, Moore (capt), Ball, Channon, Chivers, Clarke, Peters.
Scorers: Chivers (23 mins), Channon (30 mins), Peters (67 mins).

Wales: John Phillips (Chelsea), Rodrigues, Thomas, Hockey, England, J Roberts, James, Mahoney, Toshack, Page, Evans.
Substitutes: Dave Roberts (Oxford) for England, John Emanuel (Bristol City) for Page.
Attendance: 38,000.

19 May 1973: Home International Championship – England 1 Scotland 0 (Wembley).

England: Shilton, Storey, Hughes, Bell, McFarland, Moore (capt), Ball, Channon, Chivers, Clarke, Peters.
Scorer: Peters (54 mins).

Scotland: Alistair Hunter (Celtic), Sandy Jardine (Rangers), Danny McGrain (Celtic), Bremner (capt), Jim Holton (Manchester Utd), Derek Johnstone (Rangers), Morgan, Macari, Dalglish, David Hay (Celtic), Lorimer.
Substitutes: Joe Jordan (Leeds) for Macari (74 mins), Stein for Lorimer (80 mins).
Attendance: 95,950.

●

27 May 1973: Friendly – Czechoslovakia 1 England 1 (Prague).
Czechoslovakia: Viktor, Pivarnik, Zlocha, Samek, Hagara, Bicovsky, Kuna, Novak, Vesely, Nehoda, Stratil.
Scorer: Novak (54 mins).

England: Shilton, Madeley, Storey, Bell, McFarland, Moore (capt), Ball, Channon, Chivers, Clarke, Peters.
Scorer: Clarke (89 mins).
Attendance: 25,000.

●

6 June 1973: World Cup qualifier – Poland 2 England 0 (Chorzów).
Poland: Tomaszewski, Rzesny, Musial, Bulzacki, Gorgon, Cmikiewicz, Kraska, Banas, Deyna, Lubanski, Gadocha.
Scorers: Moore own goal (7 mins), Lubanski (47 mins).
Substitute: Domarski for Lubanski (54 mins).

England: Shilton, Madeley, Hughes, Storey, McFarland, Moore (capt), Ball, Bell, Chivers, Clarke, Peters.
Attendance: 73,714.

●

10 June 1973: Friendly – Russia 1 England 2 (Moscow).
Russia: Rudakov, Olchansky, Khurtsilava, Lovchev, Kaplichny, Kuznetsov, Muntian, Papayev, Andriasian, Onischenko, Blokhin.
Scorer: Muntian pen (66 mins).
Substitutes: Fedotov for Kuznetsov (46 mins), Kozlov for Andriasian (46 mins), Vasenin for Papayev (58 mins).

England: Shilton, Madeley, Hughes, Storey, McFarland, Moore (capt), Currie, Channon, Chivers, Clarke, Peters.
Scorers: Chivers (9 mins), Khurtsilava own goal (55 mins).
Substitutes: Hunter for Peters (58 mins), Macdonald for Clarke (58 mins), Summerbee for Channon (70 mins).
Attendance: 85,000.

●

14 June 1973: Friendly – Italy 2 England 0 (Turin).
Italy: Zoff, Burgnich, Sabadini, Morini, Facchetti, Mazzola, Benetti, Capello, Rivera, Anastasi, Pulici.
Scorers: Anastasi (32 mins), Capello (52 mins).
Substitutes: Bellugi for Morini (46 mins), Causio for Pulici (71 mins).

England: Shilton, Madeley, Hughes, Storey, McFarland, Moore (capt), Currie, Channon, Chivers, Clarke, Peters.
Attendance: 60,000.

●

20 March 1974: Football League 5 Scottish League 0 (Maine Road, Manchester).
Football League: Clemence, Storey, Nish, Martin Dobson (Burnley), McFarland, Todd, Stan Bowles (QPR), Bell, Bob Latchford (Everton), Trevor Brooking (West Ham), Dennis Tueart (Manchester City).
Scorers: Bell, Brown own goal, Tueart pen, Brooking, Bowles.
Substitute: Hector for Latchford.

Scottish League: Jim Stewart (Kilmarnock), Jim Hermiston (Aberdeen), Jim Wallace (Dunfermline), Jackie Copland (Dundee Utd), Rikki Fleming (Ayr), Peter Millar (Motherwell), Jim Brown (Hearts), Derek Parlane (Rangers), Donald Ford (Hearts), Davie Robb (Aberdeen), Rab Prentice (Hearts).
Substitute: Derek Johnstone (Rangers) for Robb.
Attendance: 11,471.

CHAPTER FIFTEEN

Howe sad

Bonuses for winning the Double were £15,000 for most of us, a fortune to men averaging basic pay of £100 a week, although I saw nearly half of it taken by Ted Heath's Conservative government. Fair enough, something like £3,000 disappeared in normal income tax, but the loss of £4,000 on surtax was a choker. The remaining £8,000 went more than halfway to buying a lovely three-bedroom house for £14,500 in Parkgate Crescent, Hadley Wood, next to the common and Beech Hill Park golf course.

It wasn't long before the feelgood factor began to fade. In fact, word soon reached me there was acrimony and tears before bedtime on the club's end-of-season jolly while I was otherwise happily employed on a spot of 'overtime' on behalf of England.

The lads were licking their lips at the prospect of a fortnight in the sun. Seven days in Torremolinos followed by a week in the Algarve appeared to be an itinerary which offered them the best of both worlds – the first week with wives and girlfriends, the second left to their own devices. There's no point being coy about it; a group of fit, suntanned professional footballers were not going to have to exert themselves to attract plenty of interest from the bikini brigade in Portugal. However, the Arsenal ladies, led by Peter Marinello's model missus, Joyce, and Charlie George's other half, Sue, were no mugs and kicked up a stink over plans to pack them off back home halfway through the party. They rebelled, making life murder for Bertie Mee and the club's officials. Petticoat power won the day and everyone returned after a week in a five-star hotel, their mood hardly enhanced by a lot of unseasonal rain in Spain.

TRUE STOREY

I say everyone, but as the Arsenal contingent were packing their bags, those of us who had been on international duty – myself and Bob McNab, plus the Northern Ireland pair, Pat Rice and Sammy Nelson – were flying out the other way, and so it was the four of us ended up on our own in the Portuguese sunshine.

I thought I'd earned myself another little holiday, so I treated myself to a fortnight in Majorca with Bob and Jimmy Curran, my old flatmate from Cockfosters, before reporting back for pre-season training in an odd mood.

I should have been happy and enthusiastic, given what we'd won, but while I was enjoying myself in Majorca that July, Don Howe walked out to take the manager's job at West Brom. I thought Don's decision made no sense and it has never been satisfactorily explained as far as I'm concerned, although I suspect money, inevitably, must have played a large part.

Bertie Mee was manager in name, but our coach was the motivating force. If chairman Denis Hill-Wood and the directors couldn't see that, then they were fools.

It was understandable, I suppose, that Don wanted to strike out in his own right and, okay, he had emotional ties to the Black Country, but West Brom were a struggling bottom-six sort of outfit and Don had just coached Arsenal to fabulous success never achieved before in the club's long and illustrious history. I would have thought the challenge to push on and establish Arsenal as England's finest team in the 1970s, and the immediate lure of competing in the European Cup, would have proved irresistible.

I was surprised, to put it mildly, and couldn't understand how Don could walk away from 'his baby' after all the time and effort he had invested in fostering such a winning mentality in us. Certainly, the feeling at Highbury was that the Double would be the gateway to further glory and riches – rather than an end in itself.

But Don clearly had his own agenda and took two other good men with him to the Hawthorns, physiotherapist George Wright and youth-team coach Brian Whiteside. Mr Hill-Wood went ballistic, accusing West Brom of raiding Arsenal and sniping: 'Loyalty is a dirty word these days, I suppose.'

We got a cracking replacement physio in Fred Street, who knew exactly what I was about and was impressed by my high pain threshold.

I was sad to say goodbye that month to 'Sammy' Sammels, who left for £100,000 to Leicester and the promise of some bruises from

HOWE SAD

me the next time we saw each other, while Steve Burtenshaw was promoted from running the reserves to first-team coach.

Burtenshaw was a pleasant, softly spoken chap who certainly knew his stuff on the training ground. Technically, you couldn't fault him but none of the lads feared him, and several of them knew he'd never give them a hard time if they slacked or put on a few pounds round the middle eating crap food. As we'd never been the best pure footballing side, we needed that kick up the backside from Don or another disciplinarian to keep us focused and on track.

Eddie Kelly and I were both in the team which launched the defence of our First Division title in 1971–72 encouragingly enough on 14 August with a 3–0 home win over Chelsea, the new European Cup Winners' Cup holders. Our FA Cup hero Charlie George was out for two months, recovering from a knee injury which required a cartilage operation, and we followed the Chelsea win with a hard-fought 1–0 victory at Huddersfield. Consistency was a failing, however, and we'd lose a cluster of matches, then win a few in a bunch before struggling for points again as rivals rose to the challenge of bringing the champions down to earth. Every match against us seemed to be their cup final.

Don Howe greeted me with a smile at the Hawthorns in early September, but he had a long face at the end of 90 minutes when we'd done a job on them, winning 1–0 with a goal from big John Roberts, and I'd helped to neutralise Jeff Astle, 'Bomber' Brown and Asa Hartford. Don cannot have helped but admire our professionalism that day, after all he'd been instrumental in it in the first place, but already it was noticeable West Brom were struggling for goals and it was going to prove a long, hard winter for them. We were to complete the double over Don's team, 2–0 at Highbury in December, by which time they were adrift at the foot of the table.

There was another old pal's axe at the end of September when 'Sammy' came calling with his new Leicester teammates, and I was almost sorry for him after we'd won 3–0. I say 'almost' because I was preoccupied afterwards with a thigh injury which forced me off and caused me to miss a month's football.

Deep into December came a sensational swoop in the transfer market which caused further ructions and left me out in the cold following another confrontation with the manager.

Bertie's idea of a Christmas present for Arsenal was to lavish a club record fee of £220,000 on Alan Ball, from Everton. It must have seemed like a great idea at the time because Bally was quality through and through as a footballer, we'd never had the largest first-team squad, 'Sammy' had departed and one or two injuries had kicked in. But it would have been a better signing before the season started in my view because Bally's idea of how he wanted the game played, everything channelled through him in midfield, was distinctly at odds with our preference to hit early balls up to the twin strikers, Raddy and Ray Kennedy. We would have benefited from adjusting to each other.

Bertie thought Bally would take us to a new level, but it was the start of the slippery slope instead.

The idea of having a World Cup winner on board excited some people and while nobody could question his talent, and Bally was a popular lad, he was just the wrong player for Arsenal. The size of his wage packet was a source of jealousy in the dressing room and none of us were impressed when his dad, Alan Ball senior, remarked: 'Alan didn't want to move south, but Arsenal guaranteed him £12,500 a year.'

He was initially a wrong 'un as far as I was concerned because five days after signing he had taken my place in the team, making his debut in a 1–1 draw at Nottingham Forest on 27 December.

Nothing was said to me on Boxing Day about being dropped to accommodate our new superstar. But my radar was twitching and seemed to pick up a few little whispers from the lads. That's the way bad news often travels in football; you're always the last to know – as Steve Burtenshaw was to discover himself, cruelly, in time. On the journey up to Nottingham, I started to harbour niggling doubts and Bertie confirmed my fears just before the match when he simply told me that I wasn't playing and would be on the substitutes' bench. Bally got the number eight shirt he'd requested and Eddie Kelly switched to wear my cherished number four.

Eddie was blessed with great talent, but he could be an idle little bleeder, moping about and existing on a diet of lager and crisps, and he once admitted Don pinned him up to the dressing room wall and told him straight: 'Peter Storey is not as good as you as a football player but as a competitor and in terms of attitude he is 100 per cent better.' I wouldn't argue with that.

The Forest players that day – a young Martin O'Neill, Peter Cormack and their dashing winger Ian Moore – could count their blessings that my services were not called upon. Normally, I was cool and detached, of course, but now I was boiling mad, bloody furious

HOWE SAD

beneath my usual mask of composure. I might very well have done some damage if I'd got on the City Ground in the mood I was in.

I'd been carrying the remnants of my thigh injury for a while and maybe my level of performance had dropped off, but I bitterly resented the manner in which I was jocked off. In the four full seasons which culminated in the Double campaign, I had missed only eight League matches, and I thought I was entitled to greater consideration. If Bertie had told me earlier in Christmas week that Bally was in for the Forest trip and Eddie was getting my shirt, I would have been very disappointed, but at least I would have been spared the rumour mill and all the nudge-nudge, wink-wink stuff among the lads.

Suddenly, it seemed as if I was no longer good enough for Arsenal – but there was no question of my being left out by England.

In fact, Sir Alf Ramsey was so concerned that a lack of bread-and-butter League action would have a detrimental effect on my international football, he wanted me to leave Arsenal. Never one to beat about the bush, Alf told me straight: 'You really might be better off somewhere else, Peter.' I thanked him sincerely for his advice and left him with the impression that I would act on it, but there was never the slightest chance I was going to ask for a transfer. Arsenal was my club.

Three successive League draws over Christmas and the New Year prompted a crisis meeting in January 1972 when Frank McLintock raised the matter of Steve's reluctance to put the boot in and impose discipline.

Frank knew things were drifting, that certain individuals looked as if they were eating too many pies, while others were cheating by hurling themselves into tackles rather than trying to stay on their feet.

He called a players' meeting, read the riot act and was very harsh on Ray and Raddy, virtually accusing them of cowardice in the face of the enemy and allowing defenders to bully them when they had previously been the men who could dish out the punishment.

Ray and Raddy held their hands up to the criticism but when I was subjected to a little dig, I couldn't bite my tongue and shot back at Frank: 'And how fucking well do you think you're playing, then?' To give him full credit where it's due, Frank immediately admitted that he hadn't been pulling up any trees.

While I was big enough and ugly enough to look after myself, Bally's money became a recurring issue. As I mentioned, the majority of us were on £100 a week basic, which we knew was well below the going rate at a club such as Liverpool, where we heard the likes of Tommy Smith, Emlyn Hughes, Ian Callaghan and Peter Thompson were on £180–£190 a week.

Arsenal's financial policy was 'low wages, big bonuses; treat 'em mean to keep 'em keen' – but Bally blew that out of the water with his £250 a week.

Bertie and the club secretary Ken Friar had asked him to keep quiet about his salary, but his dad let the cat out of the bag and then there was no point in him denying anything.

Frank and George Graham led a deputation demanding a general wage rise, and Bob McNab pointed out to the manager that the other quality players he fancied, such as West Ham's England skipper Bobby Moore and Francis Lee, the Manchester City and England forward, would laugh in his face if they were offered £100 a week to join the club. Bertie found a minute to stop burying his head in the sand to hold his hands up in horror and say: 'No, no, no.'

The discrepancy between what Bally and the rest of us took home every week caused a lot of unrest and friction. It wasn't Bally's fault; he'd just negotiated the best he could for himself – but we were bitter that Bertie and Ken thought they could get away with it. The dispute reached such a pitch that we had team meetings after training on a Friday morning when the notion of going on strike was seriously discussed.

Things got that bad, and never really went away the whole five years he spent at the club before the Southampton manager Lawrie McMenemy paid £60,000 to take him to The Dell in 1976. In many ways signing Bally was Bertie Mee's downfall. Before he arrived we had been more of a team.

During good spells, Bally's money wouldn't be so much of a talking point – because we enjoyed those bonuses – but in lean times the issue was guaranteed to rear its ugly head. •

As luck would have it, I was only out for a couple of months before returning in a blood-and-thunder FA Cup fifth-round tie at Derby's Baseball Ground mudheap on 26 February.

Eddie collapsed with ligament damage inside the first ten minutes and I had a serious battle on my hands trying to stop Archie Gemmill running the show. The little Scot was as game as anything, and kept popping up for more... a real Jock-in-the-box. Despite the undercurrent of violence, much of it undetected by referee Pat Partridge, the match was played at a breathtaking pace and Charlie George scored twice before Derby forced a 2–2 draw with two minutes left on the clock. There was aggro on the terraces too and Charlie, who was baited unmercifully throughout by the home fans, did nothing to cool things down by racing over to them flicking V-signs after his goals.

Derby were a quality side on their way to replacing us as champions, although I'd been a frustrated spectator a fortnight earlier when Charlie had also scored twice against them in a 2–0 win at Highbury, one a magnificent diving header, the other from the penalty spot, as we closed to within four points of League leaders Manchester City.

The attritional nature of the cup-tie at Derby might have been made for me and following a 0–0 draw after extra-time in the replay in front of a bumper 63,077 crowd shoehorned into Highbury for a Tuesday afternoon kick-off, foisted on football because of power restrictions just like the previous winter, we eventually made it into the sixth round with a 1–0 win in a second replay at Leicester's Filbert Street when Ray scored after seizing on a poor back-pass by John McGovern.

Was the double Double really on? Charlie's purple patch extended to scoring the only goal of a bitter contest at Ipswich in mid-February, more notable for a mass brawl involving 20 of the 22 players on the pitch. Quite how the referee managed not to book someone was a mystery, one he was summoned to explain in front of the authorities, who accused him of 'tolerating outrageous behaviour'. We were more interested in retaining our League title, victory at Portman Road improving our unbeaten run to a dozen matches – seven wins and five draws.

March proved disastrous, however, beginning with three successive away defeats at Manchester City, Newcastle and Leeds in which we failed to score and conceded seven goals. After that we knew the championship would be finding a new home, but our season was far from over.

Alan Ball scored the only goal against Orient in front of 31,768 fans at Brisbane Road to take us into the FA Cup semi-finals, but a different and much more prestigious knock-out tournament suddenly assumed greater importance.

Arsenal's first ever venture into the European Cup had started back in September when we were drawn to play the little-known Norwegian club Stromsgodset, a tie which didn't exactly set the pulses racing. It certainly did nothing for me because I sat it out and watched the lads stroll to a 7–1 aggregate win. Bertie rang the changes and could afford to go on the offensive against the Scandinavian minnows. With the tie effectively already settled by a 3–1 win in Norway, only 27,176 turned up at Highbury to see the return leg – understandable, perhaps, on the back of three League defeats.

I was itching for us to be drawn against one of Europe's top teams, such as the mighty Ajax, Inter Milan or Benfica, just to see how we measured up to the best the continent had to offer, but there was a distinct sense of 'just another professional job to do' when we were pitted against Grasshoppers Zurich in the second round, rather than a notion of glamour or any semblance of a threat.

Now I couldn't play in Switzerland because I was injured, and I watched as Ray and George Graham wrapped up a 2–0 win. At last, I made my overdue European Cup debut against the Swiss at Highbury on 3 November in a routine 3–0 victory. I concentrated as much as I needed to but found my mind straying to Saturday's match against Liverpool at Anfield, where I knew I would have to be at my best to nullify John Toshack and Steve Heighway. I wasn't that successful either because the Kop celebrated a 3–2 home win.

Back then, the European Cup existed solely for League champions. Group stages were unheard of; this was straight knock-out football, and after two rounds the field had been narrowed to eight clubs – the holders Ajax, ourselves, Benfica, Celtic, Feyenoord, Inter Milan, Standard Liege and Ujpest Dozsa.

The competition went into hibernation for the winter until mid-January, when we pulled out the plum quarter-final draw – Johan Cruyff's Ajax. When I'd confided to a friend that this was the one I wanted, he had warned me: 'Be careful what you wish for, Peter', as if this were the worst draw in the world. Maybe it did reduce Arsenal's chances of becoming champions of Europe, but I didn't care, preferring to see it as an opportunity to test myself against Cruyff and his Dutch international colleagues, who were among the most gifted footballers on the planet. If you're scared of a challenge like that, you have no right to be a professional footballer. Take the soft options in life all the time and you learn nothing, you demean yourself. I applauded Bertie's reaction, when he said: 'I'm very happy with the draw. Ajax's kind of football is known to us but we have a great respect for their ability.'

It was a classic tie, because as much as we fancied our chances against them, we knew the Amsterdam club felt they had a score to settle because of 1970, when they had proved so strangely tentative at

HOWE SAD

Highbury and we had knocked them out in the semi-finals en route to winning the Fairs Cup.

There were two months to wait between the draw and the first leg on 8 March. Despite all the football in the meantime, our ultimately fruitless quest for the double Double, it sometimes seemed like two years to me. Ray silenced a 65,000 crowd in Amsterdam by giving us the lead, but Ajax enjoyed the last laugh with two goals from Gerrie Mühren, the second a dodgy penalty when one of their players ran into Frank and collapsed on top of our skipper.

Despite Bally and Raddy being suspended for the return leg a fortnight later, we sensed we could win – and so did the majority of the 56,145 crowd buzzing inside Highbury, creating an electric atmosphere. Bertie was never a gambler by nature but just for once he elected to go for broke from the word go and attack Ajax with two wingers – Geordie Armstrong and the talented yet wayward young Scot, Peter Marinello.

I have it on good authority that it took me 14 seconds to put Cruyff into the Highbury terracing, but my memory has failed me for once on that score. Fourteen seconds? That long!

It's the sort of urban myth that has surrounded me, like the time I allegedly launched myself at a cross and missed the ball, only to carry two rival defenders into the back of the net; or when I was supposed to have rounded on a bloke barracking me and silenced him with the challenge: 'You – outside after the game.'

That was the skipper, incidentally. Frank learned after the match in question that his critic had a reputation as a hardman, but Frank showed immense bottle by tracking him down to his boozer and sorting him out.

What I am 100 per cent sure of, however, is that the Ajax tie was barely 60 seconds old when Marinello robbed the Holland right-back Wim Suurbier and went clear on goal. But our George Best lookalike shot too close to their keeper and a golden chance went begging.

Despite keeping Cruyff and Co on the back foot virtually all night, we went down 1–0 and 3–1 on aggregate. Marinello has never lived down that miss; someone is always guaranteed to bring it up at get-togethers. Mind you, the goal that clinched the tie for Ajax wasn't very clever either. Their keeper Heinz Stuy smashed a huge clearance downfield and the ball bounced off the retreating George Graham's head and left Bob Wilson totally isolated and powerless. George tried to make light of it afterwards, telling the lads how we should have marked him tighter because we knew what a beast he was in the air, but I didn't think it was that amusing. I forced a tight smile; I knew George felt self-conscious and was trying to lighten the mood but I hated losing, absolutely loathed it with a passion and I looked around the dressing room for teammates who felt the disappointment as keenly as me.

Sometimes when you are on a roll as a team, you think the good times will never end. We had just missed an opportunity to reach the semi-finals of the European Cup, yet certain individuals were behaving as if it wasn't that big a deal and almost seemed to be saying: 'Never mind, we'll be back again next year.'

That was a huge error of judgement. When the moment comes to be a winner you have to reach out and grab it.

Now we returned to concentrate on the FA Cup as our last chance of silverware and history repeated itself, our semi-final with Stoke ending in a draw – just as it had 12 months earlier.

It was 1–1 at Villa Park that April when an incident occurred between myself and Bob Wilson, in which it has been claimed I swore and spat at him while he lay writhing in agony on the ground.

Despite his educated background, college scarf and duffle coat, Bob was never a soft touch. I considered him brave, reckless even, the way he dived in head-first at opponents' feet, but I felt he had a tendency to over-dramatise his knocks. He was forever holding an arm, leg or some other part of his anatomy after a challenge, looking for sympathy. I thought he needed a priest to administer the last rites on a few occasions, rather than our trainer.

I'll let Bob take up the story now, as he later related it in my testimonial programme:

> It was a tight game, blow for blow with Stoke. Then I injured my knee – the cartilage trouble that almost ended my career – and as I lay in the goalmouth I knew something serious was wrong. But my lasting memory is of Peter standing over me glaring and yelling for me to get up. He was not interested in injury problems, just worried about Stoke scoring. It was not a callous reaction, at least not by Peter's own standards. For I have seen him hurt in a game but refusing to show it. Winning came first. Pain came later with him.

The honest truth of the matter is that I did storm up to Bob in the heat of the moment and shout: 'Get up, you cunt!' Frank reckons I

HOWE SAD

spat on Bob, but I refute that. I might have lost my temper with him, but I still respected him too much as a teammate to have done that. If I did spit, it was most certainly never aimed in Bob's direction.

Bob was taken off with a torn cartilage, Ray came on as the substitute and Raddy donned the gloves to take over in goal for the last quarter of an hour, and we worked diligently in defence to ensure Stoke didn't subject our striker-turned-keeper to too many fraught moments.

Geordie Armstrong had given us the lead shortly after the interval and 'Stan' Simpson had the misfortune to be credited with an own goal midway through the second half, although I reckon their centre-half Denis Smith got the decisive touch for the equaliser when George Eastham reminded us he still had more than a bit left in the tank.

Eastham, at thirty-five, had rolled back the years in early March to bend a close-range winner inside the near post as Stoke beat Dave Sexton's Chelsea 2-1 at Wembley to win the Football League Cup following an epic four-game semi-final against West Ham.

A year earlier Eastham had hung up his boots in the Potteries and decamped for South Africa to try his luck as a coach with the intention of going into management over there, but the Stoke manager Tony Waddington summoned him back because of an injury crisis.

It was a staggering return to top-flight football in this country and now I cursed him as he cut in from the right to create their goal with a dangerous cross which dropped just in front of Bob, who was struggling badly with his injury.

Anyway, that was the end of Bob's season and Geoff Barnett replaced him for the semi-final replay at Goodison Park, where we saw off the Potters 2-1. Charlie George and Jimmy Greenhoff exchanged penalties before Raddy scored the winner.

Now we had the chance to emulate Tottenham, who had followed up their Double success in 1960-61 by winning the FA Cup again the following year.

Lying in wait for us at Wembley were our old adversaries, Leeds, looking to win the Cup for the first time in their history and in the running to win the Double themselves. It was never going to be a classic centenary final, the teams knew each other too well, but it was a slight improvement on our League Cup final against them four years earlier in terms of entertainment – even if the result was identical.

Bally was unfortunate early on when he connected beautifully with a right-foot volley from Geordie's corner to the edge of the box, only to see Paul Reaney, perfectly positioned on the post, snake out a foot and prevent a certain goal.

Ten minutes into the second half Mick Jones got away on the right, but I wasn't worried because Bob McNab was closing in to stop him. I would have backed Nabbers nine times out of ten to emerge triumphant from a situation like that. This time Jones managed to ride his sliding tackle and whip over a cross which Allan Clarke met to score with a powerful diving header.

Later on Charlie, who had been as anonymous as he'd been eye-catching 12 months earlier with the winner against Liverpool, roused himself to hook a shot against the bar and that, effectively, was our last chance to equalise. It was a bitter pill to swallow, but we had to accept that Leeds were superior on the day, with Johnny Giles and Billy Bremner getting the better of Bally and George Graham in midfield.

Our season wasn't quite over and two nights later the scene was set for a nerve-jangling First Division title shoot-out. Derby had completed their fixtures with 58 points and were away on their holidays in Majorca while their manager Brian Clough was with his family in the Scilly Isles. Leeds needed a point at Wolves to win the League while Liverpool would be crowned champions if they won at Highbury and Leeds faltered. After Saturday's disappointment at Wembley, a few misguided punters thought we'd be nursing hangovers and feeling sorry for ourselves when Liverpool came calling. Unfortunately for Bill Shankly's side, our pride had been damaged and we were in no mood to roll over and die for anybody.

John Toshack was unlucky to be ruled offside when he had the ball in the net two minutes from time while Leeds somehow contrived to lose at Molineux in a match infamous for allegations of bribery and penalties which weren't awarded because the referee had apparently been tipped off that there was some 'funny' business going on.

So that's how the title finished up at the Baseball Ground, and our 1971–72 campaign ended on a duff note later that week with a 2–0 defeat at Tottenham. I thought finishing fifth in the League was a poor effort, considering our resources.

I thought I was immune from the slip in standards to an extent because I was still playing well, certainly well enough to stay in Alf Ramsey's England team.

CHAPTER SIXTEEN

Falling at the final fence

I was confident it was only a matter of time before I had another winner's medal to polish. However, 1972–73 proved to be another case of close... but no cigar as Arsenal finished runners-up in the First Division, three points behind Liverpool, and lost 2–1 to Sunderland in the FA Cup semi-final.

Make no mistake, we threw it away, absolutely bottled the chance of another Double from what I maintain was a much stronger position than the historic 1970–71 campaign.

At full strength, we were essentially the same team that had beaten Liverpool to win the FA Cup and clinch that Double two years previously, with the exception of Alan Ball as an automatic first choice – and that was a change that, on paper, had only made us stronger.

The manager did not inspire confidence, however, and I couldn't believe how petty Bertie could be at times.

A few days before pre-season officially started at London Colney, I thought I would drop in at Highbury to do a bit of running on my own and physical work to get myself in shape. I was too proud to be off the pace when the serious stuff started. Just as I was getting changed, who should walk in but Bally. He'd had exactly the same idea; and we went out on the pitch and had a good hour's work-out together.

Back in the dressing room, Tony Donnelly, the kitman, was packing the skips for London Colney later in the week and we asked him if there was any chance of a cup of tea.

Normally only managerial staff and those above that rank got that little perk, but there was hardly anyone else in the ground and making a brew was no problem for Tony.

After Bally and I had showered, the three of us were sitting down enjoying a well-earned cuppa when the dressing room door swung open and in walked Bertie. We indulged in some small talk with the gaffer, who appeared pleased with our enthusiasm, before heading home.

A few days later at London Colney, I spotted Tony looking something less than his usual chirpy self. He came over and said: 'You and your mate got me in right trouble over that tea', before revealing that Bertie had given him a severe bollocking over the matter and had told Tony: 'You do not make them cups of tea, they are just employees of this club.'

There was Alan Ball, a World Cup winner and Arsenal's most expensive signing, a player with over 50 international caps to his name, while I was a Double-winning first-team regular who was also in the England team.

Employees, that's what Bertie thought of us. How small can you get? It was pathetic, really.

Around the time Liverpool established themselves at the top of the table in late September, I scored twice in successive matches, against Norwich and Birmingham, when a corner bounced in off my knee. Some of the lads ribbed me afterwards that it was a 'classic scruffy Snouty effort' but I just grinned widely and shouted back: 'Bollocks! They all count.'

Despite suffering a horrible 5–0 defeat at Derby, the League champions, at the end of November, we were travelling sweetly and a fortnight later won 2–1 at Tottenham, where I scored again – this time with a header.

George Graham, unhappy in the reserves, was placed on the transfer list and suddenly left for Manchester United just after Christmas. One minute he was there, the next he was gone, not like so many of today's transfers which are flagged up and played out in the media for weeks before the deal is done. United was a good move financially for both George and Arsenal, because the club got £120,000 for him. Tommy Docherty had just been appointed United's new manager and made me laugh when he maintained: 'George Graham is in the class of Günter Netzer.' There was no emotion on my part to the news of George's departure and, no disrespect to 'Stroller', I knew that Eddie Kelly was a more than adequate replacement.

Anfield in February loomed as a massive fixture. Bill Shankly's team were unbeaten in their fortress up on Merseyside, where they had clocked up 12 successive home wins before dropping a point against Derby.

FALLING AT THE FINAL FENCE

Yet we went up there and put on a brilliant show. Bally was in his element, back in the city where he had shone so brightly across Stanley Park for Everton, and he scored with a second-half penalty before John Radford sealed the points.

The ground fell silent when Alec Lindsay blatantly tripped Geordie Armstrong in the box and Bally held his nerve in front of the Kop to stick the penalty low past his England pal Ray Clemence. There was no way back for Liverpool when Raddy broke away on the halfway line and scored a brilliant individual effort.

Suddenly we were on top of the First Division, but that promising state of affairs lasted barely a fortnight before a goal from Tony Brown did for us at West Brom. Liverpool were back in charge of their own destiny, but we hung in there doggedly to their coat-tails and reeled off four successive wins over Sheffield United, Ipswich, Manchester City and Crystal Palace.

Then Cloughie's bloody Derby beat us at Highbury 1–0 with an early goal from the kid, Steve Powell, and the rot set in.

Everything appeared to be nicely set up for us when we kicked off on 31 March, Grand National Saturday, because Spurs, bless 'em, had done us a big favour that morning by drawing 1–1 at Anfield, and we knew two points would see us regain top spot with just a handful of matches to play.

That should have been motivation enough, without the lads even bothering about revenge for the battering at the Baseball Ground before Christmas.

Derby's League form was suffering; they had just been beaten at home by Leeds in the sixth round of the FA Cup and wouldn't have been human if they hadn't been thinking about a forthcoming European Cup semi-final date with Juventus in Turin.

Powell's goal surprised us and we became increasingly anxious at failing to equalise; Frank McLintock was carried off with a torn muscle five minutes before the interval, while Charlie George ended up arguing the toss bitterly with a linesman.

Bally and some of the other lads keen on racing came back to the dressing room to discover they had won a few bob on Red Rum beating Crisp at Aintree, but they weren't in any mood to celebrate.

That was the end of Frank's season and although we had a ready-made replacement, I didn't rate him very highly.

Bertie had paid Coventry £200,000 for their centre-half Jeff Blockley in October and he was supposed to be a good player, although I never saw any startling evidence. Certainly, I thought Blockley would have to be quite a special footballer, not to mention character, to break up the partnership between Frank and 'Stan' Simpson which had served us so well and for so long.

There had been a poisonous atmosphere at St Andrews on the Saturday before Christmas when Frank had had no inkling he was going to be dropped in favour of Blockley for the Birmingham away match. Bertie should have been more diplomatic at the very least. In fact, I thought he was disrespectful, the way he treated the skipper like a kid and shied away from breaking the news to Frank that he was being dropped, and explaining his reasons, until the morning of the match in the team hotel.

The deed should have been done, calmly and rationally, back in the manager's office at Highbury well before we travelled to the Midlands. After the nine seasons Frank had given the club, that consideration was the least he deserved.

Instead, Bertie landed himself in trouble by asking Frank to step out of the lounge where the rest of us were either reading the back pages of the tabloids or getting ready to watch *Grandstand*. Out in the corridor was the first Frank learned he wasn't playing that afternoon, and he went mad, splintering the oak panelling with his fist.

Birmingham were a poor side at that particular time, scratching around the relegation zone, despite having a couple of excellent strikers in Trevor Francis and Bob Latchford.

Frank's foul mood did absolutely nothing for team morale and our powers of concentration, and Birmingham recovered from a goal by Eddie to take a point we could ill afford to surrender.

Away from our bread and butter in the First Division, we had quietly been picking our way through the FA Cup field with low-key victories over Leicester, Bradford City and Carlisle which took us into the sixth round for a London derby in mid-March against Chelsea at Stamford Bridge. It was hectic stuff to start with and we were caught cold at the back when Peter Osgood, with a brilliant left-foot volley from the edge of the box, and John Hollins punished us. Fortunately, Chelsea were just as edgy in defence and Bally and Charlie, with a really scruffy effort when their reserve keeper John Phillips cocked up, replied, all four goals in the 2–2 draw arriving in the opening half-hour.

Three nights later Highbury was heaving with 62,642 fans packed inside for the replay. Bally scored a hotly disputed penalty; Peter Houseman got a goal for them before Ray Kennedy scored to carry us over the winning line in the second half.

Nobody outside Wearside could have expected us to lose to Sunderland in the semi-final at Hillsborough. They were nothing more than a middling-to-average sort of Second Division side, although I thought the manager Bob Stokoe had a few useful performers in goalkeeper Jim Montgomery, midfielder Ian Porterfield and forwards Billy Hughes and Dennis Tueart. Their progress to Sheffield on 7 April had been unremarkable, with victories over Notts County, Reading and Luton.

Maybe we missed a trick, though, a warning sign in the fifth round, when Sunderland ambushed a Manchester City line-up boasting Mike Summerbee, Colin Bell, Rodney Marsh and Francis Lee. The Roker Park side drew 2–2 at Maine Road before completing the job in some style, 3–1 at home.

I can't quite put my finger on what went wrong that day. Arsenal weren't the sort of outfit to outwardly display any arrogance or underestimate the opposition, but we were extremely poor.

I think Blockley wasn't that fit and he had to stay off at half-time for treatment. With Frank's season prematurely terminated, we were forced to replace Blockley with a forward in John Radford. A few players switched around to try and find a system to suit the occasion, but Sunderland had the bit between their teeth from the moment Vic Halom gave them the lead.

Micky Horswill had already served notice that Sunderland were far from overawed when he cracked a volley towards the top corner which demanded an acrobatic save from Bob Wilson.

Then came an awful mistake, a crass error even worse than Charlie's against Stoke in the semi-final two years earlier, after which I had managed to dig us out of the mire.

A long, hopeful punt forward should have been meat and drink to Blockley, but our new centre-half made a hash of a routine back-pass to Bob, wafting lamely at the ball, and Halom said 'thank you very much' as he nipped in and took the ball round our keeper.

Geordie Armstrong almost equalised with a deflected left-foot shot which required Montgomery to demonstrate his lightning reflexes, changing direction to dive and tip the ball for a corner.

We fell further behind, however, when a long throw-in from the right was flicked on in the air to the six-yard box where Hughes twisted to loop a header high behind him, and Bob's despairing dive only helped the ball into the net.

Charlie replied with a scrambled goal with five minutes to play, picked the ball out of the net and raced back to the centre-spot with it, but the damage was done and there was no way back.

It was a match from which we never really looked like getting anything but a beating – and that was bloody hard to take.

You had to take your hat off to Sunderland though, and they upset all the odds again by beating Leeds 1–0 in the FA Cup final. At least that made me smile.

When it came to the crunch in our last half-dozen League matches, we simply failed to put Liverpool under pressure. After losing at home to Derby, we drew with Tottenham, Everton and Southampton, and squeezed out a 2–1 win at West Ham before bowing out lower than a snake's belly with a 6–1 home defeat by Leeds.

I scored the equaliser at White Hart Lane, straight after they had taken the lead. We kicked off and the ball came to me for a shot which zipped through Pat Jennings' legs. It wasn't the sort of goal I was likely to forget in a hurry for two very good reasons. One, it was a left-foot effort and two, Pat was very rarely nutmegged.

I know the reason for our poor end to the season – we weren't strong enough mentally. Frank was out of the team and on his way to Queens Park Rangers, and there wasn't the same sort of leadership on the pitch which had sustained us when the chips were down in 1971. With Don Howe long gone, neither was there the same sort of hard-nosed pragmatism on the coaching staff.

CHAPTER SEVENTEEN

Losing the plot

I sensed that discipline and focus were in short supply as Arsenal began to drift aimlessly, moving further away from trophies.

There were handshakes and smiles to begin with when Manchester United and George Graham rolled into town for the first match of the 1973–74 campaign. Our fans gave George a rousing reception before the kick-off, while I wanted to sidle up and tell him: 'You're going to get fuck all today, pal!'

Unfortunately, I was sitting out a one-match suspension hanging over me from previous misdemeanours so I was obliged to watch as we won comfortably 3–0 and the die was cast – United were on their way to relegation.

Mind you, we had nothing to crow about four games later when we found ourselves down in twentieth place in the table following a draw with Newcastle and demoralising defeats by Leeds, Sheffield United and Leicester.

There was unrest in the ranks at St James' Park where Eddie Kelly reacted poorly to being substituted, throwing his shirt at our trainer's bench in disgust.

We were appalling under the floodlights at Bramall Lane, conceding four goals before half-time in a 5–0 defeat, and not much better at home days later against Leicester, who beat us 2–0.

It hadn't taken Alan Ball long to get fed up and he alleged referee Clive Thomas was picking on him when he was booked against the Midlanders for mocking a linesman, suggesting the official needed glasses.

I thought if somebody in authority at Highbury didn't crack the whip we were in danger of becoming a rabble, and it was in this climate of discontent that Steve Burtenshaw was sacked, or rather stabbed in the back, on the evening of 11 September shortly after the return match against the Blades, which we managed to win 1–0. It was a night of the long knives.

The official line was that Steve offered his resignation and it was reluctantly accepted by the Arsenal board, but that was just a convenient way of trying to save face all round.

Bally felt he needed to be the central hub of the team, the main man, and that everything had to fit in with him. He was such a powerful personality that our first-team coach wasn't strong enough to compete.

Bally always got his own way, didn't rate Burtenshaw and could be a terrible moaner. He went so far as to call a team meeting at London Colney where he asked us all, quite pointedly: 'Do we want Burtenshaw as coach, or not?' It was a terrible question to ask because Steve was well liked among the lads.

Still, he was unceremoniously given the thumbs down and Bally triumphantly took the verdict to Bertie Mee and informed the manager that the Arsenal players no longer had any confidence in their coach.

Given that Bertie's position depended on having a tried and trusted first lieutenant, Burtenshaw swiftly became a dead man walking. It was a case of when, not if, he got the bullet.

The manner in which the dismissal came about was shocking, and demeaned a club of Arsenal's stature. At the precise moment Steve was issuing his team talk before the kick-off, Bertie crept into the dressing room and whispered to several of the senior players that Bobby Campbell, a well-regarded coach at Queens Park Rangers, was in the crowd and, more than that, would be taking Steve's job the following morning.

After the match, Burtenshaw was still none the wiser, walking down the corridor until Bertie stuck his head around his office door and said: 'Oh, Steve, could you pop in for a moment?'

The team didn't improve noticeably under Campbell, a big, brash Scouser who arrived with a decent reputation from Loftus Road. The fans stayed away in their tens of thousands as we struggled, while our impact in both knock-out competitions was negligible to say the least, if not downright embarrassing.

Three weeks after Burtenshaw's sacking, Third Division Tranmere Rovers pitched up at Highbury in the League Cup and emerged triumphant, 1–0. That might just have been forgivable had Bertie and Campbell fielded a team of fringe players, reserves and youth-team thrusters, but there could be no excuses for the abject failure of this line-up: Wilson, Rice, McNab, Storey, Blockley, Simpson, Armstrong, Ball, Radford, Kennedy and Kelly.

Aston Villa, then struggling badly in the Second Division, proved too good for us in the FA Cup. Ron Saunders brought his team south in the fourth round in late January on a shocking run, having not won in the League in 11 matches, but we were grateful for Ray Kennedy's equaliser to get us out of jail. Villa outplayed us in the replay, winning 2–0 with goals from Alun Evans and Sam Morgan.

I won't bore you with a blow-by-blow account of the rest of the campaign, because it bored me and it clearly bored our fans as we became the distinctly Mr Averages of the First Division, finishing tenth, winning 14, drawing 14 and losing 14 of our matches.

Although I didn't particularly dislike Campbell, I thought he shouted too much trying to establish his point of view. Mind you, whenever we were on England duty together, Rodney Marsh never had a bad word to say about Campbell at QPR and neither did Bally at Highbury, mainly, I think, because he was made captain, found himself indulged and had a lot of influence in picking the team.

I was happy to do a bit of property business with Campbell however, and it wasn't long before we shook hands over £40,000 for my house in Hadley Wood. I had snapped it up at just the right time, with prices about to soar, and spent another £5,000 on an extension to create a fourth bedroom. Bobby had been commuting to work from Surrey and fell in love with the place, but I wasn't sorry to see it go because it had never been my home, living as I was with Cathy in St John's Wood. There were no sentimental attachments in Parkgate Crescent, only curtains I had crudely nailed up in one bedroom.

Back at Highbury, Bertie clearly needed to do something to address the slide and general malaise or the 1974–75 season threatened to be another non-event, or worse.

Bob Wilson called it a day as the break-up of the Double-winning team continued. I had no quibble with his replacement, Jimmy Rimmer. Now, he was a good signing and a top-rank goalkeeper.

There were two significant transfers in mid-July when Bill Shankly paid £200,000 to take Ray Kennedy to Liverpool and Brian Kidd arrived for £110,000 from Manchester United as his direct replacement to lead our attack.

Although I think there was a suggestion the manager was unhappy that Ray was putting on weight, the switch took me by surprise.

TRUE STOREY

I had enormous respect for Ray; he was always so brave and unselfish. Quite apart from his prowess in front of goal, he made the Arsenal defenders look good because we knew we could lump the ball in his direction and nine times out of ten he could be relied on to shield it and bring teammates into play.

He was our top scorer in the Double-winning season, with nineteen goals in the League – including the very precious one at Tottenham to clinch the title.

Ray was the final purchase made by Shanks, who resigned the same day, and he could hardly have given Liverpool a better leaving present, for his successor Bob Paisley transformed Ray into an attacking midfielder who won five League championships, three European Cups, the UEFA Cup, the League Cup and four Charity Shields. And there was also the little matter of the 17 England caps Ray earned while he was on Merseyside. It was tragic the way he later became a victim of Parkinson's disease towards the end of his career after he moved to Swansea.

Despite scoring plenty of goals for us, I got the impression that Kiddo never wanted to be at Arsenal. In his mind, he was still a United player, understandably so, having been at Old Trafford for a decade and scoring a goal on his nineteenth birthday when United beat Benfica to claim the European Cup in 1968.

The gradual emergence of Liam Brady with his wonderful left foot from the youth team was a bonus, but a couple of signings were not exactly out of the top drawer.

Apart from Blockley, a second central defender, Terry Mancini, taken from QPR in the autumn at the behest of Campbell, was another player who would never have got within miles of the Arsenal team a few years earlier.

With the exception of Bally, in terms of quality Bertie's ventures into the transfer market following the Double were largely questionable. He was fairly clueless in football matters and relied on suggestions from others for his 'considered' decisions.

Even with Bally, there was a problem. Just as Kiddo was always Man United at heart, Bally was another northerner and still wanted to be at Everton. They were always his number one team – and I think it broke a little bit of his heart when he was frozen out of Goodison Park. I'm not saying Bally and Kiddo didn't try their best for the club – and with Brian you could not argue with the 23 goals he scored in his first season – it's just that they weren't Arsenal players from head to toe. And that did make a difference.

I wasn't surprised in the least when Kiddo jumped at the chance to return to Manchester, albeit City rather than United, in July 1976 after just two terms in north London.

Arsenal were rudderless in my last few seasons at Highbury; the trend was noticeably downwards.

By the middle of October 1974 we were bottom of the First Division after a 2–0 defeat at Tottenham, our eighth loss in the opening 13 matches which had seen us beat only Leicester on the opening day and Manchester City.

We flirted with trouble again early in 1975, losing three League matches on the bounce to Wolves, Derby and Everton – a nasty, barren little sequence which saw us plunge to eighteenth place in the table.

Derby were heading for another League title, this time under Dave Mackay, and hardly needed our assistance on a gloomy February Saturday. But we contributed hugely to our own downfall on the notorious Baseball Ground pitch, where both Bally and Bob McNab contrived to get themselves sent off.

Bally lost the plot after just 15 minutes when we were trailing to a goal from Steve Powell. Our midfield mainstay was booked for lashing out at Kevin Hector with one of his famous white boots while he was on the ground. Instead of keeping his trap shut, Bally continued to argue with referee John Yates, who showed him the red card.

John Radford got our ten men back in the game with an equaliser but before half-time Powell scored the winner.

The drama was far from complete, however, and we played the final half-hour with nine players after Bob took a leaf out of Bally's book and kept snarling at the ref after being cautioned for kicking the ball away.

The following Monday night, Bally and McNab did redeem themselves a little by helping us win 1–0 with a goal from Raddy in extra-time at Leicester in the FA Cup which took us into the quarter-finals. We had already needed replays to knock out York City and Coventry, and this was the second replay at Filbert Street.

Maybe, I thought, just maybe this was our year for Wembley again.

But I was swiftly disabused of that notion in the sixth round when West Ham arrived on a rainy day and beat us 2–0 with a couple of goals from Alan Taylor. Parts of Highbury were like a saturated bog and the Hammers got lucky for the first goal when the ball stopped dead in a puddle as Jimmy Rimmer came to claim it, and they took possession for a short centre which Taylor couldn't miss.

West Ham went on to win the FA Cup, beating Fulham in the final, while we were relieved that a flurry of goals from Kidd near the end of the campaign steered us to an extremely disappointing sixteenth place. Arsenal had mustered a paltry thirty-seven points, a mere four more than Luton Town and Chelsea, who were both relegated with Carlisle.

CHAPTER EIGHTEEN

From the top to the bottle

I worked so hard to get to the pinnacle of my profession and I genuinely loved playing football for the enjoyment it provided.

Often in life, you never stop to think how lucky you are; I know I never did. The future held nasty surprises in store, jobs I hated with a vengeance – such as driving a minicab – but which I needed desperately when I fell on hard times, because there was no alternative and I was skint. I had to withstand the humiliation, the sneers as passengers discovered my identity and enquired: 'I thought you were supposed to be famous?' and 'What are you doing this shit for, then?'

For now my troubles were just beginning.

The decline, when it came, was relatively swift, brutal and mostly my own fault. I lost my job at Arsenal, broke up with my second wife Cathy just months after we married and found solace in a bottle as I started drinking too much, far too much on occasions.

My life took a turn for the worse in the summer of 1975 when I paid Ind Coope brewery £5,000 for a three-year tenancy agreement at the Jolly Farmers, Southgate Road, London N1 – in the heart of working-class Arsenal-supporting territory. The brewery was delighted to sign up a legendary Highbury Double-winner and expressed their confidence that I would make a bundle out of the arrangement because having my name over the door would be excellent for business, particularly on match days. Before me, the pub had been a bit run down; I don't think many people used it.

Bertie Mee, however, was less enthusiastic. In fact, he was alarmed at the prospect of me becoming mine host, and I took the pub against his express wishes.

My master plan was to install a manager, let him deal with the casual bar staff and have all the day-to-day aggravation of running the place, while I would restrict myself to lording it – showing my face a few nights a week for a pint or two, and entertaining my guests whenever the mood took me. What could be simpler?

Although the Ind Coope people I spoke to nodded enthusiastically when I outlined my proposal after signing the relevant documents, I'm sure they must have been wary. They must have known from experience that running a big pub such as the Jolly Farmers in a less-than-posh part of north London, with live bands and DJs, required full-time hands-on dedication or the entire venture would prove financial suicide.

Bertie was no mug, either, and adamant that boozers were not an appropriate business in which footballers should dabble because of the long hours and physical effort required to keep them profitable, quite apart from the social temptations of the booze and birds. I suppose he was right, but the trend at the time was for players and boxers, too, to get into the pub game and it looked like a no-brainer to me.

It wasn't long before a handful of the other Arsenal lads followed my example. Frank McLintock had already invested in several wine bars before becoming the tenant of two north London boozers. He sold one quickly but kept the Sutton Arms in Copenhagen Street, Upper Holloway, for a decade.

Geoff Barnett preferred a slightly less hectic existence and took a pub outside London, but when Bob McNab branched out from his successful betting shop, he ventured dangerously close to Tottenham territory with licensed premises at the 'wrong' end of the Seven Sisters Road.

Eddie Kelly and his brother-in-law, Charlie Pini, had the Spanish Patriots off Chapel Street market, the scene of a nasty incident. A well-known boxing personality was staying at Spanish Pats one night when a petrol bomb was thrown through the window.

Talking of boxing, it was around this time that I was tempted to give the manager a swift jab in the eye over a harmless Wednesday night out watching the sport at a charity dinner event in the East End.

Dennis Pinching, a member of the London Ex-Boxers Association, had phoned to ask if I fancied stepping in at late notice as his guest because his original choice and friend, Charlie George, couldn't make it.

I drove to the venue, met lots of faces in the fight game – including trainer George Francis, who later helped Frank Bruno and John

FROM THE TOP TO THE BOTTLE

Conteh to world titles – enjoyed a pleasant dinner washed down with a couple of glasses of red wine and watched several decent amateur bouts in the ring.

Another guest at the venue gloried in his claim to be the Fattest Man in England, and a photographer asked if he might have a snap of the two of us together. I thought it was a harmless enough request and had no objection. I drove safely home and was in bed by midnight.

Saturday dawned, the day of a home match we were to win well, and the picture appeared in a national tabloid newspaper. I took some good-natured stick in the dressing room, and even I had a laugh when one of the lads held up the page and asked loudly: 'Who's this lump of lard with the fattest man in England, then?'

Monday morning found me back at Highbury, doing a few sit-ups on my own upstairs before training, when a message arrived to come down for an urgent team meeting. I arrived in the dressing room to find Bertie standing in front of our big mirror, to which he had attached the picture of me and Fatso with a smear of Vaseline.

Then our esteemed manager went into a rant about players being out on the town on a *Thursday* night, which was strictly against club rules before a match, and that they deserved to be fined and had let down their teammates. Never once did he mention me by name, however.

Tantrum over, Bertie clapped his hands and announced: 'That's it, all out training.'

I was fuming under my calm exterior and in no mood to let him escape so easily. 'Hang on, you're fucking talking about me,' I growled, and immediately his face started to turn red. 'You'd better check your fucking facts if you want to have a pop.' Bertie stormed off without a word.

I soon discovered that someone in the directors' box on Saturday had complained about Arsenal players out drinking on a Thursday. I couldn't believe that Bertie had seen the picture in the paper, put two and two together and come up with five without first doing his homework.

He made that big speech in front of all the lads and just tried to belittle me but he was never big enough to admit he was in the wrong, and he never had the decency to apologise.

I'm convinced the running sore of Alan Ball's wages was responsible for us looking outside the game to boost our income. Frankly, I thought the basic wage we were on at Arsenal was rubbish and that we needed to win the League and FA Cup every season to compete with the money on offer at England's other major clubs.

Pubs seemed the logical step. Anyway, what else was I equipped to do a few years down the line? Already I was pushing 30, a dangerous age for a professional footballer then. I'd left school with no qualifications and, as you will already have gathered from the Arsenal lads, I was never the most gifted or natural verbal communicator, so I knew that ruled out staying in football and chancing my arm as a coach or even in management down the ranks.

If the opening night at the Jolly Farmers was anything to go by, I'd soon be rolling in it. I threw a huge party; everyone at Highbury was invited, and the place was packed to the rafters. Charlie George had had enough, and the break-up of the Double-winning team continued in early July when the Derby manager, Dave Mackay, 'stole' him for £90,000.

Bertie effectively took his revenge when we reported back for training before the 1975–76 season by more or less exiling me to the reserves, although I felt I was fit for purpose in the First Division.

Cathy and I had been living together in our luxury flat near Lord's cricket ground for the best part of three years when we decided to get married that August at Westminster Registry Office, off the Marylebone Road.

The brewery was certainly keen for me to be married. I wouldn't go so far as to claim they put pressure on me, but it was suggested on several occasions that it would 'look better' if the Jolly Farmers were in the hands of married tenants.

The reception for Cathy and myself could hardly have been smaller, consisting as it did of her parents, my mum and dad, and her cousin, who officiated as best man. We had a nice meal together in a restaurant beneath the block of flats where we lived. Nobody from Arsenal was there because, being a Saturday in August, they had weightier matters on their minds than coming on the piss with me. There was no honeymoon either, and Cathy soon got fed up with me playing 'now you see me, now you don't'.

It seemed Arsenal could suddenly happily do without me, while I found it soul-destroying in the 'stiffs' for the first three months of the campaign.

Life at the Jolly Farmers with the manager I brought in didn't work

FROM THE TOP TO THE BOTTLE

out either, and it soon dawned on me I needed to be there to keep a sharp eye on the place, and also because punters expected to see me behind the bar. I couldn't blame them, because if the attraction was 'going for a drink at Peter Storey's boozer' and I was hardly ever there, they had every right to feel short-changed and take their custom elsewhere.

I'm ashamed to say I wrecked my marriage to Cathy and our existence together in St John's Wood because I was out drinking all the time and there were lots of other girls about. No question, it was my fault. Increasingly, I began to sleep overnight in the pub rather than go home to Cathy. We drifted into an unsatisfactory, unstable on-off relationship for two or three years without ever really living together in the accepted sense.

Meanwhile, the team were struggling and Highbury attendances had plummeted to around 23,000 by the end of October 1975, as unhappy punters voted with their feet and gave the terraces a swerve. Then injuries meant I was needed to fill in for Sammy Nelson and Eddie Kelly until Christmas.

My comeback coincided with an opportunity to enjoy a testimonial match against Feyenoord, but the horse-trading and politics leading up to the game on 9 December left a sour taste in the mouth.

There were three of us in the pecking order for the next testimonial – 'Stan' Simpson, me and John Radford; we had joined the club in successive years in the early 1960s and were hopeful of big things after the way Geordie Armstrong had been fêted.

Then, in March 1974, a crowd of over 36,000 was attracted to Highbury to see Johan Cruyff play a starring role as Barcelona won 3-1. The Dutchman was serious box office material, on his way to making history by being crowned European Footballer of the Year for a third time.

Bob McNab, quoted in *Seventy-One Guns*, remembers it well:

> I think we played Johan Cruyff six times and marked him man for man five times. The one time we didn't was in a testimonial against Barcelona for Geordie Armstrong. We thought, 'we can't mark him man for man when he has come here for an exhibition'. Well, we were 3–0 down at half-time, so the call went out, 'Snouty, mark him'. They didn't score again. If one of the opposition players was having a good

session, Peter Storey would mark him for a few minutes. He didn't like doing it, he would be swearing under his breath and snarling. He hated it that much, it made it worse for the poor bastard he was marking. Peter was a nightmare for players when he marked them man for man.

I thought Cruyff was terrific, one of the top players in the world, possibly the best. He was fast, he had everything, including superb balance and two great feet. But it was Cruyff's pace and speed of thought which really set him apart. He had the reaction time of a sprinter out of the blocks but also this great intelligence and vision to see how moves might develop two or three passes down the line.

If it was a crime that George Best never played in a World Cup tournament, then it was a travesty of justice that Johan Cruyff never picked up the World Cup. It was the only major trophy he didn't win and Holland blew it big-time in 1974 against West Germany, the host nation, in the final.

I remember thinking it might be a bit cagey, a little nip and tuck for the first 20 minutes or so.

I had just settled into an armchair in front of the telly at home that Sunday night in July with a glass of red wine when Cruyff kicked off in Munich. 'This looks interesting,' I said to myself as the Dutch strung more than ten passes together without the Germans getting a sniff of the ball. Then I was sitting bolt upright and almost spilled my wine as Cruyff took possession again and went tearing into the German box where Uli Hoeness fouled him. The penalty, tucked safely away by Johan Neeskens, was an easy decision for English referee Jack Taylor to make – even if the World Cup final was only one minute old and you also took the venue into consideration.

Holland should have gone on to win, but they lost their way. The Germans equalised with a dodgy penalty of their own and scored what turned out to be the winner on the stroke of half-time.

For many of the watching millions, myself included, Holland were the 'complete' team in 1974. Inspired by Cruyff, they made light of a so-called 'Group of Death' by swatting aside Argentina 4–0, East Germany 2–0 and the defending world champions Brazil 2–0 after earlier dismissing Uruguay 2–0 and Bulgaria 4–1.

On the big day, though, the Dutch were caught out by maybe the one type of player they lacked. Gerd Müller, who was a supreme goal poacher and lethal in the six-yard area, had no right to make anything of a poor cross to the front post, but he managed to stretch back, retrieve the ball and turn to shoot past the keeper.

So Müller went home with a World Cup winner's medal, while Cruyff had to make do with some gong or other as official player of the tournament.

Back at Highbury, when the final whistle sounded on the Barcelona game, everyone was absolutely delighted for Geordie. No player was more popular in our dressing room than the wee fella, and the club went to town on his behalf with a post-match banquet at Grosvenor House in Park Lane. Stan, Raddy and I thought that package – top European opponents and a slap-up meal in a five-star West End hotel – would be the template for others who had dedicated their careers to Arsenal and featured in the Double-winning team.

I thought it was dreadful when Geordie died prematurely, aged 56, from a brain haemorrhage in 2000 because he still had lots to offer the game as a coach.

Stan was offered a few games and turned them down because, I believe, the clubs suggested were nowhere near the level of Barcelona, yet they were still making hefty financial demands.

The three of us feared a duff benefit match against second-raters from the continent and a poor gate would leave us standing to lose more than we had to gain.

Eventually, Stan was called into the manager's office and told by Bertie that Arsenal had arranged to bring Feyenoord over from Holland in a month's time and the match was his if he wanted it, otherwise it would be offered in turn to me, then Raddy. Stan rejected the game, so I was summoned to see the manager.

Although I had given him some grief by taking the pub, I was unprepared to find Bertie in such an offhand mood after serving the club as a professional for over a dozen years. He wasn't downright nasty, but he wasn't very pleasant either as he offered me Feyenoord – take it, or leave it and drop down to number three on the waiting list behind Raddy and Stan. For a moment it crossed my mind to tell Bertie to stick it up his arse and go and see the chairman, Denis Hill-Wood, but I calmed down over the weekend after going out for a good drink with Raddy, who said he'd definitely have Feyenoord if I gave them the swerve. I needed the money, came back in on Monday and said I would take the match.

I still had the needle with Bertie and wasn't impressed when he informed me that I would have to form my own testimonial committee because the people in the club who had helped Geordie were fed up. Apparently, they had found it a fairly thankless task.

I was hacked off with the whole idea and never bothered sounding out a soul about forming a testimonial committee, so the burden fell to club secretary Ken Friar. While Geordie had enjoyed the glamour of a dinner in Mayfair, my spread was a little more mundane, as I think can be gleaned by this tiny paragraph in the Feyenoord testimonial programme: 'East Stand Restaurant: As we are holding a small buffet for the players and officials of both sides, this restaurant area will be closed from after half-time onwards (from approximately 8.25 p.m.).'

I perked up when Bertie revealed Arsenal had invited George Best to play as a guest. My old nemesis was attempting a comeback on a match-by-match basis with Stockport County in the Fourth Division, and I think Bertie fancied signing him permanently. Certainly, I knew that Chelsea were sniffing around, attracted by the thousands Bestie's name and reputation alone would stick on the gates at Stamford Bridge.

Brian Kidd was dispatched to Manchester to bring Bestie back to Highbury in one piece – but George, true to form, went on the piss and did a runner. It was very disappointing when that news leaked out and didn't help the gate.

Bestie had been wasting his time, not to mention his considerable talent, ever since New Year's Day, 1974. The United boss Tommy Docherty had persuaded him to try and dig the club out of relegation trouble then, following another typical bout of hide-and-seek, but the much-heralded comeback only lasted a dozen matches and Bestie never turned up for training following a 3–0 stuffing at Loftus Road. He was fined and suspended by the club and retaliated by announcing his retirement.

Bestie lured an extra 7,000 fans to Stockport to see him come on as a substitute and score the winner against Swansea in his first appearance for the Cheshire club, but the weekend before we were expecting him at Highbury, he played the full 90 minutes in a 5–0 defeat at Reading and had gone into hiding when Kiddo tried to track him down.

More impressive, I felt, was the article Bob Wilson penned for the programme, especially after all the stick and abuse I had heaped on him:

> Tonight Peter Storey reaps a deserved reward for fourteen years' loyal, hard-working service to Arsenal. My only regret, on a night to conjure great memories, is that too much emphasis

FROM THE TOP TO THE BOTTLE

has always been placed on the word 'hard' regarding Peter's football.

I'll be the first to admit that he is a hard player. And anyone hoping to read unknown snippets about the man that show a saintly side to his character are in for a disappointment.

But Peter is also a fine footballer, and it's this side of his game that so often suffers because of his 'tough-guy' image.

All too often, one of his tackles would capture more headlines than five accurate, penetrating passes in the same ninety minutes. In fact, people would go away and refer to his contribution to a match in terms of physical contact.

Reputations stick, however, and that's Peter's . . . the ball-winner, the Arsenal hardman. But there's more, much more, to one of the most dedicated professionals it has been my pleasure to play with.

Peter's great strength is his ability to close-mark an opponent. His concentration is frightening, his determination to win infectious. But by virtue of that sort of role, physical contact is inevitable. And I'm sure Peter would be the first to agree that he has made mistakes along the way.

George Best typified the sort of problems Peter faced by continually referring to the treatment he received when marked in certain games. But once again, such contact is unavoidable. A great forward clashing with a great defender.

Such publicity, however, keeps a player pinned down as a type. Peter Storey is a type, but in my opinion a very special type.

He is one of the most adaptable professionals I've ever known. During our great 'Double' days, he played in a variety of back-four and midfield roles. In fact, he's played in every defensive and midfield position . . . without a grumble.

I believe his game has suffered as a result. To me, Peter could have been one of the all-time great defensive full-backs. The most impressive pair I ever played behind were Peter at right-back and Bob McNab on the left.

Of course, so much more is expected of full-backs today. Pat Rice is a splendid attacking example. But I think he'd concede to Peter when it came to outright defensive qualities.

Storey won 19 caps for England, and again his adaptability shone through. Sir Alf Ramsey was quick to recognise how great an asset he is to any squad. He played him at right-back, left-back and in midfield. Once again, he did not have the opportunity to settle down in one position and make it his niche.

The point is, you don't win that many caps for your country simply because you are a 'hard man'. Internationals have that special something extra to offer. Peter Storey has that special something.

He's a man of two distinct characters. Off the field, if you met him individually, you'd find him a quietly spoken, well-mannered, almost retiring person. Straight, even blunt, but not in a noisy fashion.

But come face to face with the man on the pitch, and you have a battle on your hands. He cannot be panicked, cannot be talked off his game and is virtually impossible to shake off.

Looking back over my years with Arsenal, I'll never forget our FA Cup semi-final with Stoke City at Hillsborough in 1971. We were two goals down and time was running out. But where all else had failed, Peter pierced the Stoke defence with a cracking cross shot into the corner to pull us back into the game.

Then, with less than a minute to go, we were awarded a penalty. It was the sort of situation you have nightmares about. But Peter calmly stepped up and rapped the ball firmly past the world's greatest goalkeeper, Gordon Banks, to keep us in the Cup and rekindle our 'Double' hopes.

Such ice-cool nerve cannot be manufactured. When the chips are down and the tough moments have to be faced, Peter Storey is the man to have in your side.

The warmest side of the man is shown to Arsenal. He lives, eats and sleeps Arsenal Football Club. Nothing else matters, and if he does ever leave Highbury for pastures new – and I doubt that he ever will – he will leave a large part of himself here.

He's a one-club man, totally dedicated to his profession, proud of his achievements and insatiable when it comes to winning. Every game is a fresh challenge.

Tonight will be a memorable night for Peter and his number one supporter – his father Edwin, who rarely misses a game. I hope there are many years more for his special brand of action and his hunger for success.

FROM THE TOP TO THE BOTTLE

I thought Stan and I were treated like a bit of shit, really, being told to take it or leave it. In years to come, I was really annoyed with myself that I hadn't gone over Bertie's head and taken up the matter with the chairman.

Double standards certainly came into play when, as I'm led to believe, Bob wanted to end his career and launch a new one full-time with the BBC, but Bertie was desperate for him to stay. Apparently, among the incentives not to hang up his boots and gloves came the offer of a bumper, no-holds-barred testimonial match. Bob would have taken it too, but told us that with myself, Stan and Raddy in the queue before him, he felt he would have to wait too long.

It was an example of how Arsenal could put themselves out for an individual, but only when it suited them. I don't think it's nice what they did to us; it could be a nasty club at times.

The testimonial made me about £10,000, and I'm ashamed to say I didn't repay the club very well at all.

Four days later I got sent off at Stoke in a 2–1 defeat, some idiot on the terraces chucked a small piece of concrete which struck me on my cheek and another irate home fan attempted to attack me as I was leaving the Victoria Ground pitch.

If I was going to get my marching orders against our old foes from the Potteries, I would have put money on it for being 'over-vigilant' in my pursuit of Alan Hudson, but this one was down to a ruck with John Mahoney.

I clearly recall all the aggro from the Stoke supporters outside the ground, spitting and snarling as I climbed onto the team coach to take us back to London.

There was more trouble on Monday morning when the *Daily Mirror* splashed a big photograph of me laughing in the Jolly Farmers on Sunday lunchtime as I pulled a pint, above a tale by Harry Miller headlined 'Mee May Slap Fine On Storey'.

It stated:

> Peter Storey faces an Arsenal fine for being sent off in the 2–1 defeat at Stoke on Saturday. Manager Bertie Mee hinted at club action last night when he described the decision of referee Ken Burns against Storey as 'justified'. The former England defender, booked earlier for dissent, was given his marching orders five minutes from time after appearing to kick Stoke's John Mahoney. Mee said: 'It was against the letter of the law

and the spirit of the game. There can be no excuse. This sort of thing isn't in the interests of the game, club, players, spectators or anyone. Peter will be disciplined. He knows my feelings on this.' Storey, automatically banned from the next game – home to Burnley – was hit in the face by a stone thrown from the crowd as he walked off. Storey told me: 'I suppose the referee was right to send me off. But if he had kept tighter control, it wouldn't have happened. I went to defend a teammate. It was one of those moments when everyone lost their heads. Quite honestly the booking I got was the first of the season. Arsenal discipline me? That's up to them.'

I was a bit narked about the picture because it suggested I wasn't taking my football at all seriously, and I could well see how some fans who had just coughed up their hard-earned money to support me against Feyenoord might think my attitude was a bit of a slap in the face for them. Give Harry his due, though, there was nothing wrong with his article, even though that quote of mine for the pay-off line made me wince.

Bertie never did follow through with his threat to dock my wages, but he did leave me in no doubt that I was in his bad books.

If Arsenal were to salvage anything from this wretched campaign when 1976 dawned, we needed to do the business in the FA Cup. The draw for the third round pitted us against another First Division side who were even worse than us and destined for relegation. Wolves had ended the old year in severe distress, scoring just twice in five straight defeats and a draw, when we arrived at Molineux in early January.

Okay, so we weren't great, but I was confident we had more than enough in the tank creatively and up front in Armstrong, Ball, Stapleton, Kidd and Brady to get a goal or two. Yet we were abysmal, got turned over 3–0 and I found myself out of the side.

I returned a month later for a dismal 3–1 defeat at Norwich where Martin Peters and Ted MacDougall ran riot to leave Arsenal cemented in eighteenth place out of 22 in the table. With the bottom three now going down, the prospect of a relegation battle was rearing its ugly head, although the lads eventually finished seventeenth, six points above the trapdoor. Carrow Road was to prove my last match of the season.

Bertie dropped me for the next match, a 2–0 defeat at Derby, and I thought: 'Sod this for a game of soldiers.' I told the manager: 'I'd like to go,' and he replied, looking daggers: 'You're going nowhere.' With that, I went on strike.

He was quite within his rights not to sell me; equally he couldn't physically force me to turn up for work. After ten days of failing to report for training, the club suspended me on 8 March for a fortnight.

I told the press that I was fed up with reserve team football, felt unwanted and would never play for Arsenal again.

I wasn't looking for sympathy, which is just as well, because there wasn't any. Neither did a single teammate come to visit me in the pub and try to talk me round. I might have found that sad, but for the fact the club was in such a bad way, with most of the side very disillusioned themselves.

Later that March, Bertie announced he was retiring from management at the end of the season, explaining: 'The pressures on an Arsenal manager are sometimes intolerable, and I was not quite as motivated in the last two years as I should have been.'

I toasted Bertie's imminent departure with a large one, swiftly followed by another drink to celebrate.

Don't get the idea I didn't rate Bertie Mee at all. Yes, we did have a few major rucks, but they were spread over a decade. You have to credit him with getting the club back on its feet again and winning the Double – and you can't get much better than that. He instilled discipline in the ranks when Arsenal were in danger of falling apart and did a first-class job. I didn't dislike the bloke; I'd known him since I was 15 and for a spell, with Don Howe behind him, he was the bee's knees. But in the end Bertie got too big for his boots and lost a lot of respect in the dressing room as a direct result of the Alan Ball wages saga.

Meanwhile, despite plenty of adverse publicity over my strike action, I stuck to my guns for the remainder of the season. I wasn't fined as such, Arsenal merely sent me a letter every fortnight informing me that as I wasn't coming in to work, they had no intention of continuing to pay my wages. Fair enough. Financially, it wasn't too much of a hardship because the win bonuses most of the team had come to rely on were in short supply while the pub, initially, was doing a roaring trade.

It would have done even better trade had I paid for all the drinks I consumed. Previously, I had looked forward to and loved a good drink after matches on a Saturday and midweek match night with the lads, and I would share a bottle of wine when I went out in company for a meal. But I certainly wouldn't say that drinking had been an issue in any way before the Jolly Farmers.

My consumption rose conspicuously through a combination of things. I desperately missed the massive buzz I'd got from playing, the incredible adrenaline high when you are centre-stage and winning in front of a big crowd. I sought solace in alcohol and thought that would give me the same buzz. I was moody and broody because another marriage had gone down the pan – and I had a lot of time to fill at the pub, punters constantly popping in, keen to have a drink and a natter with me. Official opening hours were something like 11 a.m. to 3 p.m., then 6 p.m. to 11 p.m. . . . and I'd make the most of them. Sometimes there was nothing to do between closing time at lunchtime and opening time in the evening but to carry on drinking. At least, that's what I thought in my befuddled state of mind.

CHAPTER NINETEEN

Mr Nice and the Fulham trip

The long, hot summer of 1976 was fabulous for trade at the Jolly Farmers. We seemed to knock out Skol lager by the bucketload on magical nights with every door and window in the place wide open.

Customers dressed as if they were off to the beach in singlets, shorts and flip-flops and relaxed as hits such as 'Silly Love Songs' by Wings and Candi Staton's 'Young Hearts Run Free' were carried on the warm breeze along with the smell of barbecues and the sound of laughter.

Roads melted in the drought, and I splashed out almost £300 on a new 26-inch colour television.

Among my favourite regulars was a group of four or five hippy chicks smelling of patchouli oil, who lived just up the road and came in every day to sit in a corner, soaking up the sunshine, drinking cider and smoking the odd crafty joint. Occasionally they were accompanied by a smiling, well-educated bloke I was introduced to as Howard, the brother-in-law of one of the girls. Howard was always extremely polite and I looked forward to sharing a vodka or two with him, chatting about the world in general and politics, rather than the usual – Arsenal's chances at the weekend.

I was very surprised in time to discover that Howard was none other than Howard Marks, aka Mr Nice, Britain's most notorious drug smuggler. I found out he boasted 43 aliases, 89 phone lines and 25 companies as he travelled throughout the world in the cannabis export–import business. When justice caught up with him, Howard served seven years in Terre Haute Penitentiary, one of America's most infamous prisons.

TRUE STOREY

The mood that golden summer wasn't so relaxed a few miles away in north London, where my old teammate and former landlord Terry Neill resigned as manager of Tottenham after two seasons. He almost got them relegated first before restoring order to claim a decent ninth-place finish and appearance in the League Cup semi-final. Following a legend such as Bill Nicholson was always going to be a very tall order, but the signs were that he was getting a grip.

Terry's stock immediately plunged to gutter-level with the Spurs faithful a week later when Arsenal confirmed he was returning as Bertie Mee's successor, but I was pleased. 'Half a chance,' I kept saying to myself, 'I've got half a chance here.'

On the piss and out of condition I may have been, but I sensed all was not lost for me at Highbury when the phone went in the pub late one morning and I heard Terry's persuasive Ulster brogue greeting me like a long-lost brother, inviting me to come and see him in his new office.

Terry had been captain the day I made my first-team debut in 1965, we'd lived together for a spell as bachelor boys, and he knew the muscle and meanness I could provide. It was good to see the King of Blarney again, but he made no promises. He was happy to wipe the slate clean and forget about my recent misdemeanours, but made it clear I would only start the new season on merit. I was in no position to argue with that and knew it presented a huge challenge, but it was one I tackled head-on.

My 'fighting weight' had very rarely fluctuated from 11 st. 6 lb or 11 st. 7 lb when I was putting 100 per cent into my training, and my drinking was purely social, rather than potentially destructive. I looked at myself in the mirror that night after returning to Arsenal's good books and thought: 'Fuck me, Storey, you are a disgrace!' Long hours in the pub, snacking on bar food without the rigorous training to which my body had grown accustomed had seen me pile on the pounds.

I didn't bother with the bathroom scales in my little bedroom at the pub; I could sense I was pushing 13 stone.

The fixtures for the forthcoming 1976–77 season came out, we had newly promoted Bristol City at home for starters, and I knew those keen young lads from the West Country would be busting a gut under their manager Alan Dicks to put on a show in front of a big London audience. And I feared I'd be made to look like a mug unless I sorted myself out.

I very quickly got my act together, hired another manager for the

MR NICE AND THE FULHAM TRIP

Jolly Farmers and threw myself into the agony of pre-season training at London Colney alongside such ambitious, young whippet-thin Arsenal stars of the future as David O'Leary, Frank Stapleton and Graham Rix. How I envied them at the start of their careers. London was gripped by a great drought, and I can't have eased the pressure on supplies of water given the amount I used to get down my neck after those torturous long training runs. Sweat poured off me as if I were in a sauna.

Brian Kidd had returned for £100,000 to Manchester, but City rather than his beloved United, so Terry was in the market for a new striker and stunned the scene by paying Newcastle United a British record fee of £333,333 for Malcolm Macdonald.

I knew Malcolm already from our time together with England and I got on well with him. He was twenty-six and should have been in his prime but, strangely, it felt as if his best days had already gone – although to be fair he did serve Arsenal well for two seasons as top scorer, plundering forty-odd goals before succumbing to a knee injury. Famous for scoring all five England goals in a 5–0 romp against Cyprus the previous year, he fell out of favour with Don Revie after failing to find the target in his next five internationals. He was idolised on Tyneside, and I felt it was an odd transfer for him even though he had fallen out with his manager Gordon Lee, who waved him off with this bitter parting shot: 'He's not worth the money Arsenal have paid, I wouldn't have paid £100,000 for Macdonald.' I heard Lee once say: 'Stars are what you see in the sky at night, they're for astrologers', and I suspect he was jealous of Malcolm's special relationship with the adoring Newcastle public.

Supermac could run all day, especially the short stuff because he was electrifying over 100 yards, but quite what he made of the actual training and ball work itself at Arsenal is anyone's guess. Bobby Campbell's face didn't fit any more, he shipped out to Fulham, and Wilf Dixon followed Terry over from Tottenham as assistant manager.

Between the two of them, I honestly felt that training was a shambles, a complete bloody shambles.

I hated that. Eddie Kelly (quoted in *Seventy-One Guns*) hit the nail on the head when he said:

> Snouty wasn't one of these talkers, he would come in and do his training or even a bit extra, and everything he did was spot-on. He was never one to piss about in training, even in the five-a-sides he took it all very seriously.

I played a bit on the pre-season tour of Yugoslavia and Switzerland, where Macdonald scored his first Arsenal goals in a friendly against Grasshoppers in Zurich, but I was either used as a substitute or hauled off myself.

I knew I wasn't going to be in the team when the new campaign kicked off and that a place on the bench was the best I could hope for. Bristol City duly arrived on 21 August and left with both points from a 1–0 victory in front of 41,082 largely underwhelmed fans. I got on in the second half in place of Alex Cropley, a young Scottish lad who had come down from Hibs, and can remember in the bath afterwards thinking I really wasn't sure whether this comeback lark was such a good idea after all.

Just to complicate matters, I branched out into running the Starline minicab firm out of Newington Green and it proved to be a monumental financial mistake. Several drivers used the pub and encouraged me to take it over. It seemed like a good idea at the time, running 20 to 30 cabs, but the overheads were heavy and I had to pay controllers 24 hours a day.

Truth be told, I was still more interested in the pub than football. As for Eddie Kelly, he was more interested in finding another manager to play for and went to QPR for £60,000. Poor Eddie, he could have been a world-beater if only he'd put his mind to it, but he never recovered from the disappointment of having the Arsenal captaincy stripped away from him the previous season after suffering pneumonia.

I stirred my bones to come off the bench again three weeks later in a 2–0 win at West Ham, and suddenly got my break at the beginning of October when Sammy Nelson was injured.

I never particularly enjoyed taking advantage of a colleague's misfortune, always preferring to win my place on merit, but when Sammy went off in an exciting 3–2 home win over QPR, I grabbed my chance at left-back.

Three nights later I started my first match of the season in a League Cup victory over Blackpool at Highbury and stayed in the team for the following three League matches – a little sequence which started promisingly before ending in the pits.

First up, Stoke came calling and were routinely dismissed 2–0, but our defence then fell apart alarmingly on the road as we crashed 5–1 at Aston Villa, then 4–1 at Leicester.

The Villa manager, Ron Saunders, had paid £125,000 for Cropley, who delighted in our torment as Andy Gray went on the rampage against O'Leary, scoring twice.

We were nearly as bad back in the Midlands three days later at Filbert Street, where we suffered against another centre-forward of the highest quality, although Frank Worthington's goal came from the penalty spot. Keith Weller was twice on target, and I found time for a beer after the match with my old pal Jon Sammels. He commiserated with me; I think we both suspected my time at Arsenal was running out.

By far the most enjoyable match that October was 'Stan' Simpson's long-overdue testimonial against Tottenham one Saturday when the First Division was suspended, all bar one match, so Don Revie could prepare England for a World Cup qualifier against Finland.

Although Stan's benefit failed to capture the imagination of the public and only 19,000 fans turned up to see Tottenham win 2–0 with goals from John Duncan and Alfie Conn, my pal perked up that evening with a few of his trademark large brandies and cigars. The reception moved on from Highbury to a full-scale knees-up at the Jolly Farmers, where we were joined by the chairman, who arrived in his splendid Rolls-Royce, immediately called for champagne all round and kept Stan company for a couple of hours on the cognac. Mr Hill-Wood was in a different class, a real character, and I was fond of him.

I was not alone in my admiration of him; as Bob McNab said: 'I adored the chairman. He was a lovely fellow, an absolute gentleman and he always used to tell me and Peter Storey that we were his favourite players.'

I didn't envy Terry Neill, who couldn't wait to welcome back Sammy Nelson, and I reverted to my 'half-life' on the fringe. The manager was in a difficult position as poacher-turned-gamekeeper. It seemed like only yesterday that Terry had been one of the lads, comfortable in the centre of our company, sharing a laugh and a drink with the team. Now he had to pull rank, indeed it was expected of him – and it was virtually inevitable that old hands such as Stan, John Radford and Geordie Armstrong, who had been complaining loudly that he couldn't have a transfer, fell out with him.

The dynamics of the team were changing as new faces appeared and old ones left. Terry paid £50,000 to bring Macdonald's mate Pat Howard down from Newcastle and that put Stan's nose out of joint, although it soon became apparent that my pal was a superior central defender and Howard disappeared to Birmingham in time, having played only 15 games for Arsenal.

I can never think of Pat without shaking my head in disbelief at my first brush with the law – a frankly ludicrous incident which ended up with me being convicted of headbutting an elderly traffic warden.

After training at London Colney, I had driven back to Highbury at lunchtime to drop off Pat for treatment to an injury and was on my way to give young John Matthews a lift home to Hackney before returning to the pub. Turning left onto Blackstock Road, I came to a zebra crossing and saw the traffic warden shepherding a group of women and children safely over the road towards me. He was virtually on the pavement when I edged past him at 5 mph in my Honda estate car, nothing flash, and the next thing I know there's a huge thump on the roof where he's brought his lollipop stick crashing down as a mark of displeasure. I jumped out, confronted him and barked: 'What the fuck do you think you're doing, you silly old sod?' He argued that he had still been on the crossing when I'd made my manoeuvre and, technically, he was probably correct – by a matter of inches. But any more than that, of course, and I would have driven into him. The Honda's roof suffered a small dent and a few scratches but it wasn't my pride and joy. In my eyes this was a petty little ruck and I wasn't about to indulge in anything so pathetic as demanding the warden's name so I could bill him for minor repairs. We finished our row, I returned to my car and drove off, thinking no more about it.

To my surprise, a couple of policemen came into the pub to interview me over the matter. I told them my side of the story and they thought it was a joke. I wasn't laughing, however, when I was charged with assaulting the traffic warden and found guilty at Highbury Corner Magistrates Court. In evidence, the warden claimed I'd flown round the corner at 50 mph, nearly mown down him, assorted mums and schoolkids, then jumped out of my motor and stuck the nut on him! What made things worse was the fact that the prosecution managed to manufacture an eyewitness, who just happened to be an off-duty policeman, and he backed up the fabrication. I thought there and then that this was the most complete and utter load of bollocks I'd ever have the misfortune to hear in a court of law – but as I was to discover to my cost in much more serious circumstances, cheats and liars often flourish in front of magistrates, judges and juries.

I should have demanded photographic evidence of the terrible injury I must have inflicted on the poor, defenceless old boy if I had, indeed, headbutted him; I should have demanded to know why the off-duty policeman had not intervened and made a citizen's arrest – but I was confused and dazzled by the total farce of it all. I really should have appealed against the fine and conviction, but I simply couldn't be bothered.

I experienced more mixed emotions shortly before Christmas 1976 when Cathy was admitted to a private West End maternity clinic, off Marylebone High Street, and gave birth to our daughter Natalie, a pretty little dark-haired baby. I would have been happy in the normal course of events but our relationship, stormy at the best of times, had taken a turn for the worse during Cathy's pregnancy. Sadly, Natalie was not destined to repair the damage and bring us closer together.

Back at Highbury, Alan Ball left for Second Division Southampton after being dropped earlier that December. Ironically, I was the first man who filled his number seven shirt for three matches – a 0–0 draw at Derby, followed by a 3–1 home win over Manchester United and a 2–2 draw at Tottenham.

At the Baseball Ground, I exchanged pre-match pleasantries with Charlie George before catching Leighton James, their flash Welsh winger, nice and early. I got booked for my trouble, but he didn't fancy it after that. I knew he wouldn't because he carried the mental scars of how I had previously subdued him at international level.

I thought it was fitting in a way that United and Spurs provided the opposition for my swansong – I had enjoyed so many epic battles against those two clubs I had loved to hate down the years.

I knew there was not a snowball in hell's chance of staying in the side because earlier that month Alan Hudson had arrived for £200,000 from Stoke at the same time we were saying our fond farewells to Raddy, knocked out to West Ham for £50,000.

Sure enough, once 1977 was underway and Hudson had got his elegant feet under the table, I was dropped after a poor 2–0 defeat at Bristol City.

Although I was not aware of the fact at the time, I pulled my boots on for Arsenal for the final occasion the following week as a second-half substitute in place of Supermac on 29 January 1977, in an FA Cup fourth-round tie against Coventry. This was the starting line-up: Rimmer, Rice, Nelson, Ross, O'Leary, Simpson, Hudson, Brady,

Macdonald, Stapleton, Rostron. We won 3–1 to cheer a Highbury crowd of 41,078 with two goals from Macdonald and one from Stapleton.

It was a horrible season for many reasons; kicking off with football hooliganism rampant on the terraces, the England side collapsing under Revie and the pools panel sitting regularly because of winter's icy grip.

When I was left out for our first match in February, a dire 0–0 home draw with a Sunderland team which failed to score for the tenth consecutive time in a League match, I simply went AWOL again. Terry wanted me to stay in trim by playing for the reserves, I refused and he suspended me.

The team embarked on a miserable spell of seven successive defeats in the First Division, during which I could hardly suppress a laugh after we were beaten 3–0 at home by Middlesbrough and Terry complained: 'I am absolutely ashamed. This is the worst Arsenal performance since I took over as manager. We couldn't have beaten 11 dustbins.'

Within a fortnight there was another departure, this time our long-serving and highly respected chief scout Gordon Clark, who claimed that his position had become 'untenable' under the new managerial regime.

Terry had been banned from the Tottenham boardroom earlier in the season, but the clubs were not averse to doing business with each other and Willie Young arrived for £80,000 from White Hart Lane. I barely had time to say 'hello' to the big ginger-haired centre-half before I was walking out of Highbury as an ex-Arsenal employee.

I was summoned to the manager's office and Terry was very calm and professional as he told me: 'Fulham are after you, Peter. You'd better go and have a word because there's no future for you here.' I knew that as well as he did.

I'm glad he wasn't tempted to dress things up with all the old bollocks about being a 'loyal servant' or how 'all good things have to come to an end'. I didn't need crocodile tears from Terry. We both knew the score – I was drinking and not really that interested in playing for Arsenal any longer. I had a pub and an ailing minicab firm on my mind. And, in any case, I hadn't exactly been a pillar of loyalty over the last few seasons.

We shook hands, I walked out into the corridor and paused suddenly to reflect on the enormity of that moment in March 1977.

MR NICE AND THE FULHAM TRIP

I had come to Highbury in May 1961 after leaving school that Easter as a raw fifteen year old and recalled the excitement of travelling on the train with Mum and Dad to sign as an apprentice, the three of us with such great expectations. I had grown into a man at Arsenal – the critics who delighted in slagging me off would say 'a monster' – and the club had given me the chance to achieve so much more than most professional footballers dream of. I had helped win the coveted Double, the European Fairs Cup and Sir Alf Ramsey had capped me on 19 occasions for England. There had been cup finals at Wembley to savour and shudder over, and I had played over 500 times for Arsenal in all – 387 First Division starts. Success is like a drug; the more you have, the more you crave, and it was disappointing that the boys of 1971 didn't kick on and win more trophies.

But I was fulfilled; I had won as much in the game as I had a right to expect.

And now I stood outside the manager's office and it felt like a strange ending, almost embarrassing. Apart from the gaffer, there were no goodbyes because most of the first team didn't have an inkling I was leaving and were otherwise busy training for Saturday's visit of Ipswich. Just for a second, I didn't quite know what to do, before collecting my boots from the little room next to the dressing room which had been like a second home to me for so many years, slinging them over my shoulder and walking out of the ground. No regrets, no tears goodbye.

I climbed into my car, a nice metallic beige BMW, tuned in to Radio One and the first record up was Thelma Houston belting out 'Don't Leave Me This Way'. I had a little ironic laugh to myself. I was in no rush to reach Craven Cottage, but there was a warm welcome for me there from Bobby Campbell. It hadn't taken him long to replace Alec Stock as manager, but Fulham were in the shit right up to their necks in the Second Division. They had lost eight of their previous ten matches and drawn the other two. In nineteenth position, they were just a place away from filling one of the relegation spots.

The first thing Campbell did was laugh as he told me: 'You know we've got no money, don't you, Peter?' as if that were some sort of incentive to sign. I knew Fulham had paid Arsenal a nominal £10,000 to push through the transfer and Campbell had disarmed me, so I didn't ask for a signing-on fee.

I soon realised what I had let myself in for – a pub team, basically. Training at London Colney, right up until Terry Neill became Arsenal manager, had been absolutely first-class, so professional. Fulham didn't even have a training ground to call their own. Now we pitched up just off the A3 at the Decca Sports Ground in Surrey, or at the Bank of England facilities at Roehampton, and it was a joke, often sitting round a pot of tea before anyone could be bothered to stir themselves and knuckle down to some hard work.

And that's exactly what was needed at Fulham. They needed hard grafters because the plan to win promotion based around the long-lost world-class talents of George Best and Bobby Moore, and the showmanship of Rodney Marsh, was flawed.

By the time I ran out at Edgar Street against Hereford United on 5 March to make my debut for the Cottagers, Bestie was recovering from a 4 a.m. car crash in Knightsbridge which put him in hospital for several days and ruled him out of football for six weeks; Marsh had played his last match for the club and was about to have his contract cancelled before returning to Tampa Bay Rowdies and Bobby, God bless him, was doing his level best to shore up a defence which hadn't kept a clean sheet for over two months. Frankly, the back four looked as if they couldn't organise a piss-up in a brewery.

Bobby had been fighting a losing battle and later that month announced he would be retiring at the end of the season.

A few of the lads were virtually rubbing their hands in malicious anticipation when Bestie and I first clapped eyes on each other as colleagues, rather than the best of enemies. They were to be disappointed, because we were like a couple of washed-up heavyweight boxers. All the tension, bitterness and supreme physical effort of our clashes on behalf of Arsenal and Manchester United, and England and Northern Ireland was water under the bridge as far as I was concerned, but I didn't greet George like an old friend. Things had been said, bad things about me being 'a joke' and comparing my ability to his granny's.

Now, for all his unrivalled bravery on the pitch as a player in his prime, I was interested to discover if Bestie had the bollocks to make the first move.

We nodded an acknowledgement to each other, and as we walked out to begin training together, a rarity in itself, George told me: 'I didn't mean any of those things about you in the book. We just put them in to help sell it.' I stuck out my hand, smiled and replied: 'No hard feelings, then, George. Let's go to work, shall we?'

My abiding memory of Bestie at Fulham is that he wasn't there

MR NICE AND THE FULHAM TRIP

very often. I doubt whether we trained together more than half a dozen times. He seemed to have another agenda, with a girlfriend, his agent or a small coterie of personal drinking buddies. George relied on other people to ferry him about. If it hadn't been for them, I got the impression he would have struggled to keep any appointments.

Bestie's slack attitude to training was a bit insulting to the other lads, but he was a nice guy with a twinkle in his eyes and it was difficult to feel too badly towards him. George was in his element three matches from the end of the season when we played away at Oldham Athletic, which meant an overnight stay in a hotel in Manchester, his old stomping ground – or maybe that should be romping ground.

After travelling up by coach on the Friday afternoon, the players dispersed to their rooms or the television lounge while Bestie was chatting up the blonde in reception to book him a taxi. Fast forward to lunchtime on Saturday and everyone is on the coach waiting to set off to Oldham – everyone, that is, apart from our star player.

'Let's go then, driver,' ordered Campbell, looking downcast. We can't have been more than 50 yards down the drive when one of the team looked out of the back window and shouted: 'Stop, stop, he's here!' and we all looked round to see Bestie chasing us, shirt flapping and carrying his boots.

The manager greeted him like the prodigal son with one of his trademark flashing smiles and a 'Well done, George, so glad you could make it.'

Boundary Park had its revenge, however. It's one of the coldest grounds I've ever played at, with a wind which cuts through you like a knife. Bestie must have spent the night birding or boozing, probably both, because he cut a pathetic sight that late April afternoon, stuck out on the wing shivering and barely getting a look in as we went down 1–0 to a second-half penalty.

For a couple of seasons George Best was one of the best players in the world, maybe even 'the' best. But he was finished at 26 as a top-class footballer. I think the trouble started professionally the first time he walked out of Manchester United in 1972. Yes, he came back but he cut his career short. Other geniuses, such as Pelé and Johan Cruyff, enjoyed full and, more importantly, fulfilled careers, but George only had half a career. Yet for a few seasons he was definitely one of the top players in the world.

Although I played with and against him, I was never close enough to George to see him staggering around through drink; he was never a loudmouth at Fulham. I never saw that side of him and, frankly, I'm glad I didn't. Any addiction – alcohol, drugs, gambling – is a disease, but also a sign of weakness. I am convinced George started sliding down the slippery slope because he was so painfully shy as a young boy. That's not so surprising though, when you consider how he was plucked out of a close-knit family in Belfast when he was just 15 and soon caught up in the full glare of a media frenzy in Manchester and London. Papers, TV, nightclubs, shops, commercial endorsements, everyone wanted a piece of George and I'm sure he started drinking because it calmed him down and helped conquer the shyness.

I won't lie: I felt no emotion when George died in November 2005. He was 59 and had been in and out of the Cromwell Hospital for some time with a kidney infection he couldn't shift and it wasn't at all unexpected.

But I do think he should have tried harder to knock the booze on the head once and for all after his liver transplant. I believe that while George was waiting for the operation he felt so wretched that he didn't fancy a drink that much. Unless you are unfortunate enough to be an out-and-out dosser, you don't want a drink when you're feeling absolutely crap, do you? But the surgery was a success, and suddenly he felt much better. In George's world of skewed values, there was always a fear he would celebrate in the way he knew best with a trip down to his local in Chelsea, the Phene Arms, for a few large white wines and sodas. I can only speculate, but for a short while he must have felt reborn and invincible, and that little demon in his head would have told him life would be even better with a nice few glasses of champagne inside him.

I think he was out of order to drink again. I think he should have taken into consideration the feelings of the donor's family. I can't imagine they were too happy about the way the organ of a loved one was ultimately wasted.

Brian Clough knew the score. Stomach cancer took him in September 2004 but not before a successful liver transplant had given him an extra 18 months smelling the roses in his garden surrounded by the family and grandchildren he adored. Yet I heard how hard it was for Cloughie to stick to his small plastic bottle of still water when he went to functions awash with wine and champagne, and there were fans eager to share a 'proper' drink with him. The surgery gave Cloughie a second chance and he was far too shrewd and canny to toss it all away.

MR NICE AND THE FULHAM TRIP

Ultimately, that was maybe the crucial difference between the pair: Cloughie was a grounded family man; Bestie was a loose cannon.

Back at Fulham, I played a dozen matches in midfield but was nowhere near flamboyant enough to become a favourite with the Craven Cottage faithful, although five wins and three draws were enough to see the club just scramble clear of the dreaded drop by two points.

I started the 1977–78 season at Craven Cottage, but it wasn't the same; my heart wasn't in it. Mooro had left, I had lost a lot of interest and I didn't last very long – two League Cup ties against Orient, who beat us on aggregate, and precisely five League matches, none of which brought us a victory.

My final match as a professional footballer came on Saturday, 10 September, when I succeeded in getting myself roundly abused by the bulk of a crowd numbering 31,939 every time I touched the ball. No surprise there then, considering the fixture was Tottenham away. Fulham lost 1–0 to a second-half goal from Chris Jones. Spurs had been relegated the previous season but their exile from the top flight was to last only this one campaign. To be honest, I would have been disappointed if those supporters on the Park Lane End and the Shelf hadn't slagged me off as I did my best to make life uncomfortable for Glenn Hoddle and Peter Taylor, given the fact that I was one of the Arsenal old boys they most loved to hate.

I hung around until November, when my contract was cancelled and I announced my retirement. Campbell asked me gently: 'Do you want to pack it in, Peter?' and I nodded, replying: 'Yeah, I think it might be for the best.' To save face all round, we concocted a tale about me suffering from a long-term groin injury. The agreement was mutual, money didn't enter into it and I don't think I owed Fulham anything – morally or financially.

CHAPTER TWENTY

Going down

Casual customers popping into the Jolly Farmers on a Friday or Saturday night would more than likely have been struck by two groups of identical 'heavies' drinking at opposite ends of the bar. Wearing expensive black leather jackets or smart suits, flared trousers, fashionable long hair, designer watches and flashy jewellery, these were clearly not men with whom you took liberties. Crime was their profession – but one thing set them apart. One lot actually were villains while the others were policemen, the Sweeney, as in Sweeney Todd, Cockney rhyming slang for the Flying Squad.

The cops and robbers rubbed along happily enough outside their routine working hours, content to know where each other were and keen to study any new 'mugs', faces in the rival group.

Plenty of rogues seemed to live around my end of Southgate Road and several of them became regulars as word spread that I'd taken over the pub.

One particular set of faces made it virtually their second home and, while I was pleased to see them at first and enjoyed their big-spending company, the result was catastrophic. It might have destroyed my life; it certainly destroyed my reputation.

The Barry brothers lived just round the corner and were well-known on the manor. If you met them, half the time they were okay, not threatening characters at all. John, the eldest, was in prison when I took over the pub, which was the venue for a massive party on his release.

John and Tony Barry were already infamous as owners of the Regency Club in Amhurst Road, Stoke Newington, which had played a pivotal role in the murder of Jack 'The Hat' McVitie in 1967 and the subsequent sentencing of the Kray twins to life imprisonment.

I knew the story very well. Ronnie and Reggie got some of their protection racket income from the Regency and were very unimpressed when McVitie turned up, on a drug-fuelled rampage threatening the staff with a sawn-off shotgun. I heard a tale that McVitie once stabbed a man in the basement of the Regency before going upstairs and wiping the blade on a woman's dress.

Anyway, the Krays feared McVitie was becoming increasingly out of control, due to his habit of downing large amounts of amphetamines with spirits, and decided he had to 'go'. It wasn't long before McVitie was drinking in the Regency one evening when word reached the assembled group that a party awaited them in a Hackney flat. McVitie went along and fell into the trap, stabbed to death with a butcher's knife by Reggie while Ronnie pinned him to the floor. Two years later the twins were sent down at the Old Bailey, but in the same trial Tony Barry was acquitted of being an accessory to murder and walked free.

Given the history of the Barrys, perhaps I should have dissuaded them from using my pub as their local, but I will confess I was flattered by their patronage and, in a business sense, they were very good news.

My downfall began in the summer of 1978 when John Barry and one of his associates, a Scot named David Heron, hatched a plan to manufacture imitation half-sovereigns and asked me for £2,000 to buy a die – or coin press. I was naïve and didn't know whether half-sovereigns were legal tender or not. If the scheme had involved £20 notes, I would have run a mile.

Mind you, if I had been a criminal, I rather think forging notes would have been easier and more financially rewarding.

Barry and Heron were joined in the enterprise by a chap called Charlie Black, and they all gave me the impression the coins were for fake jewellery, sovereign rings, necklaces and pendants – frivolous stuff like that. It seemed like a scam to me, nothing too serious, something to rival the dodgy gear, fake designer tee-shirts, watches and perfume routinely knocked out by street traders and market stalls.

I turned them down flat; I wasn't interested. There wasn't even anything in it for me, they just wanted to borrow the money for a few weeks to get up and running in a little workshop over the road from the Jolly Farmers. Still I said 'no', but they wore me down. Night after night Barry and Heron would be in the pub, flashing the cash to demonstrate their 'loyalty' and 'friendship' and asking me: 'Have you thought any more about our little business venture, Peter?' Drip, drip, drip. I finally cracked in the face of their persistent wheedling. It was driving me crazy and I eventually went up to my safe and fished out the £2,000 in cash from my takings – £20 notes, tenners and fivers rolled up in elastic bands – and handed over the lot to John Barry.

It was the single most stupid act of my life, and there have been several contenders. I never thought about the consequences; I must have been fucking mad, mental.

One Wednesday evening in late September, around 9 p.m., Black came into the pub and said: 'I've got this die, Peter. Would you mind keeping it in your safe for me?' He might just as well have planted it there himself.

The next thing I knew I was being arrested, shortly after opening time the following morning. It must have been around 11.20 a.m. when the doors burst open and up to a dozen plainclothes members of the Serious Crime Squad steamed in.

Two of them came smiling within inches of my face and asked: 'Where's the safe then, guv?' The three of us went upstairs, I unlocked the safe and, to nobody's surprise, they fished out the die. Charlie had stitched me up like a kipper; it was all the evidence they needed.

The police stopped anyone leaving and arrested me and a few others, including Bobby Barry, a cousin rather than another brother, who was subsequently to plead not guilty and be cleared.

The little firm put together by John Barry and Heron had been infiltrated by Black. I was later to discover that he was a well-known agent provocateur placed by the police. It was a sting, a fit-up. Some months earlier, a suspected villain had walked free at the Old Bailey with the assistance of some dubious evidence from Heron. I say 'dubious', although I was told by a very reliable source that Heron lied his head off. The Serious Crime Squad had the dead needle with Heron and decided he had to go down, regardless of the fall-out. I was a victim of the collateral damage.

Shock and confusion washed over me in waves while I had my rights read to me in the pub. I learned that on the other side of the road, Black popped out of the coin workshop on the pretext of going to buy a newspaper and packet of cigarettes. Two minutes later, the other fellow there was caught red-handed operating the die. The assumption was that Black had been tipped off, of course, and that he was working

GOING DOWN

for the police. As he was never charged, it looks suspicious, although I can't know for certain.

The venture was a balls-up from the start. I saw about half a dozen of the specimens produced by the die and they were absolutely pathetic – buckled and useless. You would never have passed them off as half-sovereigns to the village idiot, let alone managed to sell them to anyone with half a brain.

I was stuck in the back of a Black Maria and taken to Limehouse police station, headquarters of the Serious Crime Squad, where it was evident they thought I was Mr Big, the financier of the coin enterprise. I asked to see a solicitor but nobody was interested in contacting anyone on my behalf and I spent from Thursday lunchtime until Monday morning banged up in a police cell before appearing before the magistrates at Arbour Square, just off the Commerical Road in the East End, where I was formally charged and granted bail.

I needed a good solicitor and I needed one fast. Ralph Haeems, an Indian guy originally from Bombay, came highly recommended and I remember driving down in a bitter, confused mood to his practice in Blenheim Grove, Peckham Rye to more or less throw myself on his mercy and tell him all about my predicament.

Ralph was an intelligent guy who had done a lot of work representing the Kray twins, very successfully at first, before Ronnie and Reggie started to overstep the mark. I think the bulk of his work involved gangsters. Initially, I was refused legal aid, but Ralph soon sorted that out for me.

Seven of us appeared in court to answer the charge of conspiracy to manufacture gold coins – but not John Barry. Two of them I had never met before, one I had seen once. I kept asking myself: 'Who the fuck are these people?' Additionally, I was accused of conspiracy to defraud persons unknown. But as there was no evidence from these persons unknown – probably because they didn't exist – that charge was left on the file.

Quite why the case took two years to come to conclusion in court is a total mystery; I haven't got a clue. A long waiting list, perhaps.

It was January 1979 when the *Daily Express* reported: 'Former England footballer Peter Storey and four others were committed for trial yesterday accused of plotting to counterfeit coins.'

I was back in the news for the wrong reasons the following month – but this was small beer.

TRUE STOREY

After-hours drinking was common in the neighbourhood and I suppose it was just a matter of time before I became due for a visit and the Jolly Farmers was raided.

It was almost 1 a.m. and we were still quite full when 20 uniformed coppers made their grand entrance and pissed in our pints – figuratively speaking. Despite my drinking, I was still fairly nimble on my toes and slipped out of the back door, leaving the new manager I had installed to face the music. However, it was inescapably my name up above the front door as licensee, and I was fined for the offence by my old friends, the Highbury Corner magistrates.

Under the headline 'Late penalty' on 22 February, the *Daily Mirror* reported: 'Former Arsenal and England footballer Peter Storey was fined £180 with £60 costs yesterday for allowing late drinking at his Islington pub.'

I sensed I was in a fair bit of trouble but had no idea how much until it was suggested I went to visit Tommy Wisbey, one of the Great Train Robbers, for some expert advice in the Trafalgar, the Islington pub which was then his haunt nearby on Southgate Road. It was Tommy's boozer in reality, but as he had played a role in one of Britain's most notorious crimes, the licence was in his wife's name, I believe.

I happily bought a round of drinks and explained in detail to Tommy and several of his entourage – all old-school villains, not yobbos – exactly what my part had been in the coin caper. You could have heard a pin drop as they listened attentively, leaning forward to catch every word, before I finished and then they bombarded me with questions to make sure I wasn't telling lies or trying to paint myself in a favourable light. They were suspicious of the £2,000 I had handed over, with the prospect of no profit in return, and I couldn't blame them.

I knew their response would be genuine and I was shocked when they told me: 'You have got no chance, Peter. You've been fitted up and you're going to go down.' They revealed the current police tactics of nailing target villains by rounding up as many suspects as possible on conspiracy charges and sticking them all in the dock, and explained how maybe a couple of faces would plead guilty to get a light sentence, but that any jury would be tempted to think the defendants were all in it together, guilty by association. It was spelled out to me: 'A couple of hands go up and that makes it look so bad for the others.'

Tommy and the chaps saw the dejection on my face, my mouth drop, but I perked up when it was suggested: 'There is another way. What you need to do is jump bail and disappear to Spain. Arrange to get some money to you for living expenses. Come back when the trial is over and claim you were scared, that people were threatening you. Then you'll get a trial all on your own with a different judge and jury, and a fair crack of the whip.'

I was bitter, in the shit and dug myself in much deeper by drinking heavily again and not thinking straight. Maybe Cathy would have acted as a sobering influence, but our marriage had long since crumbled. It struck me that the Jolly Farmers was the root cause of so much trouble and pain, when it was supposed to be providing me with a lucrative, carefree retirement. I came to hate the place for what it represented and I gave it up, or rather Cathy took it over and later bought me out. I knew I would lose my licence anyway when the thing with the coins came to court if I was found guilty.

My life had been so much richer and more rewarding in every sense at the start with Cathy, and when it was definitely all over I looked back with regret.

Our greatest indulgence had been eating out together so often it cost me a small fortune. The kitchenette in our flat was tiny, encouraging us to become regulars at a family-run Italian restaurant in St John's Wood High Street.

There were no end of attractive bistros in our fashionable neck of the woods and we enjoyed a good run for our money in most of them.

We didn't socialise regularly with other Arsenal couples because they tended to live further out of central London, but Cathy and I did become regulars on a Sunday lunchtime at a smashing little boozer, the Sir Richard Steele on Haverstock Hill in Belsize Park, where we'd often see Cherie Blair's dad, the actor Tony Booth, famous for his role as a Scouse layabout in the TV comedy series *Till Death Us Do Part* – and he often seemed pissed. The landlord was a wonderful old character called Freddie, who had attracted a showbiz crowd which also included the actor Ronnie Fraser, who was close friends with Sean Connery and Peter O'Toole, and the blind singer Lennie Peters, from the duo Peters & Lee, who had a number one hit single with 'Welcome Home' in 1973.

I used to make a beeline for a chat with Lennie, not out of any great sympathy but simply because he was an interesting geezer and I enjoyed his company. Cathy had a bubbly personality to go with her good looks and fitted in perfectly.

TRUE STOREY

We had a great holiday in Morocco at Club Med in Agadir and enjoyed some of the best live entertainment London had to offer – Frank Sinatra at the Albert Hall, Liza Minnelli at Finsbury Park and a memorable one-woman show by Shirley MacLaine.

I was given complimentary membership at the Playboy Club, where I bumped into that larger-than-life character Malcolm Allison. The Manchester City and Crystal Palace manager was going out at the time with a Bunny Girl called Serena Williams, who was almost as famous in her prime as her namesake, that fabulous tennis player, is today. Gambling didn't interest me at the Playboy, but I'd often eat there while Cathy was working in the restaurant.

I was surprised when Cathy told me she was pregnant, because we hadn't been living together for ages. After Natalie was born, it was very hard for Mum and Dad because they doted on their tiny granddaughter, yet Cathy wanted nothing more to do with me then – understandably so, given my poor behaviour – and returned all the presents they sent for Natalie. Cathy did try hard to keep us together as a couple but even on the day we were married, I had my doubts whether it would work because, among other things, I had been under a little pressure to go through with the ceremony.

That pressure, however, was like a drop in the ocean compared to the burden I felt weighing down on me now.

Tommy Wisbey's escape plan made sense, but first I needed some money quickly to skip bail and set myself up in Majorca, as there was no way of knowing when I would be appearing in front of a judge. If I was going on the run, I wouldn't last long with no money.

While I will always maintain I was the innocent victim of circumstances beyond my control in the coin conspiracy business, there can be no excuse for my next brush with crime – prostitution.

I'm not proud of it and it wasn't clever, but I was desperate and desperate men do desperate things.

A bloke I knew ran a massage parlour and when he told me how lucrative it was, I was hooked. I started scouting around for some premises to rent and settled on a cheap flat situated between a café and a newsagent's in Leyton High Street, basically two bedrooms, a bathroom and a small kitchen which I took on a six-month lease.

My contact offered me two of his working girls in their early 20s, Camilla and Lulu, and the Calypso massage parlour was born.

I arranged to meet them for the first time over rum and cokes in a

GOING DOWN

smoky pub, but I could clearly see that they were not at all bad-looking. Camilla and Lulu knew the ropes better than me and suggested they charge £10 a punter for a topless massage before offering their selection of extras – hand relief, oral sex and full sex – plus what Camilla giggled was 'a bit of tying up, whips and all that kinky stuff'. I nodded wisely and smiled politely. I'd been around the block, so to speak, a fair bit and had always found enough to keep me entertained without recourse to Camilla's kinky stuff . . . the boots, clamps and bondage she talked about enthusiastically as she ran through her potential repertoire much like a head waiter introducing you to the menu at a posh restaurant. I remember trying hard to suppress a laugh – it sounded like preparation for a mountaineering expedition.

Of course, it was all about the extras; for the girls in terms of serious money and for the punters in terms of getting their rocks off.

I had some neat little advertising cards printed and trawled the district, sticking them in newsagents' windows and telephone kiosks.

Punters called the Calypso's number, spoke to Camilla or Lulu and arranged an appointment between noon and 7 p.m.

Business was soon booming and the girls were joined by Helen, a petite blonde from Wales, who took over after 7 p.m. to concentrate on the night shift, and she proved extremely popular.

Camilla and Helen lived in Hackney, while Lulu had her own flat near Surrey Docks. I chauffeured the trio to work and often drove them home again when their shifts ended, or hired a minicab if I'd been drinking too much.

We agreed to share the £10 introduction fees 50-50, the girls kept the extras they made and bought all their own oils, talcum powder, tissues and towels. The initial signs were very encouraging, that much was evident from the £500 a week I was soon making.

So far, so good. My plan was always to get the Calypso up and running before handing it over to a manager and clearing off to Spain before the trial.

The business was beginning to take off when I was grassed up after five or six weeks. Someone informed the local Leyton police and half a dozen boys in blue raided the flat just after I had arrived. It led to one of the worst Christmases of my life.

The case was dealt with at court more or less straight away because I pleaded guilty on 22 December 1979. I held my hands up and was fined £700, with £175 costs, and given a six-month suspended jail sentence for running a brothel. I'm not sure whether the punishment fitted the crime, or was harsh, although someone said the magistrates were making an example of me as a deterrent. I was just relieved to get the case out of the way. The chairman of the bench told me: 'These are offences which the public at large deplore and treat with abhorrence.'

I was pleased that no charges were brought against Camilla and Lulu, who were in the Calypso at the time of the raid, or Helen. I felt responsible for those girls.

I was struggling for ready cash and the magistrates accepted my plea for time to pay the fine in instalments.

I knew the newspapers would have a field day with the case, and that it would be very hard for Mum and Dad, so I did my best to avoid the headlines. The shame and degradation were hard to bear.

So far, the press had contented themselves with a paragraph or two on the murky world I was living in, but the brothel business was an 'open goal' the tabloids were never going to miss.

The *Daily Express* ran with 'Football Star On Vice Charge' and readers learned:

> When former soccer star Peter Storey retired he became a minicab operator, with a brothel on the side, a court heard yesterday.
>
> Storey, 34, advertised the brothel as the 'Calypso Massage' on cards in shop windows.
>
> Magistrates at Waltham Forest, in East London, were told that during police observations outside the Calypso Massage in High Road, Leyton, they saw 50 men arriving for sex sessions.
>
> Sergeant Roy Lott said Storey, of Seymour Gardens, Ilford, Essex, had three girls working topless on the premises and they offered a variety of sex services, including intercourse.
>
> Storey drove them to work in the mornings and arranged to have them picked up at the end of their 'shift'.
>
> Storey, who played mainly for Arsenal and was 19 times in the England team between 1971 and 1973, admitted charges of keeping a brothel and living off immoral earnings.
>
> He was given a six-month suspended sentence and fined £700, with £175 costs.
>
> Mr John Cope, for Storey, said: 'He is a man of good character and succumbed to the temptations to make easy money. He is rather relieved it was stopped at this early stage.'

GOING DOWN

Storey married in 1969, but was divorced from his wife Susan in 1972.

I was labelled a pimp and a ponce, and that hurt – conjuring up images of some manipulative bastard in a dirty old raincoat threatening his drug-addicted girls with violence if they didn't go out to work the streets, and then taking all their earnings. My arrangement with those three girls on the game simply wasn't like that. Yes, of course it was illegal, but it was professional, even if I was a rank amateur when it came to the oldest profession.

CHAPTER TWENTY-ONE

Behind bars

Fortunately, I still had the Starline minicab operation to fall back on – not that the business was a great earner – and it became a matter of trying to scrape enough to get by. I was paying controllers and had to do some driving myself to make ends meet.

Obviously, all bets were off now when it came to doing a bunk to Spain – the furthest I got was Ilford. I became a nomad, living here and there in flats, and dossed down in Kentish Town for a spell.

I visited Tommy Wisbey again but he didn't have a Plan B and told me bluntly: 'Without money behind you, son, you're fucked.'

With nothing stable to fall back on and feeling under a lot of pressure, it was a very worrying time. In fact, my life was like a nightmare; nothing seemed to go right, everything went from bad to worse – and it must be said a lot of it was my own fault.

Then I jumped out of the frying pan and into the fire with another stupid, reckless decision which eventually led to another criminal conviction. I was in serious financial trouble after leaving the pub to Cathy, and not receiving any money for it, so I sold a couple of the Starline motors on which I had paid deposits because I couldn't keep up the hire-purchase repayments. Basically, a crook in Canning Town offered me £2,300 in total to 'lose' a green Mercedes and a dark blue BMW, and I took the money. It was such a silly thing to do, ridiculous if you consider I had originally paid £7,000 for the Merc and £3,000 for the BMW.

The scam was set up by an intermediary, who knew how desperate I was for money, and I went round to the home of the crook – a big, rough fella dripping with gold jewellery and rings. The following morning he sauntered into the office with a pal and a thick wad of notes. The money changed hands, as did two sets of car keys, and that was the last I saw of the Mercedes and BMW which, I have no doubt, were driven to a back-street garage and sold privately once the number plates had been changed, and quite possibly after a re-spray.

My head must have been scrambled because I had totally failed to think things through to their logical conclusion. I didn't know how I was going to get away with it and the remaining hire-purchase payments were going to come to considerably more than £2,300.

Still, I soldiered on, groping blindly in the dark until I ran out of money again, inevitably. The repayments stopped and the HP company sent round a debt collector to investigate matters at the office. I wasn't there, he wasn't happy and when the police were summoned to intervene and I couldn't produce the goods in question, I was charged with stealing the two cars and the case was scheduled to be heard at Snaresbrook Crown Court.

Theft makes it sound as if I was going out nicking motors on the streets of north London. I wasn't, of course, but that's no excuse. I knew the difference between right and wrong.

The ironic thing was that Starline had a contract with Pentonville to transport prisoners to court and back, accompanied by warders. But we got the sack because I ran the stereotypical terrible minicab firm, like something out of *Carry On Cabbie*. We were unreliable and would turn up for work in unlicensed vehicles at the jail, of all places.

I found someone to take the business off my hands, handing over the keys as I told him: 'Here, you take it, I just want out. Good luck, pal.'

Bankruptcy soon followed – as did a couple of nights inside Pentonville as a prisoner myself after I twice failed to attend the court hearing into my parlous financial state. I had moved in Ilford from Seymour Gardens to York Road and I either ignored the summons or it was sent to one of my several previous addresses. In any event, I was charged with contempt of court in my absence and a warrant was issued for my arrest. I had been signing on each week at the local police station for what seemed like an eternity as a condition of bail over the business with the half-sovereigns, and the next time I went to the Ilford nick I was driven straight to Pentonville, before appearing in front of a judge to offer my apologies.

'Football star wins freedom', reported the *Daily Express* on 5 July 1980 when their readers learned:

TRUE STOREY

> Former Arsenal soccer star Peter Storey was freed yesterday after spending two nights in jail.
>
> He was taken to Pentonville prison – not far from the Highbury football ground – after failing to appear at two bankruptcy proceedings.
>
> He apologised to London Bankruptcy court. 'Everything got on top of me,' he said.
>
> Mr Registrar-Parbury said: 'If he flouts the laws of this court he is likely to find the circumstances very uncomfortable. But if he co-operates he may find his journey through bankruptcy not quite so unpleasant.'
>
> Mr Storey, 34, of York Road, Ilford, had a bankruptcy order made against him in January on the petition of a finance company claiming £7,500. He is now a minicab driver.

I kept waiting and waiting for the conspiracy nonsense to come to trial. Eventually a letter found me, bearing the date for my hearing at the Old Bailey in September 1980.

The procedure ensures you have advance notice of the judge, and the defendants' solicitors agreed we had got an 'early result' because the Recorder of London, Mr James Miskin QC, was listed to preside. He was, by general consent, pretty fair.

Maybe it wouldn't end in tears after all and my mood of despondency was further lifted when I started going steady with Gill Ashby, a young girl I had met in the pub and who was destined to become the third Mrs Storey.

Jimmy, a colleague, interviewed Gill for a job as a part-time barmaid and took her on. A local Islington girl, working as a secretary, she was still a teenager, much younger than me. Gill was highly attractive, quite outgoing in the personality stakes and very slim with dark hair – not at all dissimilar to either of my first two wives, Susan and Cathy.

They must have met and exchanged words about me, but there was no antagonism between Gill and Cathy as far as I was aware. Cathy wasn't really living at the pub; most of the time she wasn't there as Gill became more and more a permanent fixture in my life.

On the day of the trial, I felt confident that justice would prevail as I walked up the steps of the Old Bailey, only to be met by some very gloomy faces on our legal team. 'What's up, who's died?' I joked. My mood altered when I learned that Mr Miskin was otherwise engaged and the case was up before 'Jack' Abdela, who enjoyed a reputation as a 'hanging judge'. Not literally, of course, but the defence counsel reckoned he always tended to favour the police and the prosecution.

The jury was duly sworn in and seven defendants, myself included, filed into the dock. Ralph Haeems warned me: 'You've no chance with Abdela, Peter. Plead guilty and you'll cop for a suspended sentence.'

I've always had a stubborn streak and refused point-blank. Seen through my eyes, the case against me was a complete joke. The only thing I was guilty of was naïvety and drinking with the wrong people. That's hardly a crime, is it?

The charges were itemised individually and the first four of us pleaded not guilty, but the other three held up their hands. They had been advised, like me, to plead guilty in expectation of nothing more than a suspended sentence.

Their briefs asked for bail to be extended while the case proceeded against the rest of us, and expected it to be granted as a formality. You could almost sense the atmosphere change and tension rise when the judge, His Honour Jack Samuel Ronald Abdela, to give him his full title, snapped words to the effect that he was refusing bail because of the extremely serious nature of the alleged offences, and that he couldn't understand why any of us had been out on bail in the first place. He was an old soldier, a liveryman with the Worshipful Company of Painter-Stainers and he would have got more than a funny handshake from me if I'd ever caught him on his own.

Abdela played the hardman right there in front of the jury, and I feared his reaction might influence the jury against us.

The shell-shocked trio were duly remanded to Wandsworth prison and we carried on regardless. I was granted an extension to my bail after the first day of the trial, but only if two guarantors stood surety. I had absolutely no prior warning that this condition might be sprung on me and, as I only had one immediate friend in the vicinity, I was taken to Brixton prison. I was preparing to spend the night there in a cell when word came through that Ralph had secured the second bond and I was released.

The case was scheduled to last several weeks, but Abdela was in no mood to hang about.

Virtually every time the evidence of police witnesses was questioned by our barristers, Abdela would interrupt, asking: 'Are you calling this officer a liar?'

And as for those witnesses, they were bowing and scraping and calling Abdela 'my Lord' – he was lapping it up and, I believe, he even referred to us in the dock at one stage as 'riff raff'.

It was madness, because in my eyes I was being accused of conspiracy to make imitation stuff which would be used as jewellery, but the nub of the prosecution argument was that the offence amounted to counterfeiting gold sovereigns, much the same as manufacturing £50 notes, which, I understood, carried a maximum sentence of life imprisonment.

Abdela was called upon on the Friday to make a ruling in private – and it was absolute. Regardless of whether we had been manufacturing half-sovereigns for Christmas crackers or not, we had no defence and were therefore technically guilty.

My barrister, Paul Dodgson, came to me and broke the news: I had no option now but to change my plea.

In the lift from the cells to court, Heron was laughing and joking that we'd have to try and escape or 'have it on our toes', as he put it. Court officials don't have much of a sense of humour at the best of times and Heron's jest about us running away was passed on to Abdela, who remanded us in Wandsworth for the weekend, although we had been out on bail for two years.

When Monday, 15 September 1980 dawned I thought I was just admitting to a technicality.

Some technicality. You would have thought we'd been planning to steal the crown jewels, the way Abdela got on his high horse and sentenced me to three years and two other guys, Micky and Dave, to twenty-seven months each. Heron would be dealt with later for some reason. Bobby Barry was cleared, and quite rightly. He'd been drinking in the Jolly Farmers more often than was healthy for him, but he had been nothing to do with the coins.

I didn't feel faint or grip the side of the dock when sentence was passed, only experienced a deep sense of injustice and impotent violence. I simply stared at Abdela and said under my breath: 'You fucking useless cunt.' I wish we'd been on a football pitch at that moment, then I could have gone straight over the top and broken his leg.

How Abdela later had the brass neck to describe my plight as 'heartbreaking' I found beyond belief after the way he had treated me like scum, the hypocrite.

Understandably, the press had a field day with my downfall and the *Daily Mirror* splashed a headline, 'Shame Of Soccer Hero Storey':

BEHIND BARS

Former England soccer idol Peter Storey was jailed yesterday for his part in a forgery plot.

Sentencing him to three years, Judge Abdela said at the Old Bailey:

'Believe me, it's heartbreaking to find you here. You are a man who commands the respect of thousands.' But he added: 'You financed this scheme.'

The court was told that 35-year-old Storey was persuaded to invest in a scheme to forge half-sovereigns.

When police raided the ex-Arsenal player's public house – the Jolly Farmers in Islington – they found two counterfeiters' dies. In a warehouse nearby was a hydraulic press fitted with a die ready to cast the fakes, and a pile of copper blanks.

The court was told that Storey, capped 19 times for England, had money troubles.

After he changed his plea to guilty, his lawyer Paul Dodgson said:

'He has lost everything. He has gone from being a success, to being in every way at the bottom.'

Two other men involved in the plot each got two and a half years in jail. Another two got suspended sentences.

There was more for my family to suffer in the *Daily Express*, who contented themselves with the headline: 'England Star Peter Storey Jailed' but labelled me a 'greedy crook' and went on:

The Crown had alleged that Storey put up £4,000 to start a factory producing bogus gold coins.

He had joined the conspiracy to recoup heavy financial losses, said Mr Robert Harman, QC, prosecuting.

Since his arrest he had lost his thriving pub and was now living with his parents in a council house.

Four grand? I don't know where that ever came from because I'd only ever put up £2,000. And I'm sure there had only been the one die, not two.

Wandering through the black museum of my press cuttings some 30 years later brings back a certain bitterness at the sense of injustice. But even in my darkest hours, I was surrounded by infinitely more tragic figures. At least I have had a chance to rebuild my life – and

TRUE STOREY

for that I can count my blessings. I am capable of compassion, contrary to popular belief. Next to my so-called sins in the *Daily Express* was a lurid inquest account of how the popular actress Yootha Joyce – recognised nationwide for her starring role in the TV comedy series *George and Mildred* – had been a secret alcoholic for ten years and drank herself to death as a 'lonely, tormented woman', weighing only 6 st. 9 lb when she was admitted to a Harley Street clinic.

Next to another report about me, there was a poignant story of a 19-year-old lad killed in a car crash on his way home from collecting his wedding suit in South Yorkshire.

No part of me ever died and I was never a criminal mastermind, but rather a foolish former footballer with more money than sense. But now to the public at large I became the man sentenced to three years in prison for financing a plot to counterfeit gold coins. It sounds so big-time, so glamorous, doesn't it? All I did was lend some money to blokes I thought were going to make a few quid by knocking out cheap imitation jewellery. I wasn't exactly in the Howard Marks league; I was never going to damage the Bank of England's gold reserves or send the Dow Jones Index plunging.

I left court heading for Wormwood Scrubs locked in a 'cattle wagon' with barred windows. When we arrived I had to strip naked, part with my expensive suit and put my clothes and shoes in cardboard boxes. My prison-issue replacements consisted of dark blue denim-type trousers, light blue shirt, underpants, black socks and shoes.

Micky, Dave and I were given a meal before the three of us were banged up together in a cell measuring about 8 ft square containing one double bunk and a single. You couldn't swing a cat in there, it was so cramped.

A couple of days into my sentence, I spotted Heron and knew the Mighty Jolly Farmers Mob was four-handed inside. A fellow inmate passed me a well-thumbed copy of the *Daily Mirror* and said: 'I thought this might interest you, Peter.'

Under the headline, 'Coin Faker Is Jailed', I read:

> The mastermind behind a forgery racket involving former England footballer Peter Storey was jailed yesterday.
>
> David Heron, 50, of Hackney, London, was given three and a half years at the Old Bailey after he admitted conspiring to forge half-sovereigns.

BEHIND BARS

Storey was jailed for three years on the same offence on Monday.

For most of us, the Scrubs was the worst type of prison we could be held in until the authorities decided to transfer us somewhere appropriate – an open prison in my case.

I knew I'd missed a trick with the food when one old-timer informed me the clever ones made out to the screws that they were either vegetarian or Muslim. That way, apparently, they got better quality, fresher food produced in smaller batches rather than the stuff churned out for the bulk of the inmates in industrial quantities. I thanked the old lag and made a mental note about vegetarianism if I was ever inside again, but said I thought I might struggle to convince anyone I was a bona fide Muslim. Fuck it, I did feel rough but I hadn't entirely lost my sense of humour.

The first couple of weeks were dire, being inducted into prison life, settling into the sheer bloody mind-numbing routine, and nothing at the Scrubs was worse than being locked in that cell for virtually twenty-three hours a day, permitted just one hour's recreation which consisted of little more than walking round and round in circles to stretch your legs in the prison yard.

I had a personal bucket in which to relieve myself and slopped out each morning. We were also temporarily uncaged to collect our meals from the canteen, but had to return to our cells to eat. It was a twilight world in which little privileges, like being able to leave your cell door open just a crack, seemed important.

I didn't have a job to relieve the monotony and felt more useless than ever. The prison was jam-packed, but the workshops were closed because there weren't sufficient staff to supervise the inmates.

Understandably, working in the kitchens and cleaning, the two jobs which were available for a little bit of extra pocket money, were jealously guarded. The smokers were desperate to land them so they could afford the tobacco which might kill them if the boredom didn't get to them first. Cigarettes were one vice which never appealed to me.

Gill and I had a strong relationship and I didn't live in any fear she might leave me while I was banged up. She sent some money in to supplement my small weekly allowance and my one luxury was to order a daily newspaper, usually the *Daily Mail*, which I would read from back to front before giving it away or swapping it for the *Mirror* or *Sun*.

TRUE STOREY

The boredom was oppressive, with very little reading material and so many hours a day to fill. Forget any images of prisons with TV sets in the cells and inmates playing snooker. There was none of that for us in that filthy holding pen although, joy of joys, after a month my application for a transistor radio was granted by the governor, which was big of him. On rare occasions we got to see a film.

Gill visited once a week when the prisoners were ushered into a large room with tables and chairs. She would buy tea and cakes through a tiny hatch in a wall for us to share and we'd chat, but it was a far from cosy arrangement. Mostly those 60 minutes sped past as we urgently discussed all our hopes and fears for the future, but on a couple of occasions that hour felt like a life sentence because I was depressed and morose, and I'd watch the second hand ticking away on a large clock while Gill did her best to remain upbeat and coax some life into me.

The other highlight of the week was to be taken down to this little counter where you could buy your own branded toothpaste, shampoo and soap, rather than relying on the harsh, basic prison-issue stuff. Tobacco and sweets were also on sale; Mars bars were very popular.

It was pathetic how small childish things, such as a bar of chocolate or a tiny radio, were highly prized items.

Once a week we were supposed to queue up for a bath or a shower, but sometimes an inmate would cheat, spot your name on the rota and steal your slot. That happened to me a couple of times, and then I had to wash myself all over from a basin of water. It was a wretched existence in a dirty, smelly, sweat-stained environment.

I didn't encounter any trouble inside, no grief or violence at all on account of my 'star' status. I suppose there must have been some homosexuality going on, but had anyone been stupid enough to make advances in my direction he would have been greeted with a swift kick in the bollocks – or worse. Ninety per cent of the inmates were just mugs, me included, I suppose; the only real danger was likely to come from the major criminals, category A prisoners, but they were on a different wing and we never fraternised.

The category Bs were mainly re-offenders and I was classified as a category C, among mainly first-time offenders deemed not to be a threat to society, men who were typically guilty of fraud, silly stuff like fiddling VAT and stealing from their own firms.

I'd been in prison for six weeks when my solicitor paid a visit to inform me that the car theft charges had been switched from

Snaresbrook to the Old Bailey, but there was no hurry, nothing of any immediate concern because the case had yet to be scheduled on a list giving 12 months' advance notice.

More significantly, he insisted that in his opinion there were good grounds to appeal against both the sentence and conviction for conspiracy, and he asked me: 'Shall I ask for bail?' I was in a fatalistic mood, resigned to doing at least a year inside and felt about as lucky as a one-legged man in an arse-kicking contest. 'Yeah, suit yourself,' I replied with a lack of grace and enthusiasm.

I didn't get my hopes up and thought no more about it, but one rainy afternoon several days later I was halfway through watching an old Norman Wisdom film (talk about piling on the punishment) when my name was called out and I was marched off to the governor's office, where I was informed that my application for bail had been successful and that I was free to leave Wormwood Scrubs.

Gill was waiting outside in a car and we drove swiftly to the flat I had been renting in Kentish Town, shared a shower and made love all night.

We had a rude awakening the following morning, an urgent telephone call from Gill's mother with a message from my solicitor telling me that the business with the stolen cars had been plucked out of thin air and was due to be heard in a matter of hours. Basically, if I wasn't in court number three at the Old Bailey on time, a warrant would be issued for my arrest.

Was that vindictive or what? Either the Crown Prosecution Service or the police, maybe both, had it in for me big-time. It was, quite frankly, unbelievable. I had been on bail for car theft for eight or nine months and, suddenly, it's sprung on me the day after I have temporary respite from a three-year prison sentence.

I jumped in a car and broke several speed limits on my way to the Old Bailey. I'm surprised I wasn't nicked for speeding. Of course, there had been no time to hire a barrister, but a solicitor was brought in from another court to plead on my behalf. He stood up and explained how unprepared the defence was to proceed, and why. The judge took a sympathetic view and postponed matters.

CHAPTER TWENTY-TWO

Video nasty

When I was at Arsenal, I'd get free seats and also buy maybe a dozen tickets for each home match and give them to people I considered friends.

When I came out of prison, I felt I could have been living in a cardboard box on Oxford Street and these 'friends' would have crossed the road to avoid me rather than give me the time of day. I felt like a leper.

Danny Ward is a good guy, but that wasn't always the case. He had a bad attitude as a youngster and fell foul of the law. He'd worked as a driver at the Starline minicab firm, but owed me nothing; I hadn't given him tickets to watch me play or done him any favours.

Fortunately, Danny became a reformed character who enjoyed helping people who were in trouble and when he heard what a mess I was in, he came to the basement council flat in Islington where Gill and I had moved with the offer of a little driving job, supplying a newspaper clippings library in Palmers Green.

'It's nothing special, Peter,' he said, almost apologetically. 'And I can only manage £40 a week.' But the work meant the world to me; it really kept me going.

Twice a day I would collect a sizeable bundle of nationwide regional morning and evening papers from the office Danny and his brother John ran in Holborn, just off Fleet Street, and deliver them to the library in north London.

I will be forever grateful to Danny and John, a useful amateur footballer who played in Rod Stewart's team when the singer had a full-size pitch marked out in the grounds of his mansion in Epping.

Thanks to the Wards, I was earning an honest wage and the dark question I had been asking myself, 'unemployed, or unemployable?' began to recede. Gill was working as a secretary and we lived as normally as we could with two court cases, the coins and cars, hanging over us, plus the threat of me being banged up inside again.

At least we had fallen on our feet with the flat; it was very nice, in a quiet square of terraced houses. The property was unfurnished when we first moved in but Gill put a lot of effort into making it feel like our own 'proper home'. I had lost virtually all my money, however, and there was absolutely no chance of me treating Gill to the sort of high life I had enjoyed at first with Cathy. Those expensive Italian meals out, long boozy Sunday lunchtimes, concerts and shows were a thing of the past; we were penny-pinching instead and eating out was a luxury we could not afford.

I stayed out on bail for nine months and was confident the counterfeiting nonsense would finally be rejected by three judges hearing the appeal in the Royal Courts of Justice in the Strand, just a few hundred yards from my newspaper collection point.

My junior barrister was enthusiastic because at his chambers a Queen's Counsel, Louis Blom-Cooper, who did not normally touch legal aid cases such as a mine with a bargepole, had been shown Abdela's judgement and didn't like it one bit. So now I had a QC leading the fight on my behalf.

My Silk unfortunately didn't convince the appeal judges, and it was all over very quickly. Abdela's cronies upheld the original ruling, I looked across the court to where Gill sat biting her lip and slowly shook my head, before steeling myself for a trip in a Black Maria with Heron, Micky and Dave to Wandsworth prison.

It was there that I was stunned to bump into Howard Marks again briefly. He seemed remarkably unconcerned by either his environment or predicament. Howard was the same old easy-going charmer inside and made me laugh when he sauntered across a landing and said: 'You'd better make it large ones for both of us, landlord, and go easy on the tonic!'

Howard was as cool as they come, and I admired his bravado. He must have known he was going down for years and years, yet the prospect seemed to faze him as much as losing a few bob playing cards.

I was locked up in Wandsworth for two months before being allocated a place at Springhill Open Prison, Aylesbury.

By an odd coincidence I'd been to Springhill the previous year with Tottenham legends Dave Mackay and Alan Gilzean to play for a team of old professionals, managed for the day by Malcolm Allison, against the prison XI. So I was familiar with the place and relieved to find it was a world away from the crushing oppressiveness of the Scrubs or Wandsworth.

The trouble with the stolen cars was eventually resolved in about five minutes flat at the Old Bailey without a trial on 29 April 1982. At last I met Mr Miskin, the man down to originally preside over the business with the half-sovereigns, and found him to be every bit as reasonable as I had been led to believe. I pleaded guilty and received two six-month prison sentences, which ran concurrently, so there was no damage done there to my future liberty.

The headline in the *Daily Express* ran 'New shaming of ex-England star' and readers learned:

> The shame of former England soccer star Peter Storey was described at the Old Bailey yesterday.
>
> Storey, 36, the former Arsenal and Fulham defender, admitted two charges of stealing cars he was buying on hire-purchase.
>
> His counsel, Mr Victor Levene, said: 'It is tragic that a man who had such an illustrious career should have this sort of downfall.'
>
> The court heard that since he gave up the game five years ago Storey, with 19 caps for England, had been convicted of living off prostitution, keeping a brothel and conspiring to counterfeit coins.
>
> Storey is now serving a three-year jail sentence for the coins case.
>
> When his playing career ended, he had been running a pub in Southgate, North London. He lost that and is now bankrupt.
>
> Mr Inigo Bing, prosecuting, said Storey sold a 1973 Mercedes he had bought for £7,000 for £1,800 cash. A BMW which cost him £3,000 went for £500.
>
> In a statement to police, Storey said he needed the money to get out of financial trouble.
>
> The Recorder of London, Mr James Miskin, QC, praised Storey's football ability. He said there was no point in extending his jail term and imposed a concurrent six months' sentence. Storey is due to be released next February.

VIDEO NASTY

The *Daily Mirror* published their account of proceedings under the headline: 'Judge's Mercy On Fallen Star' and had Miskin telling me: 'You ran into trouble and adopted this means of putting your sticky fingers on ready cash.'

I kept my hands out of trouble and my head down at Springhill and was preparing to serve the rest of my sentence when Gill came to visit and calmly announced that she was pregnant, and told me I'd better ask the governor for a day release pass because there was no way she fancied becoming a mum without a ring on her finger. Or as Gill put it, quite succinctly: 'We've got to get married. It's bad enough putting up with you, Peter, but I'm not being held responsible for another little bastard!'

I was genuinely delighted I was going to be a dad again, at last.

The governor reassured me that there would be no problem being released temporarily on compassionate grounds, providing I didn't blot my copybook, and I went back to work at my little job, cleaning the local sports centre.

Springhill wasn't a holiday camp, more like an army camp, but the regime was considerably more relaxed than the suffocating atmosphere of Wandsworth. At first I slept in a wooden dormitory containing a dozen beds, before being moved to another, smaller hut with a toilet and shower, where I enjoyed the privacy of my own room.

When my spell as a cleaner ended, I moved to a workshop assembling double glazing before applying for, and landing, the job I really wanted – outside in the fresh air, gardening.

I also managed to regain some fitness by captaining the Lags XI football team from midfield in Springhill's local league fixtures, going to away matches in a prison minibus.

Gill and I married shortly before our first son, Peter, was born on 4 November 1981. The wedding was a low-key affair at a church in Islington. Nobody from Arsenal came. I wasn't sufficiently close to any of my old teammates to feel I wanted them there. I was released from Springhill for the day and Dad drove me to our flat, where I changed into a suit. One of Gill's relatives was best man and her mother hosted the reception at her flat near the church. I restricted myself to a couple of drinks, having been warned by the governor that I would lose privileges if I returned legless. The party ended abruptly when Dad tapped his watch in the early evening and said: 'Time to go, son.' I kissed the bride, the third Mrs Storey, and he drove me back to prison.

I must have been in Springhill for six months when my legal team launched a fresh appeal, this time to be heard at the House of Lords. Mr Blom-Cooper was adamant that Judge Abdela's ruling had been faulty but, unless challenged, it would be enshrined in law and the details of my conspiracy conviction would set some kind of a precedent.

I was released on bail and not obliged to attend the hearing, but felt crushed again when I phoned my solicitor for the verdict, only to be told: 'Sorry, Peter, it's not gone our way', and received instructions to hand myself in at the Royal Courts of Justice. 'In and out like a fiddler's elbow,' I thought to myself, but it was no laughing matter.

Pregnant again, Gill was beside herself with grief and felt the nightmare would never end. I kissed her and baby Peter goodbye, packed a bag and caught the tube to the Strand.

Instead of being returned to Springhill, as expected, I was carted off to Wandsworth. I knew I didn't have much longer to serve and at least I had the relative 'luxury' of a single cell. I was resigned to completing my sentence in south London but after a couple of months was told I would be transferred back to the open prison.

On my arrival for a second term in Buckinghamshire, the governor asked: 'What's wrong, Peter? Didn't you want to come back here to us?' I was totally perplexed before he explained how he'd received a phone call from a clerk at the Royal Courts of Justice, informing him of my failed appeal at the Lords, and had replied: 'You can send Storey straight back here.'

Instead, I had had to endure another two months in the Wandsworth fleapit. Make no mistake – someone had it in for me, somebody was being fucking nasty.

My second son, Anthony, was born on 3 December 1982, and I was released on parole in time for Christmas. My emotions were all over the place that festive season. Before the complicated tale of crimes and punishment, I'd been running a successful pub with Cathy, my second wife. Now I was on the dole, married to Gill and father to a couple of smashing little nippers. One moment I felt elated by the sense of freedom, the next depressed at living in a council flat in Islington, signing on for unemployment benefit and worried by the burden of having to provide for my young family.

Friends were in short supply, but one did pop up in the shape of Martin Wengrow, a devoted Arsenal fan whom I'd first met in my early 20s. Word had reached Martin that I was in dire straits and he

VIDEO NASTY

invited me to his clothing business in Great Portland Street. Martin was in the rag trade and let me have some cheap stuff to knock out on market stalls. It was bloody hard work at first getting established, but I kept at it. I'd let my mum and dad down, Gill too, and there was no way Peter and Anthony were going to suffer now, I told myself.

My career as a high-profile England and Arsenal footballer already seemed like a lifetime ago. It was almost as if it had happened to somebody else. I wasn't interested in the First Division results as much as in a new fashion for girls – tartan kilts, which were beginning to sell like the proverbial hot cakes. I regularly stocked up on those kilts by the vanload from Martin to sell on my pitches, particularly one lucrative site in Portobello Road.

Business was booming in the early '80s; tourists discovered the pound was exceptionally cheap and flooded into London to take advantage of the exchange rate. I seemed to be making money hand over fist, so quickly in fact that one summer found me only working weekends – yet still earning over £4,000, which was frankly unbelievable for just two days' hard graft.

I would kiss goodbye to Gill late on a Friday and sleep overnight in my fully-laden van in Portobello Road, waking at 5 a.m. to set up my stall and be ready for the first early-morning tourists eager to snap up anything in tartan they could lay their hands on. Apart from kilts and skirts, scarves and children's wear were also very popular.

I spent Saturday nights in my own bed with Gill and was up in the small hours heading for Petticoat Lane, another venue which proved a fabulous earner on a Sunday.

After a few years I was back on my feet and, as the money rolled in, I could afford to purchase a larger two-bedroom flat from Islington council under their 'Right to Buy' initiative. I paid £20,000 for the property in Elmore Street, off the Essex Road.

I became a father again on 4 September 1987 when our third beautiful boy, Jamie, was born – but it wasn't long before my life descended into chaos once more and led to another prison sentence.

By the end of the decade, the recession had started to bite, the exchange rate wasn't so attractive to tourists and things went downhill in terms of both my market trading business and my personal relationship with Gill.

There wasn't a tipping point, one particular incident when I thought: 'Fuck me, we're in trouble here, this marriage is not going to last.' The deterioration of our relationship was a slow, painful process. I was out working all hours while Gill got herself a secretarial job at the Islington Business Centre, and it was during this period that Gill started to go out more without me and we grew apart. I was thoroughly fed up and we split up.

Sadly, shit happens, and while Jamie was too young to absorb all the backbiting, shouting, recriminations and rubbish which exploded at home when the marriage hit the rocks, I hated the fact Peter and Anthony were exposed to the negativity at such a tender age.

Not long afterwards, I was at a party where I met a Frenchwoman, Danièle Scorcelletti, who was to become my fourth wife.

I didn't appreciate it at the time, but Danièle was my soulmate. She struck me immediately because of her looks – taller than Susan, Cathy and Gill, she was a delectable blonde – but very quiet and easy to talk to. There was an intellectual side to Danièle which I found very appealing.

Gill moved out with all three boys and went to live in Spain with her new fella. Danièle was still married, but living apart from her husband, Mario, and I moved into her place in Richmond. We discovered that years earlier our flats in St John's Wood had been barely 150 yards apart and, by an uncanny coincidence, on the day I married Cathy at Westminster Town Hall, Danièle was getting hitched to Mario in the same registry office. Uncanny.

We joked about fate bringing us together, but it was no laughing matter when I soon survived a bizarre brush with the police as a suspect in a murder inquiry.

Gill and the boys returned from Spain to Elmore Road, where she was unnerved to discover a car-load of 'heavies' parked over the road from the flat on consecutive days. They eventually summoned the courage to hammer on the door shortly after Gill returned from work one teatime, introduced themselves menacingly as the Murder Squad from Loughton in Essex and demanded to know my whereabouts. She told them I didn't live there any longer, but could be found in Richmond, and was simply given a message to pass on that I should contact them at my earliest convenience.

If tracking me down was such a big deal, I don't know why they didn't come straight over to the badlands of suburban Surrey. Perhaps they'd lost their map, or maybe it was nearly opening time.

Gill called me on my mobile and I contacted Loughton CID, who arranged to meet me at 7 p.m. the following evening at Richmond

VIDEO NASTY

police station. I was still none the wiser in the interview room where two detectives started throwing their weight around attempting to intimidate me. Then a photograph of a smiling fella in a dinner suit with a pretty blonde on his arm was casually flicked over the desk in my direction.

'Who's this then, Peter?' I was asked. 'You know him well, don't you?' I racked my brains, but the face didn't ring any bells. The boys from Essex insisted that not only did I know him, I had, in fact, threatened to kill him. They told me he was a notorious ladies' man and that I'd got the hump when he'd started going out with one of my girlfriends. I remained a picture of innocence and the cops must have been convinced that I was telling the truth. They revealed the fella had been found executed, gangland-style, with a bullet through the back of his head in his car in Epping Forest. Something to do with drugs, I believe.

Why my name was ever dropped into the frame is another mystery. But what I do know is that had I still been living in Islington, those Murder Squad heavies would probably have jumped out of their car and handcuffed me in the street. That was a scary thought.

Things became complicated on the domestic front. I split with Danièle, rejoined the family and bought a place in North Chingford, where we lived for three or four years.

The property boom had worked to my advantage, that flat in Elmore Road going for £100,000 and enabling me to buy the house for £150,000. I had married Gill for love, very definitely, and when the boys were born I felt sure the marriage was solid. We got back together for the sake of the children, really. It started when I just popped round to see the boys and say hello, although I argued with Danièle over making the most of my visiting rights. We were understandably both a bit wary of making another go of it, but Gill and I enjoyed a couple of decent family holidays in Lanzarote, and I was a proud father, out and about with the lads in playgrounds or simply mucking about in Epping Forest. But most of the time I was working, and working bloody hard. It was exhausting.

I could have done with another fresh start at work in 1990 because the markets had gone down the pan. I went out in 'style' after a ruck with a female traffic warden in Soho saw me convicted the following year of using foul and abusive language, a crime which resulted in a 28-day suspended prison sentence.

It was the end of a long, hard and not particularly profitable day on a stall in Rupert Street and I was busy loading up my estate car with a mountain of unsold stock when this snooty warden turned up and pointed out I was parked on double yellow lines. 'Yeah, I know, love,' I said. 'Sorry. I'm getting packed up as soon as I can and then I'll be away.' Obviously it was more than her job was worth to show a little latitude and I began to lose it when she said sniffily that she wasn't 'my love' and spoke to me slowly, as if I were some sort of little kid with learning difficulties: 'No, you don't seem to understand, sir . . . yellow lines, motor car, parking offence.' I knew I wasn't going to win this battle, so I left a few cardboard boxes of gear on the pavement and simply drove off round the block and came back, expecting her to have shoved off. But she was lurking down an alley and when I parked illegally again to reclaim the boxes, she pounced and started writing out a ticket. With that, I swore at her and drove off. I thought nothing more of the incident, but a fortnight later I was working the same pitch in Rupert Street when two cops arrested me on the spot and took me to Vine Street nick, where I was charged with bad-mouthing the woman but also, much more seriously, reckless driving.

When the traffic warden had filed her official complaint, I was told she had sworn blind that I'd mounted the kerb and tried to run her over. That was absolute rubbish, complete bollocks. Once I got a solicitor involved and the prosecution realised I would fight the reckless driving charge all the way, it mysteriously disappeared from the charge sheet and I held my hands up to the swearing.

That unhappy little episode proved the final nail in the coffin of my roller-coaster career as a market trader, but I couldn't keep out of trouble.

Foolishly, I chased the easy money, broke the law and paid for it in jail. Again.

Jimmy, my old colleague, resurfaced with an enticing plan to go to Holland, buy some blue films and run off about 50 copies, netting us a very handsome profit from the pornography industry in the West End. So we decided to put this marvellous idea into action. Jimmy had done some business with Ron O'Sullivan, who ran a chain of Soho sex shops, and convinced me that O'Sullivan would happily buy anything we could supply him with in terms of serious blue films.

I've been in more than my fair share of trouble but certainly not on the scale of O'Sullivan. It wasn't long before his life changed dramatically.

VIDEO NASTY

Better known now, of course, as the proud father of snooker star Ronnie 'The Rocket' O'Sullivan, Ron was sentenced to life imprisonment in 1991, with a recommendation he serve 18 years for murdering Charlie Kray's bodyguard in a Chelsea nightclub with a knife.

I was introduced to Ron in a pub, where we said hello and had a few drinks together. He seemed like a nice fella. I left the financial arrangements between us and O'Sullivan to Jimmy, who told me how we could turn £200 into £2,000, and that was enough for me – I was hooked.

Early one bright October morning, I drove my Suzuki Jeep down to Dover, where we caught a cross-channel ferry to Calais, and motored up to Rotterdam. Unfortunately, Jimmy's ability to read a map didn't match his talent behind a bar and we ended up taking the wrong turning off a motorway into a prohibited slip road at the docks.

The Dutch cops didn't need to be Van der Valk to have their suspicions aroused by two admittedly dodgy-looking geezers driving a British-registered motor around docks infamous for drug smuggling. Four plainclothed detectives in an unmarked police car flashed their headlights and pulled us in. An honest explanation that we had merely lost our bearings appeared to satisfy them; they laughed and waved us on our way.

'Fuck me, Jimmy, that was close,' I said to my companion, but he was laughing too. 'No sweat, Peter.' That was easy for him to say – I was melting.

We eventually found what we were looking for, a wholesale warehouse on a large, scruffy industrial estate on the outskirts of Rotterdam. Inside, it was an Aladdin's cave of pornography with some seriously perverted hardcore stuff on offer. Jimmy knew the score better than me and selected 20 titles which he felt would be appreciated by 'London's connoisseurs'. Describing Soho's voyeurs in the same vein as recipients of fine imported wine made me grin.

I fished out £200 cash to pay for the videos, which were stacked into a big brown-paper carrier bag, and we drove the Jeep round to the back of the warehouse and packed the films carefully inside the spare tyre. With that, I filled up with petrol and drove back to Calais, where we squeezed onto the late Dover ferry. Once on board, Jimmy and I headed straight for the bar, repeating that meaningless phrase 'sweet as a nut' to each other and grinning like idiots. My sense of relief was such that I could have murdered a gallon of lager, but I settled for a couple of leisurely half-pints knowing we still faced the drive from Kent to London. The last thing we needed now was for me to cock up the entire operation by getting pulled over for drinking and driving.

My heart sank the moment I drove the Jeep down the ramp and was shepherded urgently towards a shed. I thought we might bluff it out, but one look at the faces of the customs officers on duty that night told me everything I needed to know: Jimmy and I were fucked.

We stood there like lemons as the Suzuki was pulled to pieces – it was like watching locusts, or rather piranhas going at a piece of meat. It dawned on me that those friendly Dutch detectives must have tipped off the English authorities that the Jeep and its occupants were suspicious. The game was up when the spare tyre was fed through an X-ray machine, the films were discovered and we were arrested.

'Soccer Ace On Porn Charge' reported the *Daily Express* on 11 October. I pleaded guilty the following month to importing twenty obscene tapes, was jailed for four weeks and did my time in Canterbury, passing the time in the prison workshop.

The minicabbing game looked the best option when I came out, and I went to work in Islington for a firm run by Tommy Adams in Roseberry Avenue.

Tommy was a member of Britain's most notorious crime family and later ran his own personal black cab, bugged by MI5, who discovered he was running large-scale drugs deals out of it all over London. Tommy's A Team were feared and respected by many in London's underworld throughout the 1980s and '90s.

When the law eventually caught up with Tommy in September 1990, he was jailed for seven and a half years for smuggling cannabis worth £2 million, and also fined the small matter of £1 million.

I had no beef with Tommy though, and was just relieved to be earning. In fact, I got on well with Tommy socially, I thought he was a pleasant fella – although you couldn't describe us as close friends and he certainly never involved me in any of the drugs stuff.

The Adams family had a big reputation, and everyone in Islington knew it. Tommy himself was an enthusiastic football fan, still playing Sunday League parks stuff as a centre-half of the traditional 'no-nonsense' variety. On one occasion, Tommy was involved in an old boys' match and recruited me to play alongside him at the back with Terry Naylor, the former Tottenham defender.

VIDEO NASTY

My former Arsenal teammate Eddie Kelly's brother-in-law Charlie Pini got in touch to ask if I was interested in joining his little crew chauffeuring Arabs around the capital for two or three months during the summer. I was glad of the work – it made a change from driving in some dodgy areas of north and east London, occasionally unsure whether my late-night fare would do a runner or charmingly vomit all over the back seat and put me out of the business for the remainder of the shift.

I drove minicabs for nine months of the year and, for the other three, top-of-the range limousines containing members of the royal family of the United Arab Emirates from Abu Dhabi. When my employer changed to Khalifa bin Hamad al-Thani, the emir of Qatar, summer would find me commuting from home in Chingford to a succession of addresses in Highgate, Hampstead and Holland Park where the sheikh had conveniently based three of his wives. Next stop was very often another H – Harrods, for the girls to indulge in some heavy-duty retail therapy.

Then came a bloodless coup d'état in 1995 while Sheikh Khalifa was staying in Geneva, Switzerland and found himself deposed by his son Hamad bin Khalifa. The people I was working for were potty, suddenly declared themselves 'fed up' with London and moved the entire entourage, including us drivers, into a five-star hotel in Istanbul on the Bosporus, flying to Turkey in their personal 747 jet.

Seven of us were working-class Englishmen, a mixture of drivers and security men, and for the first few weeks we lived the life of Riley, feasting on the richest food imaginable in one of Turkey's most fashionable hotels. Although the wages were good, and I know Gill appreciated the money I was earning for her and the boys back home in Essex, boredom quickly set in, working eight-hour shifts seven days a week. A few of us might venture out to a nightclub, but there was nothing for us to get attached to in Istanbul. I was homesick and yearned for a plate of honest to goodness fish and chips or bacon and eggs. I started to turn my back on the sumptuous free meals in the hotel restaurant, preferring to eat with local Turks, who smoked like chimneys in a nearby café. The gig with Sheikh Khalifa ended after a year and I couldn't wait to get back home – but not to Gill and the boys.

It sounds callous, I know, but I'd been in touch with Danièle again throughout my time in Istanbul. Too much had happened with Gill and there was no going back to her, either in a physical or an emotional sense. She found another fella and I returned to live with Danièle in Richmond, and have been with her ever since.

I couldn't break away from driving jobs to make ends meet and my next venture with a pal saw us rent a couple of Ford Galaxy people carriers and ply our trade with customers at the airports, Heathrow mainly, but it never took off. We simply weren't busy enough. I returned to minicabbing with a firm in Old Street before I bumped into Keith Fitch, a friend from my time in Turkey. 'How's your luck, Peter?' he asked. 'Pretty crap, same as usual,' I replied – but my despondency soon lifted when Keith suggested I get a van and join him in the courier business for a company in Kentish Town. It was a cracking little job for a couple of years. I'd get there early in the morning and then sort out the 70 or 80 parcels which needed to be dropped into a manageable route and I was away, sometimes finishing as early as 3 p.m. and earning £700 a week.

The year 1996 found me happy with Danièle, making a bob or two, with a small circle of immediate friends – although none of them were from my Highbury days – when the twenty-fifth anniversary of Arsenal's Double-winning season arrived and one newspaper got it into their heads that Peter Storey was the big story because, it was suggested to me, I was 'a recluse'. A reporter offered me £2,000 to speak, but I wasn't interested. The courier work was going well and I wasn't short of a bob or two. I had a fair idea of how I'd come out of the piece in the tabloid – some sort of freak, maybe football's answer to Charles Dickens' faded old bird in *Great Expectations*, Miss Havisham. Once I heard the word 'recluse' mentioned, alarm bells started ringing.

I just wanted to get on with living my own life. It had been a disaster since I'd finished football and the wounds were too fresh for them to be opened up again for public scrutiny all over the nation's breakfast tables.

A few days later, I was leaving home in Richmond at 7 a.m. when suddenly this reporter came charging across the road, holding his arm out to shake hands. 'Hello, Peter. I'm so-and-so from the so-and-so and we're still very keen to do your story and there's two grand in it for you,' he smiled, nice as pie.

I told him I'd think about it on my way to work and he took my mobile phone number. Thirty minutes later the phone rang and I had to disappoint him. 'Sorry, pal,' I said. 'I have given it some more thought, honestly, but I'm just not interested.' He was far from

VIDEO NASTY

unhappy, though, and replied: 'That's no problem, we've got all we need now to run the story.' A fortnight later the paper exposed me, alongside a big picture of the reporter shaking hands with me in the street, as the Arsenal Double-winner who didn't mix with his old pals but, in fairness, it wasn't a rotten type of tale, not as bad as I had feared.

CHAPTER TWENTY-THREE

French renaissance

Regrets? I have more than a few, naturally. Who doesn't, if they're honest? Certainly, I would like to have been a considerably better husband and father. I'm sorry for any pain and suffering I may have caused those closest to me. As for my crimes, I've been vain, foolish and naïve – but I never deliberately set out to hurt anyone.

I've been content living a peaceful life with Danièle since 2004 in a beautiful rural part of south-west France – in the Lot Valley off the beaten track between Cahors and Toulouse. The climate and gentle pace of life suit me. When the sun's out, I can put my feet up in a hammock in two acres of garden, which is also popular with our Border Collie dog, three cats and goat, Valentin, who saves me from having to get the lawnmower out too often.

I try to improve my mind by reading as much as possible and enjoy a decent glass of red wine, especially when I'm in the kitchen, where I'm happy to get stuck in. I like cooking and have developed my culinary skills over the years. I won't boast I have a 'signature dish', although I do love to cook duck, and mussels with garlic.

Danièle bought the place for a few thousand pounds in 1987 before we met because her long-term plan was always to retire to the French countryside. Basically, it was an ancient, derelict barn without a roof, consisting of little more than four walls. Inevitably, that has meant an extensive renovation schedule, but we've taken our time and gradually done up the old place.

Next to the barn stands a magnificent water tower, dating back to the seventeenth or eighteenth century, and our next project is to convert it into a studio where Danièle can produce more of her watercolour paintings.

FRENCH RENAISSANCE

We manage to tick over financially with the income from Danièle's house in Tangier Road, Richmond, which is rented out to a high-flier in the City of London, while I made £20,000 a decade ago by selling some of my England caps and four medals – the European Fairs Cup gong from 1969–70, my League Championship and FA Cup winner's medals from the Double campaign the following season, and the FA Cup runners-up medal from 1972.

I never met the private collector who wanted those mementos – the deal was done through an intermediary – but he was welcome to them. I don't need tangible reminders of my modest place in English football and my achievements. My memories are enough and, anyway, that £20,000 came in very handy at the time.

Sorry if that sounds less than romantic and a bit hard-nosed, but that's just the way I am. Anyway, I've still got a few England caps here in France, stuffed away in a cardboard box somewhere.

A wild tale surfaced in the press in May 2008 that I had personally just flogged some stuff and made £28,000. Under the headline 'Cautionary Storey with a sad ending', I was perplexed to read: 'A sad footnote to a career gone wrong. Peter Storey, Arsenal's one-time hard man, has sold his medals from the historic 1970–71 Double-winning season on eBay. His nine-carat gold FA Cup winner's medal and Football League winner's plaque fetched £28,000. After leaving Arsenal, Storey fell into a spiral of crime, and served a prison term.'

Chance would be a fine thing. Clearly, someone had just turned a profit on my gongs, and good luck to them. I wouldn't have the foggiest notion about selling anything on eBay. For one thing, Danièle and I don't even possess a computer.

Football still interests me – but in a casual sort of way, which is a bit strange I suppose, given how totally driven and fixated I was with results and winning in my professional career.

The last match I saw in the flesh was Arsenal against Aston Villa in the final season at Highbury, where I sat on my own and was happy to pay for the privilege of watching a classic attacking performance and a 5–0 home win. It was April Fool's Day 2006 and Emmanuel Adebayor opened the scoring before Thierry Henry weighed in with a couple of goals.

I certainly don't feel deprived or cut off from the game in my neck of the woods because French television regularly screens three Premier League matches on a Saturday, one after the other. Danièle would think I was losing my marbles if I sat down to watch that lot. So would I, come to that. Then there's all the French league football, of course, plenty of stuff from Serie A in Italy plus continental midweek action from the European Cup.

I do, however, always make a point of trying to watch Arsenal, because they are capable of producing the most attractive football, as much as for any sentimental attachment.

It's a bit churlish to be critical when Arsène Wenger is striving for perfection, but while the midfield men are all very comfortable on the ball, I think there is 'softness' there at times and they can be suspect and exposed when a bit of real defending is required against top-class opponents. For all Wenger's many attributes, getting his team to stop opponents and making life uncomfortable for them is not one of his strongest points.

I am not really equipped to talk about hard men in the game today, because there aren't any. Roy Keane was the last of a breed which has become extinct and since he hung up his boots with Celtic in the summer of 2006 the game has changed in favour of attackers. Tough guys and rugged tacklers have been victimised. If I were playing today, the chances are I'd be sent off inside five minutes for giving some foreign striker a stern look. I'm sure the referee would interpret that as malicious intent.

Wages of at least £100,000 a week seem to be the going rate for a top Premier League player, and it's nice work if you can get it. But I'm not resentful, because the world of football has not so much moved on from my era as virtually changed beyond all recognition.

I do, however, take issue with the fact that clubs seem to feel the need to carry a professional playing staff of about 40, and particularly that some of these characters are more than satisfied to pick up their £50,000 every week without getting remotely close to a first-team start. That's a ridiculous state of affairs. I would frankly be embarrassed to receive that amount of money *not* to play, and would be banging on the manager's door wanting to know why I wasn't considered good enough to get in the team – or demanding a transfer to a club where I could play. Those bulky squads are ludicrous.

Everything certainly wasn't better when I was enjoying the vast proportion of my football with Arsenal and England in the 1970s – but it is perhaps worth recalling that we won the Double in 1971 with basically 14 players on pitches far inferior to today's 'carpets'. Including our little run in the Fairs Cup, we played 64 matches that season. Bertie Mee and Don Howe certainly knew their best team on

FRENCH RENAISSANCE

any given Saturday, and if you had asked Bertie about rotation, he'd most likely have thought you were quizzing him about the vegetables in his garden at home.

It's a dangerous game too when the Premier League clubs can only afford to pay these gigantic salaries because of all the money they receive from television. With the overkill of so much football on TV, it's absolutely vital that the clubs keep match ticket prices affordable to the working-class man and his kids, or else even more fans will join the ranks of armchair supporters like me.

I very rarely have any contact with my former Arsenal teammates. Bob McNab rings me two or three times a year for a natter from Los Angeles while Sammy Nelson, who lives in Brighton, invites me to old boys' get-togethers at corporate functions which he runs with Charlie George – but I don't feel obliged to go to these things. If I lived in London, it might possibly be different, but geography dictates it's by no means a simple journey from my remote village in France. Several years ago I went to the National Exhibition Centre at Birmingham for a big do where several members of the 1966 England World Cup squad signed memorabilia and the organisers were keen to invite a few former Arsenal players. I thoroughly enjoyed my couple of days in the company of 'Stan' Simpson and John Radford, but I haven't kept their telephone numbers. It was also good to meet up with most of the surviving members of the Double-winning squad at the Emirates at a do for Bob Wilson – but I slipped quietly away after the dinner, before the speeches and serious drinking began, to catch the last train back to stay with my dad, Edwin, in Farnham.

I live my own life with Danièle, a remarkable and talented woman, and I am content with it.

I do make sure I get back over to England a few times a year to see my dad, and nothing beats it when my three sons – Peter, Anthony and Jamie – drive over to join us and we go up the local pub for Sunday lunch and a few pints.

Mum passed away in 2002, but Dad is an independent sort and lived on his own before settling into sheltered accommodation a couple of years ago. I'm as proud of him as I am of the boys.

Peter, the eldest, worked nights and weekends stacking shelves at Sainsbury's in Woodford Green to pay for himself to study psychology at the University of East London in Stratford before taking a masters degree in child psychology and working in research, funded by the

Government. Now he is a primary school teacher and shares a flat with Anthony in Wanstead.

The great love in Peter's life is Arsenal Football Club. I first bought season tickets for him and Anthony at Highbury when they were schoolkids and now they pay for their own seats at the Emirates Stadium.

Anthony is not so academically inclined, but has achieved a lot in other areas. He passed his City and Guilds exams and is a tiler for a large firm in east London and seems to work all over the City and at Heathrow airport. He was a good amateur footballer too, but knocked it on the head because the clubs he played for took the game so seriously, demanding a level of commitment and regular training at night which would have left Anthony knackered when he got up in Chingford for work the following morning.

Jamie also likes football, but he's not so keen as his elder brothers and is more into music. He has played guitar in a few bands but, just like Peter, he knows the world doesn't owe him a living. In fact, he inherited Peter's job at Sainsbury's so that he can fund himself through college to become a paramedic. Meanwhile, Jamie has had a job helping make up the notes for doctors at Whipps Cross Hospital.

When I'm not with Danièle in France, I'm more comfortable in an environment I'm familiar with – enjoying a leisurely pint or two with Dad and the boys.

There's no Natalie, though, never has been. I could spin a sob story but, to be honest, most of the time I don't think of her. I don't carry around an image of Natalie in my head. I expect she's married, maybe with children of her own. It's probably for the best that we leave things the way they are. Having said that, I'd never reject her if she did want to meet me again after all these years – I just think that's unlikely.

Back in the pub on a Sunday afternoon it's even better if Arsenal are playing on the telly. Someone in our party compared me to the tremendous little dapper midfielder Cesc Fabregas last season, and wondered how we measured up as players. I just smiled and replied: 'No contest – I was much more handsome.'

And that's the truth.